Searching for Evil

...and the perfect donut

By

Richard A. Nable

This book is a work of non-fiction. Names and places have been changed to protect the privacy of all individuals. The events and situations are true.

ISBN: 1-4107-7688-3 (e-book)
ISBN: 1-4107-7689-1 (Paperback)
ISBN: 1-4107-7690-5 (Dust Jacket)

This book is printed on acid free paper.

1stBooks – rev. 08/26/03

I would like to give special recognition and thanks to my parents, Ann and Dan Nable, without whom not only would this work not be possible, but neither would I. No one could ask for better parents or role models. You are the foundation on which my life is built.

To my loving, dear, charming, patient and understanding wife Kim (who is in fact God's gift to mankind) and our adorable, talented and brilliant children, Erin and Austin. You are the center of my universe, my inspiration and my anchor. I am truly blessed.

This book is dedicated to all those men and women throughout history who have joined and who will join in the fight against Evil. It is a task not relegated to a few, but to any and all who wish to make the world a better place.

In particular, this book is dedicated to the "sheepdogs" of the world. Who are the sheepdogs? The following paragraph explains. It is paraphrased from the book, "On Killing" by Lt Col. David Grossman. The book is a must for any police officer and for any civilian interested in the psychology of violence. Moreover, the following paragraph is the essence of police work distilled.

"Most of the people in the world are as sheep: gentle, decent, kindly creatures who are essentially incapable of true aggression. There is another human subspecies that is a kind of dog: faithful, vigilant creatures who are very much capable of aggression when circumstances require. There are also wolves (sociopaths) and packs of wild dogs (gangs and aggressive armies) abroad in the land, and the sheepdogs (the ideal soldiers and policemen of the world) are environmentally and biologically predisposed to be the ones who confront these predators."

The ideal police officer is the protector of all that is good in the world. We guard that tenuous line between order and chaos. Without us the world would perish. Our charter is a sacred one, and those who choose to don the mantle of the Soldier or Police Officer must be ever willing, ready and able to protect the sanctity of our office, be ever vigilant in our endeavors and remain true to the expectations of those whom we serve. We are Conservers Of Peace. There is no nobler cause.

Table of Contents

In Service

"In service" is a police term that means basically, I'm on duty and ready to answer calls for service. For the purposes of this book, it is an introduction. My primary intent in writing this book is to offer entertainment to both police officers and civilians alike. If you are not careful, you might even learn something, but that would be a wholly unintended side effect. All the stories you are about to read are true and I had a direct involvement with the majority of them over the course of my sixteen years as a street officer for a major metropolitan police department in the Southern United States.

I was born and raised in the state of Georgia and went to the University of Richmond, VA, where I received a bachelor's degree in biology. Immediately after graduation I made the conscious decision to make a stark departure from my intended career goal. I applied for a position in several police departments near where I had grown up. In less than three months, my journey as a police officer had begun.

For the five years prior to this writing, I have also been a training officer. My duties include not only working the street on a nightly basis but also training both new and veteran officers in a variety of police related curricula including criminal and traffic law, search and seizure, use of force, officer survival and tactics, vehicle pullovers, courtroom testimony and the list goes on and on. I am a certified firearms instructor and general weapons enthusiast and I am SWAT certified. I am a nationally certified driving instructor and teach not only basic defensive driving but also high speed and pursuit driving.

I am an active member of the Georgia Association of Law Enforcement Firearms Instructors, The Association of Professional Law Enforcement Emergency Vehicle Response Trainers International and a lifetime member of the National Rifle Association.

Police work is something I have always loved and have devoted my life to, so it seemed to me to be only natural to write a book about it. I tried to write in a manner that would be understandable to a large audience but I do occasionally revert to "cop talk". To make things easy to understand, I have included a chapter entitled "Pig Latin" in the back of the book that hopefully will explain any terms not familiar to the reader.

I have tried to incorporate a broad variety of my experiences coupled with some philosophy and personal perspective that I hope will be both entertaining and enjoyable, and perhaps even a bit educational.

Chapter 1

Stupid Dog

One unique thing about being a training officer is that when you are teaching recruits one on one rather than in a classroom setting, each poor soul is a captive audience. They each in turn are subject to my countless rants and raves on politics, morality, justice and responsibility as well as my rambling, random, philosophical jaunts and pompous pontifications.

A familiar tangent that I like to go off on is the parable of the Stoic dog. (Please note that "stoic" is capitalized indicating that in this reference, the dog is not necessarily stoic but the reference to the dog is what is Stoic.) In case the reader is not familiar with the parable, I will gladly repeat it here. Though the details often change with the storyteller, the core lesson remains true to the original. The parable is commonly attributed to Zeno, an ancient philosopher and the founder of, you guessed it, Stoicism. The word stoic comes from the Greek word "stoa" which essentially means porch. So Zeno was pretty much a guy like any other guy who liked to sit on his porch (or the porch of the Parthenon) and talk about stuff. My version of his story is as follows.

There was once a police officer who liked to take his dog to work with him. Occasionally the officer would get out of his car to walk around and perform some "community oriented policing". Sometimes he would take his dog to walk with him, but on occasions would leave the dog to guard the car. Since it got too hot inside the car to leave the dog locked inside, the officer would sometimes chain the dog to the bumper of the squad car.

One day when the officer left the dog chained to the bumper, he forgot to set the parking brake and the car slipped out of gear. Since the car happened to be parked on top of a hill, the car began to roll. At this point the poor little doggy was faced with a choice. Though all he really wanted to do was stay on top of the hill until his master returned, his destiny was to go down the hill with the car. If he chose to fight the car and try to remain on the hill, then he would likely be strangled and would inevitably be dragged down the hill anyway. If he chose not to fight the car, he could run and jump onto the trunk and enjoy the ride to the bottom. Despite the wants, desires, dreams, or hopes the dog had of staying on top of the hill, the only sure thing was that he was going to the bottom. How he got there was up to him.

Riding on the trunk, the dog would be both exercising his free will and autonomy while at the same time yielding to necessity, yet if he chose to resist, his sorrow would be grossly compounded without changing the eventual outcome.

We humans have one distinct advantage over Fido. While we too may be tied to metaphorical leashes, our Creator has endowed us with something the dog is not so fortunate to have; that is the gift of reason. If we choose to do so, we can realize when we are the victims of unalterable circumstance and choose to adopt an attitude that allows us, and those around us, to cope with the situation in the best possible way. This philosophy is repeated in a common prayer, "Lord, grant me the Serenity to accept the things I cannot change, Courage to change the things I can, and Wisdom to know the difference."

Often times Life's journeys take us to places we never intended or wanted to go. How we behave along the way, what we learn and how we use that knowledge are the things that are important; not where we start or where we end.

With that being said, I find it odd and "unreasonable" that Evil fights when hopelessly outnumbered. That Evil continues to do evil even when there is no reward. And why, if something makes perfect sense, do politicians and police department administrators avoid it like the plague. Perhaps we are more like dogs than we realize.

The next parable to which I often heartlessly subject my students has reached cliché status. I am, however, still amazed at the number of students who hear it for the first time from little ole me. It is an age-old parable whose theme is human nature. That of course would be the parable of the Frog and the Scorpion.

In this parable, a dastardly, diabolical and sociopathic scorpion is pacing up and down on the shore of a river. He desperately wants to cross but cannot swim. He looks and looks for a way to cross, first upstream and then down, but to no avail. Then, alas, he spies a frog on the opposite bank.

The scorpion turns on all his charms for the altruistic, naïve, liberal, but well-meaning and basically good amphibian. He pleads with the frog to come and carry him across the river on his back. The frog, apprehensive of strangers, (especially those darn scorpions) is hesitant to come to the scorpion's aid and asks the scorpion, "How do I know I can trust you not to hurt me?"

The scorpion replies, "If I sting you while crossing the river, we will both drown. Where's the sense in that?"

The frog asks, "How do I know that you won't try to hurt me before we cross the river?"

The scorpion replies, "Because I want to get to the other side. If I hurt you before we cross, I will not attain my goal."

The frog asks, "How do I know that you will not hurt me when we reach the other side?"

The scorpion replies, "Because when we make it across the river, I will be too grateful to hurt you."

In the frog's mind the scorpion makes sense so he agrees to give him a ride. Half way across the river, the scorpion stings the frog. The frog is perplexed by this development and in his dying agony asks, "Why did you do that? Now we will both die."

The scorpion replies, "I don't know, I guess it's just my nature to sting frogs."

It is unfathomable to me why so many people are just like that frog. Human beings seem to be unique in the animal world in that even when our instincts scream to us that a person should be avoided, we will place ourselves in harm's way, or fail to contact the appropriate authorities or take the appropriate measures when others are in harm's way, for fear of being construed as insensitive, racist, or politically incorrect.

The frogs of the world live in their own separate reality that defies all reason and logic. Their deep-seated fear of violence and aggression causes them to cling insanely to illusions of peace and blindly ignore the repeating lessons of history. They fool themselves into believing that the scorpions of the world think the same way as the frogs. One glaring and infamous historical lesson occurred on September 30th, 1938 when the British Prime Minister, Neville Chamberlain, returned from a meeting with Chancellor Hitler. At that meeting the Munich Pact was signed and essentially gave away a good portion of Czechoslovakia to Germany with little input from the

Czechs. Mr. Chamberlain stood in front of 10 Downing St. and said, "My good friends, for the second time in our history, a British Prime Minister has returned from Germany bringing peace with honour. I believe it is peace for our time…Go home and get a nice quiet sleep."

In a lesser known speech to the British Parliament on October 3rd of the same year, Minister Chamberlain added, "With regard to Signor Mussolini,…I think that Europe and the world have reason to be grateful to the head of the Italian Government for his work in contributing to a peaceful solution." I think we all know how badly the scorpions stung the frogs in the years that followed.

For a more intimate and down to earth example, imagine a lone female who in an office building or apartment building summons the elevator. The elevator door opens and inside is a poorly dressed, unkempt, "suspicious" looking male subject that makes that hair on the back of her neck stand up and causes that queasy feeling in her stomach. How many women in today's society would look at the man, and then listen to their "gut feeling" and even though that gut feeling may be wrong, say "no thank you" and wait for the next elevator? How many women in today's society would take a deep breath and, ignoring all the red flags, climb into a closed metal box with a creature that by all instincts is quite likely a natural predator of women?

Sometimes violence is necessary, inevitable and unavoidable. You can be dragged into it on your leash, kicking and screaming and unprepared or you can hop onto the war chariot and ride gloriously into battle. Despite your wants, desires, dreams or hopes for peace, sometimes you cannot avoid being dragged down the hill into conflict. How you get there and what you do once you arrive is up to you.

Don't make the mistake of projecting your values, morals and thought processes into the minds of others. Don't ever think that there are not people out there who are stone cold Evil. Understand that there are people who will kill you just for the sick pleasure they derive from watching you bleed. There are people who will beat you, rob you, violate you and murder you for something as insignificant as the color of your skin or your hair, your politics, your religion, or your nationality and the list goes on and on.

It is senseless for decent people to try to understand the mind of Evil. Just accept that these people exist and do your best to avoid them or contain them. Don't be the frog who becomes convinced that the scorpion will change his nature because it makes sense to the frog. Don't let your natural aversion to violence give your enemy the edge he needs to defeat you. Evil is evil and that's all there is to it. To fully understand it you must become it and the cost of that is too high.

Following that line of reason, any laws or policies that are directed at the effects of Evil rather than at the Evil itself, will do minimal good for a free society. Banning the tools of Evil will do nothing to stop or contain the Evil. It will merely require Evil to adapt. Laws do not control anyone who chooses not to obey them. Laws are simply society's way of legitimizing the punishments for certain behaviors but they are not capable of controlling those behaviors.

Somehow we have grown to believe that if we make something illegal then people will quit doing it. Make guns illegal and people will quit shooting each other. If that were true, then making murder illegal would prevent it from happening, and we all know that is not the case. That is why legislating morality never works. Does making sodomy illegal do away with homosexuality? Should it? The best way to change the world is to raise your children to be moral, decent and good and to strive to that ideal yourself. For in a world full of moral, decent and good people, what need would we have for laws?

When the philosophy that drives our legislation is one that assumes that laws exist primarily to control people, then we begin the slide down the slippery slope to Totalitarianism. The only thing that can control a person is that person. Therefore, I feel the need to repeat that ideally, laws should only exist to provide a fair and just application of punishment for those who choose not to control themselves in accordance with the prescribed behavioral guidelines of the society in which they live.

Unfortunately, there are many politicians who in certain places have greatly limited the ways in which people may defend themselves, but so far you still have the basic right of self-defense. I would caution you to beware of those politicians and lobbyists that will try to convince you that there is honor in being a victim. Most of those politicians have never had the misfortune of being a victim. They live with armed security guards, surveillance cameras and large fences that virtually eliminate the threats that ordinary citizens face

5

every day. I am reminded of the words of Benjamin Franklin that have been repeated throughout the years by great champions of freedom from Abraham Lincoln to Ronald Reagan, "Those who would sacrifice freedom for security deserve neither."

Now let me tell you about a very unique community. This particular community is governed by a strict totalitarian dictator. In this community, no citizen is allowed to possess a weapon of any kind. The ruler tells the citizens when they can eat, when they can sleep and what they can watch on TV. The ruler strictly limits the number and type of tourists he allows into his society and censors everything that goes in or out. He governs the citizen's work and their recreation and literally controls every moment of their day. This community has the highest ratio of Police to citizens of any community in the world. This community was created for the sole purpose of eliminating crime yet it has the highest crime rate of any community on the face of the planet. This community exists many times over across the United States and the world abroad. It is called a prison.

One thing we may learn from prison is that no matter how strict the rules are and no matter how closely you watch Evil, you will never stop Evil from being Evil. Evil is its nature and it cannot change. No matter how much you love it, pet it, squeeze it, talk nice to it, teach it or want it not to be Evil; Evil will always be Evil. As much as good people cannot comprehend why some people are bad, evil people cannot comprehend why some people are good. Recognize that the two have always and will always coexist, and take steps to deal with Evil.

The ancient Chinese philosopher Confucius, is credited with saying, "The exemplary person is one who seeks harmony, not sameness" and that, "it is the person who extends order in the world, not order that extends the person." While many have twisted this concept to apply it to socialist endeavors, its core truth is one from which we can all benefit. If we endeavor to reach a harmony with those with whom we exist rather than to force one another into a sameness, the result is a metaphorical symphony rather than a monotone; where individuals are free to be themselves, not to the detriment of one another, but to the benefit of all. If your behavior does not adversely affect me, or any of the other good people in the world, why should I have any interest in forcing you to change it?

In The gospel of Thomas, Jesus Christ said, "I have cast fire upon the world. Look, I watch until it blazes." While many take the term "Fire" to mean his Word, perhaps that fire is the differences that manifest themselves across the races, religions and countries of the world. If you believe in God as the Creator of all and the ultimate source of morality and humanity (which incidentally, I do) then you must admit that God created all the races and peoples of the world. If he is in fact the all-knowing, all-seeing Creator, then he must have had a reason for creating the world the way that he did. While fire can be both a detriment and a benefit depending on how it is put to use, the same may be said of humanity. If we seek to maintain a harmony rather than a sameness, then the Fire will be a life giving warmth rather than a destructive force and perhaps that was God's intent all along.

My final literary reference will be a bit more uplifting. Again the piece I have chosen is one that has been repeated time and time again. Its poignancy may not be apparent at first but if you take the time to reflect upon it, perhaps you will realize how grand an intellect it took to create such a masterpiece. To fully appreciate it, I must add that the author, William Ernest Henley, was plagued by illness for most of his life, which among other things resulted in the amputation of a limb. When he wrote the following poem, he was in an English hospital suffering from tuberculosis. His illness would eventually result in his death in his early fifties. As you contemplate this work, compare the author's attitude to the prevailing attitudes in our current society and ask yourself if you would have the strength to view the world as did Mr. Henley. The title of the poem is Invictus. (Which in Latin is pronounced in-WIK-toos.) The word translates to (masculine, singular, nominative form of) unconquered, unconquerable, invincible.

<u>Invictus</u>

Out of the night that covers me,
Black as the Pit from pole to pole,
I thank whatever gods may be
For my unconquerable soul.

In the fell clutch of circumstance
I have not winced nor cried aloud.
Beneath the bludgeonings of chance
My head is bloodied, but unbowed.

Beyond this place of wrath and tears
Looms but the Horror of the shade,
And yet the menace of the years
Finds, and shall find, me unafraid.

It matters not how strait the gate,
How charged with punishments the scroll,
I am the master of my fate:
I am the captain of my soul.

- William Ernest Henley

Chapter 2

The Civilized Mind

The Greek philosopher Socrates posed the question, "What is Justice?" After hearing all the answers from his students and deciding that those answers were less than adequate, he offered the conclusion that "Justice is a well-ordered soul." While I do not disagree with that lofty assumption I would like to offer a differing, perhaps augmentative, perspective. I believe that Justice is the inevitable product of the Civilized Mind.

The civilized mind is one that is not plagued by hatred, anger, politics, or jealousy. It is not swayed by selfish ambition nor is it a slave to those irrational emotions. That's not to say that in the civilized mind these things do not exist for that would be unattainable at this point in our evolution. It is to say, rather, that in the civilized mind these things are recognized for what they are, they are controlled, and their effects are attenuated by rational wisdom.

A clue that you are dealing with an uncivilized mind is that in the face of factual argument and reason, the uncivilized mind resorts to emotional attack and accusation rather than the defense of logic and empirical evidence. I expect this behavior from my three-year-old son. Whenever I explain to him what is going to happen if he does something he is not supposed to do or that he cannot have something that he desperately wants, he thinks for a moment and then says, "You're mean."

We see much the same tactics from any number of different groups. If you use reason to show some people that their position on a particular matter or their reasoning might be flawed, they often resort to the rhetorical equivalent of, "You're mean." Another popular debate strategy for this type of intellect is the "I'm rubber, you're glue" defense. At that point in the debate you may as well quit. You have won and will likely never convince the other party of it because they are obviously unwilling or unable to comprehend.

Likewise, in our current environment concerning an impending attack on the terrorist, dictatorial regime in Iraq, we see news footage everyday where pacifists and anti-war demonstrators call the U.S. racist for threatening war with Iraq.

Now if a rational person were to look at the situation they would find that accusation to be quite odd. The United States is arguably one of the most (if not the most) integrated societies that the world has ever known. Virtually anyone from any country or race, religion etc. can come here and be free to make of themselves whatever they wish. Iraq, on the other hand, is predominately of one race and one religion where outsiders literally need to fear for their very lives by just being there. That, my friends, is the definition of racism.

Now, I am not saying that if someone opposes war with Iraq that they are automatically an imbecile or are uncivilized. I merely point to some of the arguments being made as being indicative of people who think with the crowd because that's what their particular crowd is thinking. Logic and reason are as strange to those types of people as calculus is to a monkey. I will never slight someone for their opinion as long as they legitimize it by knowing why they have it. I can "agree to disagree" and leave it at that. People who try to force their opinions on others are to be feared.

The aforementioned philosophies find a natural place in police work. I tell my students in the "use of force" class, that once a suspect is under control, the confrontation is over. There is often a lot of unused energy after a physical battle or pursuit that officers channel into an "ass-whippin'" for the suspect. Emotions like hate and anger can easily worm their way into our consciousness and if we are not careful, they can cause us to lose control. We need to train ourselves ahead of time to find a more acceptable outlet for that energy. Too many otherwise good police officers get fired, sued or arrested simply because they did not have a channel for that energy.

A good analogy may be found in the game of football. Football is by its very nature a violent game. The players regularly muster violent, angry energy to attack the opposing team but for the most part are conditioned that when the opposing player is down and the ref blows the whistle, the violence ends. Once the quarterback is sacked, it is quite rare to see the "sacker" continue to beat the quarterback until his energy is expended. In the rare cases in which that happens, someone is usually there to break up the fight and the players are disciplined.

It would be ridiculous to suggest that the players should first attempt to reason with the quarterback to get him to relinquish the ball to the opposing team without all that pesky violence. Football games would take forever if teams had to dispatch diplomats and issue ultimatums before finally reaching a consensus on taking action. That is not the way the game is played.

Likewise, when a cowboy in a calf-roping contest breaks out of the gate to pursue the calf, he has no hatred for the animal…he just does his job. He pursues the calf, ropes it, tackles it, slams it to the ground and then ties it up. Once the animal is secured, he throws his hands in the air to signal he is done and the time clock stops.

When pursuing criminals, we as police must adopt these attitudes. It is the criminal's job in the law enforcement rodeo to run away from the police as fast as possible. It is the police officers job to chase them, slam them and handcuff them (rope them). When the job is completed, the game is over and that's all there is to it.

Sometimes there is a personal conflict between officer and perpetrator and that's fine until it clouds the officer's judgment. That's when the officer has to realize that he may have to "tag out" and let another officer handle the problem if possible. There is no perpetrator in the world worth going to jail for.

There's nothing wrong with being mad. Anger is a perfectly natural, necessary and acceptable human emotion in its proper parameters. Use the anger to channel the energy you have to accomplish the task at hand. It will help you run faster, fight longer and hit harder when the circumstances warrant. However, if you let it control you instead of controlling and using it, your rage will eventually get you into trouble. Therefore, in conclusion I submit the following;

The Civilized Mind is a prism that refracts the light of humanity.

The Civilized Mind is secure in its beliefs and can allow others to be secure in theirs.

The Civilized Mind is kind and caring, open and rational, and capable of peaceful coexistence.

The Civilized Mind realizes the value of emotions without becoming a slave to them.

The Civilized Mind is not plagued by regrets for past actions or remorse for lost opportunities.

The Civilized Mind knows that there is no malice in simple disagreement, no threat in non-conformity, and that being an individual means being individual, and every individual is an integral part of Humanity as a whole.

The Civilized Mind cannot hold a grudge.

The Civilized Mind is color blind.

The Civilized Mind does not prefer violence and is in fact docile and peaceful by nature, but recognizes that sometimes violence is necessary and unavoidable to protect the innocent and contain Evil.

The Civilized Mind has the wisdom to realize when violence is necessary and the fortitude to perpetrate that violence in order to protect the greater good.

In short, Justice is the water that flows from the fountain of The Civilized Mind.

Chapter 3

Smackdown

Now that we have dispensed with all the foofy, philosophical stuff, let's move on to something a bit more concrete. One of the necessary and perhaps most important aspects of searching for Evil, is violence. One of the most difficult things to make people understand, especially when those people are by nature non-violent, is that violence is sometimes the only language that Evil understands. Certain forms of Evil cannot be talked to, reasoned with, or rehabilitated. Certain forms of Evil can only be subdued and contained.

The law enforcement philosophy of use of force (or violence) is simple but should be explained. We have a use of force continuum (or confrontational continuum to be politically correct and as euphemistic as possible). In my department, the current use of force continuum is as follows:

1. Officer presence
2. Verbal commands
3. Empty hand control techniques for passive resistors
4. Chemical agents
5. Empty hand control techniques for active aggressors
6. Impact weapon
7. Lethal force

In other departments, the use of force continuum may differ or may be phrased differently but will likely be similar to ours. Over the last few years, some departments have also included stun devices. Ours is not one of them.

One of my fellow instructors, who is currently a lieutenant in our department, uses a philosophy he calls "measured aggressiveness". It means simply that you implement a level of force that is appropriate to the situation at hand. No more and definitely no less.

When police officers use force, they should in theory use the maximum amount of the particular level of force they have chosen. What that means is that if I am authorized to hit you, then I hit you as hard as I can. I don't give you a little slap and see if that works and then move up from there. If I am authorized to spray you with a chemical agent, I don't spray just a little and see if you comply, I spray you with the whole can.

If I am authorized to shoot you, I don't fire a warning shot, then aim for your pinky etc.; I aim for center mass and fire. If that doesn't stop you I will aim for your head and I will shoot until I perceive that the threat is gone. That is the standard operating procedure for use of force encounters.

An officer's use of force must necessarily be greater than the force that is being used against him or her. Theoretically, if you use the same amount of force as your adversary, then the confrontation is a draw. In confrontations with Evil, a draw is unacceptable. In every conflict there is a victim and a victor. Sheepdogs have to be the victor. You should always fight with one goal in mind and that is to win. The only way to win is to control the adversary and stop the aggression. The best, safest and most effective way to do that is to use more force against Evil than Evil is using against you. The longer a confrontation continues, the greater the likelihood that all those involved will become injured. Therefore, a quick and forceful smackdown is the safest for all involved. (When considering force on the low end of the scale that rule is not so apparent or important. The higher the level of force, the more important that rule becomes.)

What civilians must realize is that any confrontation involving a police officer is an armed confrontation. At least one person in the confrontation (the officer) has a lethal weapon. If the officer is somehow incapacitated then the officer must assume that his assailant will disarm him. It is therefore feasible to postulate that what constitutes deadly force against a police officer may actually be less than what constitutes deadly force against someone who is unarmed. Can a police officer who has just been inundated by a chemical weapon or knocked nearly unconscious by blunt force trauma, afford to wait and see if his attacker is going to leave or if he is going to attempt to use the officer's weapon to "finish the job"? We cannot afford to wait and see if Evil is going to kill us after we can longer defend ourselves. We don't get the luxury of do-overs.

There are many lethal weapons in the world that are not firearms. If you deploy a lethal weapon against an officer, or anyone for that matter, then that person is allowed to deploy a lethal weapon

14

in self-defense. If you approach me and threaten me with a weapon, (a rock, a brick, a tire iron, a baseball bat, a knife, etc. etc.) or something that I perceive to be a weapon (like a realistic toy gun), then you can expect me to shoot you. I will keep shooting you until I perceive the threat to be eliminated and I will be justified. (Just because my weapon may have a longer range, better accuracy, or more power than yours, doesn't mean that I am not allowed to use it.) If you die as the result of your actions, tough titties. If not, that's ok too. That rule is the same for anyone regardless of whether or not they are a police officer. Everyone in the United States, thus far, has a right to defend themselves.

Though the topic of the use of force could occupy an entire volume, I feel that I have presented the bare basics. Too often, officers either do not know or are not capable of committing the appropriate level of violence. Many officers tend to use the least amount of force available. They often pay for that mistake with unnecessary injury or even with their lives.

That is why education and training are so important. I will always prefer diplomacy to violence and would rather talk for twenty minutes if it will avoid a twenty second fight. Sometimes, however, Evil gives us no choice. When it comes time to lay the smackdown on Evil, you must know what you are allowed to do and you must do it without hesitation to the fullest of your capabilities. The moment a perpetrator you are placing under arrest pulls away, he is resisting. For your safety and theirs, they need to be controlled both immediately and powerfully. That prevents the fight from escalating, thereby keeping injuries minimal, and keeps the encounter safer for everyone involved.

With this basic concept explained in much the same way (though a bit abbreviated) as I explain to my students, I will recount an incident that occurred with one of my trainees. This incident replays itself across the nation on a daily basis and can be seen regularly on the police reality TV shows.

I had just finished giving a soliloquy not dissimilar to the preceding paragraphs when my trainee and I were dispatched to a domestic violence call. I repeated my admonitions that should someone need to be taken into custody, control should be established quickly. The trainee said she understood. Theory and practice are often two different animals.

When we arrived at the apartment that was the epicenter of the disturbance, we were met outside by a lone female whom I recognized. She was a crack addict who had a history of fighting with police. She said she had been arguing with her boyfriend and wanted us to do something about it.

We walked upstairs to the apartment to consult with the other half of the dispute and interviewed them one at a time. The man was calm, lucid and melancholy while the woman was excited and appeared to be under the influence of something. After my trainee had determined that the female was the primary aggressor, she decided to place her under arrest.

By that time we had moved to the outside stairway. My trainee told Evil to put her hands against the wall and that she was under arrest. That information did not sit well with Evil. Evil backed away and began exhibiting obvious signs of resistance. I sat back, acting as a cover officer, and was glad to be evaluating what had the potential to be a good performance.

The officer tried at first to reason with Evil to no avail. I hinted that Evil should be taken into custody and reminded the trainee of our conversation only minutes before. She nodded her head and grabbed Evil's wrist. Evil pulled away. I was expecting a smackdown, but the trainee just kept the quaint little tug-o-war going.

Evil began to escalate the encounter while the trainee played "catch-up". Often when I have a trainee who is undergoing a stressful encounter, I will attempt to increase that stress level by yelling commands or doing whatever seems appropriate to the situation at hand. At first glance, this may seem cruel, but it is a vital training tool and gives the trainee considerable insight during the post-encounter debriefing. In this case, Evil began yelling and fighting and the trainee just kept using minimal force to counteract Evil rather than maximum force to contain and control Evil.

The encounter blossomed into a full-fledged wrestling match where Evil began banging its own head into the concrete stairs, while the trainee impotently tried to contain it. At that point I had to step in and Evil was immediately subdued with no further injury to herself or to anyone else. My trainee stated in the post-encounter debriefing that she now understood what I meant. Nonetheless, she earned a failing grade that day. (Grades are not given, they are earned.) My only hope was that when she was tested again at a time when I wasn't around to assist, she would not fail.

#3.2 Evil Avalanche

When dealing with anyone over whom you have legal authority there is a general rule that many people seem to forget. For your authority to be recognized and respected it must be evenly and fairly enforced. This concept applies not only to the police officer dealing with Evil, but also to parents dealing with children or to UN security councils dealing with rogue nations etc. etc. If the authority figure sets a rule or a guideline but then does not enforce it, the authority figure becomes impotent. Think back to the last time you saw an unruly child in a grocery store or a mall. The mother tells the child that if he doesn't quiet down, they are going to leave. The child doesn't quiet down and the mother doesn't leave. That tells the child that mommy has no real authority and does not need to be obeyed. The rest of the world works in exactly the same simple way. Perhaps if our politicians understood this, little embarrassments like the Viet Nam "conflict" would have had a different outcome.

If you point your gun at Evil and say, "Stop or I'll shoot," when you have no intention or justification to shoot, what will you do when Evil refuses to comply? If you don't have a plan "B" then you are screwed. What you are doing in essence is saying, "Stop, or I'll be forced to tell you to stop again." Since Evil perceives no legitimate consequence for failing to comply, what motivation for compliance is there? When we tell our children that if they don't eat their dinner, they cannot watch TV and then we allow them to watch TV after not eating dinner, is it any wonder that they become unruly? When we tell Saddam Hussein to get rid of his weapons or we will tell him to get rid of his weapons again, what are we thinking? There is a time for talk and a time for a smackdown.

When you are exercising your lawful authority over Evil, do not be afraid to plainly state the consequences for failing to comply with your lawful order. Give warnings if you like, but if you give a "final" warning, be prepared to follow through. There is no place in the exercising of authority for threats, there are only promises, and you are only as good as your word.

A prime example of this philosophy in action was on a loud party call that I had to respond to. There was no backup available so I had to proceed to the fifth floor of the apartment building to handle the call by myself. The party had spilled out of an apartment and was occupying half of the entire fifth floor. It was out of hand. I located the person throwing the party and informed him that we had gotten a complaint. I explained to him the law that he was breaking and that he would get one warning. I explained in certain terms that if I received another call to the location and the party was still in violation, then he would be charged accordingly. He stated that he understood and I left.

Surprise, surprise, surprise. An hour or so later I got a return call. The party was even bigger and louder than before. When I located the owner, he was even drunker than before and instead of being Mr. Agreeable, he turned out to be downright Evil. I won't bore you with the details but it wasn't long before Evil was under arrest for a panoply of violations of the state criminal code. I went to handcuff him and of course he resisted so I slammed him to the floor. About that time Evil junior showed up and jumped on me. I couldn't fight both of them and since I had one side of the handcuffs on Evil, I quickly put the other on Evil junior. Then I separated myself from the fray.

That maneuver apparently took them by surprise because they quit fighting. I picked up Evil and Junior was forced to follow. I walked him over to the stairs and instructed them both to walk down in front of me. Junior grabbed onto the handrail and refused to move and Evil egged him on. I told them both that if they didn't walk down the stairs, I would have to force them down the stairs. They didn't believe me and challenged my authority. I offered them a final warning that did not change their demeanor. I then grabbed Evil by the hair and dragged him down the first flight of stairs. Like the dog chained to the bumper of the car, Junior had to follow or risk injuring himself and his father without changing the eventual outcome.

They stumbled and fell to the first landing and started cussing at me and threatening me. I picked Evil up by the head and gave him a chance to walk down the next flight of stairs on his own. I believe his response was something like, "F@#% You." I made good on my promise and precipitated another Evil avalanche. After the third verse of this song, Evil and Evil Junior both underwent an extreme attitude reversal and walked the remaining flights of stairs with no more resistance. From that point forward they were perfectly compliant and I never had another problem out of them. That, my friends, is the definition of discipline. While I do not necessarily recommend throwing your children down the stairs, the underlying principle is the same.

Something that is always hard for anyone to do is to remain emotionless when making good on your promises. It is always a good idea to avoid name-calling or any other behavior that may make people think that you are personally involved with the situation. Remember, it's not personal. It's business.

#3.3 Happy New Year

Oddly enough, I have another story that involves stairs. It is an incident that occurred one New Year's Eve when our shift was running a little short. Most of our units were making arrests or answering other calls so I had to handle the domestic dispute without even the faintest hope of any backup. I was hoping that the situation could be handled quickly with no action taken. That was not the case.

When I arrived, I spoke with the complainants. They were a man and wife who had been out for a New Year's Eve celebration. They returned home to find that their roommate had broken a window and some furniture in an alcohol induced frenzy. They apparently had had difficulties from him before and this was the "last straw". They were adamant about wanting to prosecute and wanting him out of the apartment because they were afraid that they might become the targets of his violent behavior.

I tried not to let my irritation show as I informed the rather muscular, tattooed and shirtless individual that he was under arrest. He turned away from me without saying a word and put both arms out perpendicular to his body as if preparing to perform a swan dive. I seized the opportunity to get one handcuff on him and as I was manipulating his arms to get the other handcuff on, the fight began. I would like to note for those who may not be aware that most fights begin when you put your hands on Evil.

We wrestled our way to the doorway of the second story apartment. Our little dance was precariously close to the concrete stairs leading to the ground floor. Consequently, it wasn't long before the fight went down the concrete stairs to the ground floor. Thankfully, I landed on top of Evil rather than vice-versa. We struggled back to our feet and began slamming each other into walls and doors. I still had a good hold on the handcuffed arm, which may be the only reason that I eventually won the altercation. I remember seeing several apartment doors open and then shut again despite my winded grunts for assistance. It's always reassuring when the citizens ignore a police officer in need.

At one point, I had Evil at a distinct disadvantage. I was on top of him with both of his arms twisted and pinned behind him. His face and mouth were very bloody and I could see that he was about to try to spit in my face. Like a good pO-lice, I had my leather gloves on and I promptly freed up one hand to put it over his face. He tried to bite me but he only bit glove. A few good downward thrusts with that hand caused his head to strike the concrete hard enough that it fazed him momentarily. It was just long enough for me to use my last bit of energy to get him handcuffed completely and turn him face down on the concrete. He was still struggling but it was then much easier for me to hold him down.

After taking a minute or two to regain my strength and catch my breath I was able to blurt out over the radio that I needed another unit. There were none available but there was a supervisor nearby who started right away. The supervisor was a very large female officer. She was a pretty good supervisor but not well equipped for street work. She arrived quickly but could not gain access to the gated entry of the apartment complex. She was just about to ram the gate with her patrol car when a resident opened the gate for her.

By the time she arrived I was so exhausted that I could not feel my arms and I felt as though I was about to pass out. She asked what I needed her to do. I told her to just sit on Evil while I regained my strength. Since she weighed about 350 pounds, sitting was enough. After a few minutes, I had regained sufficient strength to take control of my prisoner and transport him to the public hospital to get the thirty some stitches required to stop the bleeding in his face and have the concrete contusions on the back of his head treated. Evil didn't say much after being subdued.

I need to make the comment here that wrestling with a perpetrator alone is generally not a good idea. In this case it worked out okay, but it could just as well have turned horribly wrong. If you are not 110% sure you will prevail in a hand-to-hand confrontation, then it should be avoided. Police have the habit of not wanting to run from a fight. It's not the macho thing to do but sometimes it is the smart thing to do. The basic premise of the "Contact and Cover" principle is to have at least one cover officer. If you are the only officer there, then sometimes it is better to be "cover" than "contact". There's no perp worth dying for. Remember, if Evil lives to run away, then he will go to jail another day. A tactical withdrawal should always be an open option.

Furthermore, when engaged in hand-to-hand combat, properly executed sensory overload on your adversary will facilitate your victory. What that means is that you cause as much sensory stimulation as you can for your adversary and he will become confused and then weak, allowing you to take control. Do not strike an adversary in the same place over and over again. He will focus on that spot in his body and will become numb to the strikes. The immediate effect of the repeated pounding is minimal, but hours or days later, there may be heavy contusions or even broken bones and ruptured organs which will undoubtedly be pointed to as "police brutality".

Instead, strike in multiple locations all over the subject's body and use verbal commands and any other implement lawfully at your disposal to provide the maximum amount of sensory input. When your adversary's brain attempts to process all the information coming in from all the different impact sights and other areas of input (like eyes and ears), his brain literally overloads like a 5 amp circuit under a 20 amp current. Victory is normally achieved much more swiftly and without as much risk of severe or long-term injury. Our specific intent is not to wound or to punish (though they may be secondary effects), rather, **our goal is to control.**

One more thing… While stitching up Evil the doctor said, "Man, must've been a good fight. What happened to the other guy?"

I just said, "Oh, he came out all right."

Evil didn't say a word.

#3.4 Anybody Home?

Recently, I was talking with a lieutenant in our department. He was a marine for a few years before joining our department. After spending four to five years as a street cop, he worked for about nine years on the SWAT team before returning to the patrol division as a shift supervisor. During our conversation, he paused for a moment to think and then said, "I just realized something. In my entire career I have only been in a handful of situations that were scary enough for me to want to call for backup. You were there for two of those and both times we came out okay. That's pretty good."

One of the times he was speaking of involved a generic, knock-down, drag-out fight between the two of us and a representative of Evil who quite possibly could have been the twin brother of The Incredible Hulk (though they probably had different fathers since our guy's skin wasn't green). That fight ended with a few bruises on all parties, some ripped uniforms, and a couple of big dents in the fender of my patrol car.

This story is about the other time. We happened to be working beats that were adjacent to one another and, as a result, often responded to serious calls together. (That made us beat partners.) Our dispatcher directed us to start for an address in an affluent neighborhood. The anonymous caller only said that there was a woman in "distress" at the house at that address. There was no further information.

He was the primary unit and I was the backup unit. We parked our patrol cars at the bottom of the long and winding driveway in the hopes that we could approach the house on foot and unnoticed. The house was on a large, dark, wooded lot and was not visible from the road. The driveway wound around the front of the house from left to right before terminating in a garage on the far right side. We crept quietly up the driveway, not wanting to announce ourselves to any potential Evil until we were ready. About half way up the driveway, there was a small parking pad. On the parking pad was a car that had a broken windshield and a smashed out side window. The glass on the ground led us to believe that the damage was fresh.

The scene was eerily quiet and there were no lights inside or outside of the house. We slowly worked our way to the front door.

Since we had not used our flashlights at all, by the time we got to the front door, our eyes had adjusted to the darkness well enough to see that the front door was slightly ajar. The area the house was in was a very deep valley. That meant that even if we had decided to call for backup at that point, our portable radios would not have transmitted from that particular location.

We carefully pushed open the door. There was a faint light coming from an unseen room on the main level that allowed us to make out the general floor plan of the area immediately inside the front door. The foyer to the "Brady Bunch" era, ranch style home was large and opened into several other rooms. In the middle of the foyer was a staircase leading to the full basement. The opening for the staircase was surrounded by a solid wood wall about four feet tall. The stairs went from our right, down to our left.

On the right edge of the foyer was hallway that led away to some other part of the house. We surveyed the situation for a moment and decided to announce our presence. The primary unit called out, "Police…is anyone here?"

The response we got was the unexpected barking and snarling of two rather large Doberman pincers who came to greet us from that long hallway. We met their barks and raised them a snarl. The dogs moved away from us, around to the other side of the wall that surrounded the staircase. At some point while we were directing our attention toward the dogs, a young man (early twenties) poked his head around the corner from the hall to the foyer. He yelled something like, "What are you doin' in my house?"

The primary officer engaged the alleged resident while I covered the still snarling canines. The man was visibly nervous and agitated and screamed for us to leave as he ran for the stairs right in front of us. The primary officer grabbed the man by the arm and the fight was on. The sight of the struggle made the dogs very angry. They both began advancing on our position. Meanwhile, the man was dragging my partner down the stairs.

My partner screamed, "Watch the dogs!" and continued his struggle on the stairs. At times like those you have to trust your partner's abilities and follow his lead. Circumstance had dictated what my partner's job would be in this encounter. My partner dictated what my job would be. That's the way police work. I concentrated my attention away from the fight and toward the two dogs I now refer to as "Zeus and Apollo", after the old TV series Magnum PI. I drew a mental line between the dogs and me. If they crossed it, they died.

My partner continued struggling with the man. I heard the both of them crash into the hollow core door at the foot of the staircase. I moved to the top of the stairs to where I could see both the staircase and the dogs. My partner was out of sight at that point, so I went sideways down the stairs. The dogs didn't follow.

Just inside the door at the foot of the stairs, the basement floor had given my partner the stable platform he needed to subdue Evil. After he was handcuffed, we pulled him to his feet. I held onto Evil while my partner checked the rest of the basement. In one room, there was a young female hiding in the shadows who offered no resistance. In another room, behind the air conditioning and heating unit, was another young man who was also trying to hide. When our search was complete, we had five rather suspicious looking characters in custody that had all been haphazardly concealed throughout the basement.

All five subjects were rounded up, as were the multitude of controlled substances lying about that they had each been ingesting (LSD, mushrooms, cocaine etc.). The man who had dragged us down the stairs turned out to be the son of the man who owned the residence. His dad was away on business so Evil thought he would take the opportunity to throw a little party.

The odd twist was that when we finally contacted the father, he informed us that his son was not allowed in that house because of his criminal tendencies. In addition to the multitude of drug and obstruction charges we had on Evil, the father prosecuted him for trespassing.

After the investigation was completed, we could only assume who had made the initial 911 call and why.

#3.5 Encore

In every jurisdiction, there are, over the course of history, certain individuals who embody the term "revolving door justice system". These individuals are arrested time and time again for whatever their preferred Evil may be. They are jailed, they get out, they commit crimes, they get caught, they go to jail again...and the cycle repeats.

One such individual came to my attention one night when I performed a maneuver I call the "Evil Turnaround". That maneuver exploits the inherent guilt and paranoia that certain forms of Evil cannot seem to shake. The mechanics of the maneuver are this: I simply drive slowly down the main road that runs through my beat. Since it is the main road, most of the Evil traversing my beat drives on that road at one time or another. I wait for a group of cars to pass me in the opposite direction, then, I make an abrupt and deliberate u-turn as if I have a purpose and I speed up to join the group of cars that just passed.

"What could that possibly accomplish?" you ask. Well, if one of those guilt-ridden, paranoid, representatives of Evil is in that group of cars, he will often take evasive action. I have experienced only moderate success with this maneuver, but it is fun to employ when things are slow and I am out "fishing". The most common reaction of Evil is that he simply makes an abrupt turn into the nearest street or parking lot to see if I am following him. A less common reaction that I have only seen once or twice, is that Evil immediately tries to flee in his car.

If a car immediately speeds up and takes evasive action, then that's all I need to tell me that he's up to something. Most Evil is a little more subtle and requires some extra work. If I see a car that seems to make one of those abrupt turns off the main roadway, I normally pass right by the vehicle. I make it a point not to look at the car after it turns and act as if I am going on my merry way. Then, I either watch my rear view mirror or turn off the roadway ahead and wait to see if the same car returns to its original path. If it does, I get suspicious.

On one night in particular, I hadn't tried the Evil Turnaround in a long time so I thought I would give it a shot at the next available opportunity. Much to my amazement, on the first try I got a bite. I turned around on a group of cars heading north (out of the city) and almost immediately, an older model, beat-up, Lincoln Town Car made an abrupt left turn into residential district.

I nonchalantly drove by the street where it had turned. Out of the corner of my eye, I noticed that the car had pulled into a driveway of a vacant house and had quickly turned out its headlights. I knew that particular house was vacant because I had been to calls in that neighborhood before and had noticed that it had a "For Rent" sign on it that for over six months had apparently attracted no one.

That particular neighborhood had no streetlights and was very, very dark. I took advantage of that darkness and sped around the block to creep up behind Evil. I parked my car a few houses away from where I had seen the Town Car park and I got out to approach on foot.

It only took me a minute to get to a vantage point where I could see the silhouette of the Town Car as it was backlit by the streetlights from the main road. I could also see the shadow of a man standing next to the Town car. I watched as he cautiously walked out toward the main road as if he were looking for someone (like me). Then he hurried back to his Town Car and jumped in the driver's seat.

That was my cue to run back to my patrol car and jump in my driver's seat. I drove with my lights off, back toward the suspected Evil just in time to see the Town Car pulling out of the driveway, heading back toward the main road. I must have startled him when I came up behind him in the patrol car and turned on all my lights at once. He slammed on the brakes and stopped in the middle of the road, just before reaching the main road.

He exited his car quickly and so did I. All those little alarms were going off in my head as he limped around the front of his car and opened the hood. I ran around the back of my car to approach him from the passenger side. I could tell he was still in front of his car but I could not see him since the hood was raised. As I got closer to his car, I yelled for him to step out where I could see him and to put his hands up. He did neither.

I moved closer and was fully expecting an assault. As Evil came into view, he was fiddling around with something under the hood. I challenged him again to put his hands up. He did not acknowledge me and kept fiddling. I closed the distance between us to make contact and told him in no uncertain terms that if he made any sudden moves, I would shoot him. I crept up behind him and grabbed his shirt collar forcing him head first into the engine compartment. I told him to give up his hands and he finally complied. I quickly handcuffed him and sat him on the pavement.

I asked what he was doing and he made up some story that was 100% bovine excrement. After all the investigating was done, the only Evil I could find was that he had a suspended drivers license, no insurance, and he smelled like he had been smoking crack.

He was a very large man and I was glad that he chose not to fight. In retrospect and for reasons that will be clear in the next few paragraphs, I think that his decision not to fight me was based upon the fact that he was recovering from both a recently sprained ankle and a stab wound to the chest that was about a week old. Nonetheless, I arrested him, impounded his car, and took him to jail, with nothing more than a little unused adrenaline.

A few weeks later, I was patrolling in the same area and was stopped for a red light on another side street at its intersection with that same main roadway. There was very little traffic on the road at that time of night, so I was surprised when I heard the sound of screeching tires. I looked in my rear view mirror and saw the headlights of a very large car barreling toward my rear end. The car stopped about two feet prior to impacting my bumper. I sat as if nothing had happened and watched as the light blue Lincoln Town Car made a right turn. The car went down the road about fifty yards and turned right, into the parking lot of a closed real estate office.

By that time, my light turned green. I nonchalantly made a left turn and as soon as I was out of sight of the aforementioned parking lot, I made a u-turn. I went around the back side of an apartment building and got out to surveil the parking lot and the car that had almost hit me.

I got out my binoculars and watched as the driver of the car walked around the parking lot looking for something (like me). It was at that point that I had the startling realization that that was the same guy I had arrested weeks earlier in a spookily similar situation.

I called my beat partner on the phone and told him that I was getting ready to stop a guy that I thought might try to run. I gave him the description and even remembered Evil's name. The officer I had called immediately recognized the name as someone that he and other officers had chased several nights earlier. He had been driving that same light blue Town Car and had driven off the roadway into some muddy grass while trying to flee from officers. That night he put up a good little fight before being smacked down by at least four beat officers. His car had been impounded and he had been taken to jail that night as well.

Anyway, it wasn't long before that crappy old Town Car was back on the main roadway, heading north. I snuck in behind him and blended into traffic, waiting for the backup unit. When the backup unit advised me that he was close, I went ahead and activated my emergency equipment. As expected, the appearance of blue lights was all Evil needed to prompt him to take off.

He blew through a red light and turned left down a side street. His car would not go very fast, but it was fast enough to be dangerous. He negotiated a few more curves and ran over a few curbs before I realized that he was heading back to his own house.

He made the last sharp left turn into his driveway with two patrol cars hot on his tail. He parked precariously in the middle of his carport and leapt out of his car to try his luck on foot in the yards of his own neighborhood.

I yelled his name as I ran after him telling him that it was useless to try to run. He ignored me (surprise) and ran into his back yard and then into the adjacent back yard. I caught him just as he was about to jump a chain link fence. I grabbed him by the neck and slung him to the ground. He tried to get backup so I jumped on him and the fight was on. My backup was right behind me and between the two of us, we had him handcuffed in a matter of seconds.

I was trying to catch my breath before telling our dispatcher that he was in custody. Simultaneously, my dispatcher began dispatching cars to handle a 29 (fight) called in by a resident of the same neighborhood. The caller told dispatch that there were some men fighting in his back yard. He couldn't see them but he could hear the fight and "…it sounded like a good one." I told dispatch to disregard the fight call, that it was a result of the chase, and that Evil was in custody. Once again, his car was impounded and he went to jail for a laundry list of charges.

Let us now move forward a month or two to a Friday night just before 2300 hours. I was working a part time security job on my off-night and was listening to the police radio. I heard a unit pull out on a 54 (suspicious person) in a shopping center that was a couple of blocks away from my location. It was near shift change and I knew that there would probably not be any backup available for him so I casually started for his location.

Within minutes, the officer blurted out that he was in pursuit of the suspicious person. Following his announcement, the radio became clogged with all sorts of units trying to transmit. Some were asking for a repeat of his location while others were verbally acknowledging the pursuit. The result was that no one could transmit clearly, including the officer in pursuit.

I went in the direction that the officer had said he was going. Within moments, I found his patrol car with the blue lights on. His car was stopped on the roadway near a Ford Taurus station wagon that had crashed into a tree. Both cars were empty. I jumped out of my car and ran into the front yard where the wrecked car was. I yelled for the officer but heard no response. I detected a hint of pepper spray wafting through the air and assumed that they were close.

I walked toward the rear of the house and noticed that the smell of pepper spray was getting stronger. I yelled out again and heard a muffled response from the woods to my right. I ran into a kudzu patch and down into a ravine. At the bottom of the small ravine was a creek that was about eight inches deep. As soon as I got to the creek, I could see the officer about twenty yards ahead of me. The officer was coughing and was struggling to handcuff a rather large, shadowy piece of Evil.

I ran toward the officer and made it about ten feet before I discovered that the creek became about three feet deep. I was running on adrenaline at the time, so my unexpected bath only slowed me down for a second. I ran up to Evil and gave him a swift kick in the ribs. That was enough to make Evil put his hands behind his back.

I finished the handcuffing job that the first officer had started. That officer fell to the side to recover from his massive energy expenditure and the residual effects of his own pepper spray. As is often the case, the pepper spray had a greater effect on the officer than the perpetrator.

I dragged Evil through the creek, carefully retracing my steps to make sure Evil experienced the same thing leaving as I did getting there. When I got him into the light of the front yard, I recognized him as the same scumbag we had fought so many times before. At least he had the sense to get rid of the Town Car.

He was a classic example of the kind of Evil that never learns. He does not think rationally and he has a steadfast rule; no matter what, he always fights the police. Guys like him are not the exception. They are everywhere, and police have to deal with them every day. We all have to understand that these scumbags exist and that we, the police, are the ones that have to keep them in control. Not everyone we arrest needs a smackdown, but some people understand and comply with nothing less. There's a time for talk and a time for action. In the police world, that time is usually dictated by Evil or by the civilians we encounter, with little or no regard for, or input by, the officer.

Chapter 4

You Can't Run, But You Can Hide

Now it's time to "cut to the chase" – foot chase that is. This chapter deals with foot pursuits. Based upon my observations in my own little corner of the world, when pursuing Evil on foot, it often chooses to hide rather than run. I first began to make this realization a few years into my career and began taking mental notes in an attempt to prove or disprove the theory. Several years afterward, I came across an FBI study and some independent work done by police officers across the nation that supported my own observations.

For a quick explanation of what I long ago began referring to as "Nable's 100 yard rule", we must first look at the "fight or flight" response. This response was first documented and given its name by a Harvard physiologist named Walter Cannon. The fight or flight response is an innate self defense mechanism shared by most higher animals that causes some very unique things to happen to the body. Bear in mind that the basic purpose of this instinct is to create a condition of body and mind that will most effectually facilitate survival in an actual or **perceived** life or death encounter.

The process is initiated when the brain perceives a threat and stimulates the release of certain chemicals into the bloodstream. Many police officers refer to this as the "adrenaline dump".

The adrenaline dump causes several things to happen. First, the respiratory rate increases to allow for the intake of greater amounts of oxygen to fuel the muscles needed to engage in a fight or in a flight. Blood flow to the areas of the body least likely to be used in the encounter (such as the digestive tract) is curtailed. In extreme circumstances the body will also evacuate the bladder and/or the bowels, perhaps to discard unneeded weight and to provide an olfactory deterrent. Blood flow to the extremities, like fingers and toes, also decreases so that in the event of an injury to less vital muscles, there is little blood loss. Blood flow to major muscle groups is consequently increased since these are the muscles most needed for rapid escape or for mortal combat.

One of the most important consequences of the fight or flight response is the loss of fine motor skills. Since the body shunts the blood away from the little muscles in our hands and the increase in energy causes uncontrollable shaking, it becomes very difficult to do simple tasks such as reloading a pistol or even holding it steady. Other tasks are nearly impossible, like finding the door key for your car or putting a key into a lock.

By its very nature, the fight or flight response completely bypasses the rational mind. The pupils dilate and our awareness intensifies. Fear becomes the dominating emotion. Irrational thought processes are the inevitable result. People just cannot think clearly when suffering the effect of the fight or flight response. The effects of this condition were perhaps best stated by the 18th century British statesman Edmund Burke, "No passion so effectually robs the mind of all its powers of acting and reasoning as fear."

Then we have what I call the "wounded deer" phenomenon. Many hunters will tell you that after they wound a deer, the deer will often sprint to escape immediate harm but then circle back around to familiar ground and perceived safety rather than running headlong into unknown territory.

Since the response in a fleeing perpetrator is fueled by much the same instincts as that of the wounded deer, the perpetrator will often times not travel far before circling back to where it started. Since many pursuing police officers are suffering from a lesser degree of the fight or flight response, they often outthink themselves. They use their rational minds to try to decide where Evil went and they think that since it wouldn't make since to run around in circles then Evil wouldn't do it.

The best way to catch Evil is to think like Evil. If Evil suffers from the effects of the fight or flight response then he is not thinking rationally and will do things that just don't make sense. As long as the pursuers remain cognizant of that fact, they can use it to their advantage.

Another noticeable behavioral pattern in fleeing-Evil is the tendency for making right hand turns. Often times the fight or flight response will elicit an initial left turn followed by subsequent right turns to effect the aforementioned circling behavior. Evil tends to keep right when traversing open spaces or corridors and often gets confused when forced by obstacles to make left turns. I would be interested to see if this pattern is stimulated by our country's "keep right" attitude which would mean that suspects in the UK would show a proclivity for circling to the left. I tend to think that it has more to do with brain physiology (i.e. left brain vs. right brain and all that) than with environment but can't really say either way.

The fight or flight response causes the body to expend massive amounts of energy very quickly. Consequently, when the effects of the adrenaline begin to wear off, the body becomes extremely fatigued and must rest. If Evil thinks it is out of sight of its pursuers, then it would only be natural to assume that it would find somewhere to rest and recoup the lost energy.

Whatever the reason, in my experience these phenomena happen all too often to be ignored. The following stories are but a few in the literal hundreds that reside in my repertoire.

A story that is one of my personal favorites began one night during our shift change from evening watch to morning watch. I was just coming on duty when we received a call on a vehicle accident (signal 41) involving a police unit from another jurisdiction. Radio was gracious enough to advise not long after, that the 41 was the result of a police chase of which we had not been notified. Information soon trickled down the line that the Evil being chased happened to be armed robbers (two of them) who upon being wrecked by the pursuing officers, had proceeded to shoot at the officers before fleeing on foot into an apartment complex.

My trainee and I arrived without too much delay and learned that a two man unit from a neighboring jurisdiction had located a vehicle matching the description of one that had been taken in a home invasion robbery minutes earlier. The high-speed pursuit with the nearly new Mercedes four-door began when the officers activated their emergency equipment (blinkie-blinkies and woo-woos) some twenty miles from their 41 location. The pursuit proceeded into our jurisdiction where for reasons known only to the pursuing officer, he decided to perform the P.I.T. maneuver (Pursuit Intervention Technique) in an unfamiliar area, without advising the appropriate jurisdiction, and without any backup units anywhere close.

The P.I.T. maneuver was performed (and subsequently functioned) flawlessly. Evil spun around once before crashing into some bushes and causing a surprisingly minimal amount of damage. The two perpetrators promptly exited the vehicle and began firing pistols at the officers who for reasons known only to them, never fired back. (Perhaps one of those curious stress responses or a simple lack of training or preparedness.)

The officers took cover. Evil fled. No one pursued. I was the first officer at the scene followed closely by several more units from my jurisdiction and tons of officers from the initiating jurisdiction including detectives and even some off-duty units. I directed my people to set up a relatively small perimeter but it wasn't long before the shift commander for the other jurisdiction arrived and took over.

In my personal opinion, if competence were water, that particular commander was the Sahara. Only a feeble attempt was made to coordinate with our department and that commander proceeded to set up a perimeter that was nearly two miles square. I tried to point out that in that particular area, there were formidable natural barriers (including dense brush, creeks and cliffs) outside of the apartment complex where Evil was last seen and that in all likelihood, Evil was in unfamiliar territory and not equipped with a whisper quiet VTOL craft or the latest illumination or night vision technology. Taking that into consideration, Evil was most likely to be (you guessed it) within 100 yards or less of where it was last seen.

Next occurred a phenomenon all too familiar during foot chases in the dark. Units began hearing things in the woods that they were sure were the perpetrators. These auditory hallucinations happened over a vast expanse of ground causing units to run from one location to another with no concrete evidence of the presence of Evil.

Please understand that in the dark, in the woods, whether the terrain is familiar or not, it is IMPOSSIBLE to walk (much less run) without making noise. It is also highly likely that if you run through the woods in the dark it won't be long before you run into something that will cause you great pain. If you don't believe me, go outside tonight and try it.

Nevertheless, police seem to regularly disregard "Ocham's razor", which postulates that the simplest explanation or theory is likely the correct one, thinking that Evil is somehow capable of traversing great distances with stealth and speed that could not be matched by the most accomplished woodsman in broad daylight.

Frustrated, I sat back and manned my little section of the perimeter and repeated my suggestions to the command hierarchy several times. Three hours went by and the SWAT team and K-9 and multiple miscellaneous ground personnel turned up neither hide nor hair of the elusive Evil.

The K-9 officer on scene decided to do one final sweep of the apartment complex before calling it quits. I congratulated her on her insight and within 10 minutes, one half of Evil was located hiding on the second floor balcony of an apartment less than 100 yards from where he was last seen. He was taken into custody without incident.

I still maintain that the second half of Evil was likely in a similar position and could probably see or hear us take his compatriot into custody, but the search was called off and everyone went home as if catching part of Evil was as good as catching the whole.

Good leadership is a rare and precious thing.

#4.2 ...But I Looked There!

Next I will take you to another night on the morning watch in the middle of an otherwise uneventful shift. An off duty officer had been alerted to some suspicious activity in her apartment complex and, when she went to investigate, found two representatives of Evil in the act of stealing an automobile. It just so happens that they had used another stolen vehicle as their method of transport to that particular location and were attempting to leave in both.

If I remember correctly, one vehicle wrecked or in some other way became unusable so Evil united into one car and fled South on the nearest limited access freeway. Officers gave chase and the vehicle wrecked while attempting to exit the freeway a few miles away. (I am glad that most of the soldiers in the Evil army don't understand basic physics. If they did, then they would know that the average vehicle will not make 90 degree turns at 60 mph.) The closest officer could see the wreck and could see both representatives of Evil as they ran from the car but could not see where they went when they entered the woods.

We had the luxury of being able to spare six or eight officers for the subsequent search and set up a perimeter quite quickly. I asked the officers close to the 41 scene if they had searched the immediate area fully and they assured me that they had. We began a thorough search of the outlying area, which included a large field with very little room to hide and a narrow strip of woods adjacent to the roadway, that we were assured had been checked by the first officer on the scene.

Probably two hours passed before we gave up. The initiating officer decided to do one more sweep of that narrow section of woods and guess what? Within fifty yards of the wrecked, stolen car he found both Evils covered up by pine straw where they had been quietly waiting the entire time. Both were taken into custody without incident but with a considerable amount of time and energy wasted.

#4.3 A Different Kind of Blinky Blinky

My next story takes us back in time to the early 90's. It was a dark and soon to be stormy night. The air was pleasant and calm. A call came out on a shoplifter at a local discount store who was being chased by employees. Several units were close by and we saturated the area. Since no one had the Evil in sight, I did what I often do to catch Evil. I found a nice dark spot to hide and watch for Evil to go by. I am amazed by officers who think that when they are searching for a perp in the dark, they will somehow find him by driving around in their marked police cars with all their lights shining brightly as beacons in the night that scream out, "I am the police, this is where I am. Please hide from me now."

My preferred approach is to meet Evil on his terms: Hiding in the dark. This time I didn't have to wait long. As I turned off all the lights on my car and turned down the nearest side street with no street lights, I saw something that at that point in time, I had never seen before. I saw little red flashing lights that looked to be very close to the ground. I could tell that they were moving away from me. I sped up to investigate.

I started laughing when I saw that it was a person matching Evil's description who had little lights in the heels of his shoes that lit up with every step he took. While still in the car, I called out to radio my location and direction of travel. I drove as far as I could and jumped out on foot to continue. My pursuit led through the backyards of a house or two. I was keeping close to Evil but not gaining.

As I rounded the corner of a house no more than fifty feet behind Evil, I ran smack dab into another officer. I said, "Where did he go, he was right in front of me?"

The other officer never saw him so we checked a hedge that separated us. There was no sign of Evil. I was stumped. I knew that I was right behind him yet he had somehow disappeared. As usual, all the other officers left as quickly as they had arrived, so I just waited.

In the dark I sat waiting for my eyes to adjust so I would not have to use my flashlight. I would like to make the point here that most officers who work at night use their flashlights way too much. If you can see without it, don't use it. It gives away your location to "the enemy" and offers little in return. Also, on a more subtle note, if you are engaged in a foot chase in the dark with someone who very likely doesn't have a flashlight, then you need to use your flashlight as little as possible so that you can see things from Evil's point of view and act accordingly.

When running like a scared jackrabbit, decisions are split second and are based on the sensory information at hand. If you come behind the jackrabbit slowly and with an implement that significantly changes the sensory input, then you will have a different perspective than the jackrabbit and therefore make different assumptions about where to run. So if you are searching or chasing someone in the dark, use your light only periodically and as necessary. Make judgments about where to go with your light (or night vision) turned off.

Back to the story. I walked around the house where Evil was last seen. I moved very slowly and did my best not to make a single sound. I turned off my radio. I looked intently at everything that I could see and identified every object in my field of view to my satisfaction before continuing. I had gone almost completely around the house when I saw a dense dark object behind the bushes along the side of the house. I stopped and stared at it for a long time before deciding that it was not shaped like anything that should be next to a house, so probability was high that it was Evil.

I slowly and silently crept to within about twelve feet of the dark, amorphous blob. If the blob was in fact Evil, I fully intended to ensure that his imminent, near death experience would be accompanied by a blinding white light. So with my pistol in one hand and my 40,000-candlepower aluminum Mag light in the other, I illuminated the suspected Evil and barked, "Don't move!" As it turned out, it was Evil and I scared the snot out of it. I told Evil to stand up slowly or I would shoot it (even though I wouldn't - it just sounds good) and Evil, trembling, complied.

He was so scared that even though my commands were characteristically deliberate, loud, slow and simple, he had difficulty processing the information. I told him to put his hands on the wall and he put them behind his back. I told him to kneel and he stood up etc. Eventually he calmed down enough to comply and I took him into custody without incident. Most perps are cowards and idiots. Scare them badly enough with a surprise attack and they will melt. However, I caution you not to grow to expect this reaction because if the day ever comes that you meet the worst kind of Evil, Evil that has no fear, Evil will be the one with the surprise.

#4.4 Holding Down The Fort

Next, we move to a cold winter night when a call came in on a hit and run accident that left a woman injured but thankfully, not too seriously.

When the responding officer arrived at the scene, the vehicle that caused the accident was there but the driver had left on foot. Subsequent investigation revealed that the perp vehicle was stolen and eventually led to a foot chase of the driver that went off and on for almost 6 hours.

Most of the "foot chase" was really a game of catch-up. We would get word of Evil's location and go try to find him but we never really got our eyes on him well enough to put a plan into action.

Finally, the thorough investigating by the responding officer, coupled with information learned after capturing the passenger of the stolen car paid off. We learned that our perpetrator had called his girlfriend to come pick him up at a nearby school. We converged on the area of the school just in time to find Evil, his girlfriend, and his sister. Evil's girlfriend was captured as all three subjects tried to flee the scene. In the following confusion, Evil once again became a fugitive and this time took his sister along for the ride.

A short foot chase was abandoned due to lack of manpower. My trainee and I responded to the location shortly thereafter to conduct a thorough search on our own. The investigating officer was preoccupied taking names and information for whatever report he had to write. He also had to stand by with Evil's girlfriend while she received minor medical treatment for injuries sustained in her escape attempt. I asked the officer where Evil was last seen and he pointed me in the right direction. I took off in that direction and told my trainee to try to stay close and to keep his eyes open.

I found a fence dividing the vacant lot I was in from the upper middle class residential neighborhood on the other side. I found a suitable place to climb over and landed in someone's back yard. (Another officer had scaled the same fence a few yards away and was in someone else's back yard.)

As luck would have it, we had calculated correctly in determining Evil's path. Our suspicions were confirmed not just by a freshly broken wooden privacy fence but also by a neighbor who saw us outside and said that he had just seen a young man and woman running through the neighborhood. We decided to fan out and do a careful search of the neighborhood. I had already lost my trainee, but really wasn't concerned as there were more pressing matters requiring my immediate attention.

I holstered my flashlight and surveyed the area. Knowing that perps on the run usually follow the line of least resistance and best visibility (for them to see where they are going) and tend to "keep right", I decided that I would follow the well lit residential street about seventy five yards and begin my search near the dead end. I ran straight down the street and in between the two houses that were directly in front of me.

As a rule, if time permits, when there is a possibility of encountering violence, I like to empty my bladder at the first available moment before proceeding. Often times in life threatening or extreme stress situations, part of the fight or flight response results in an involuntary evacuation of one's bladder. While perfectly natural, such a function can be an embarrassment and a hindrance. Also, I like to have every advantage possible and that extra pound or so of urine is always nice to get rid of.

I remember thinking while urinating on the bushes of the house to my right, "wouldn't it be funny if I was peeing on the bush where the perps were hiding?" I double-checked and wasn't – darn it.

I started out of the light that was on the street side of the residences into the pitch black that was their back yards. I went slowly to give my eyes time to adjust and to avoid thrusting myself headlong into an ambush or another foot chase. I made careful advances, trying to stay hidden in the shadows and making a point not backlight my form against the distant streetlights.

As I made my way with my radio off into the back yard of the first house, I could make out a row of trees on the rear of the property and what looked like a children's combination swing set and play fort about fifteen feet away between the house and the trees. I thought at that point that I heard talking. It was low and muffled but it was definitely talking. I thought for a moment that the sounds might be coming from my radio but an instinctive feel of the on/off button confirmed that my radio was not the culprit.

The next logical assumption was that someone near me was talking. As I crept nearer to the play fort, the sound became more intelligible and I could make out that it was two people whispering. At that point I thought that perhaps I was far closer to Evil than I had intended to be. I froze in my tracks and listened. It was apparent from the conversation that Evil was unaware of my presence and was very close - probably in or around the play fort.

Master Sun states in "The Art of War" that when you are weak, feign strength and when you are few pretend to be many - a good premise to work from when facing the unknown. I quietly reached for my flashlight, which is held in a non-Velcro holder because Velcro makes way too much noise when you're trying to be sneaky. I illuminated the play fort while simultaneously yelling my cherished expletives. Evil was indeed there, hiding in a small enclosure under the fort and was disoriented by the sensory overload caused by my yelling and the bright light focused on their faces. I had the male come out first. I blocked the entry to the area where they were hiding and had him move backwards on his knees with his hands extended towards me. I handcuffed him immediately, and proned him out while directing the female to do the same.

Both were compliant and later stated that they thought there was more than one police officer there at the time or they might have tried to escape again. I turned them over to the investigating officer, rounded up my trainee, who incidentally had given up the search, and went back in service.

#4.5 Physician, Heal Thy Self

Though I preach the principles of foot chases (as described earlier) almost to excess, I will freely admit that on rare occasions, I have some sort of mental lapse that causes me to disregard those principles. The result is usually either that Evil gets away completely or the pursuing police have to work much harder to apprehend it.

An incident that illustrates my point occurred early in a morning watch shift. It began with a call on a 29, 51/4 (a fight with a person stabbed and an ambulance enroute). I was the backup unit. The primary officer and I happened to be together when the call came out. We were at the scene in less than two minutes. When we arrived we found a young man (late teens, early twenties) lying in the parking lot. His mother was with him attending to the non-life-threatening, but still very painful, stab wound that he had in his abdomen.

Both parties told us that the person responsible for the wound was another young man who was a friend of the victim. They gave us a description of that night's Evil and pointed us in the direction he was last seen heading. They also added that after stabbing the victim, Evil had actually stabbed himself in the abdomen as well.

While the primary officer stayed with the victim until paramedics arrived, I went searching for Evil. I drove towards the rear of the apartment complex and began a slow search in my vehicle. It only took about two minutes before I came upon the building where Evil was resting in a stairwell. He saw me coming and took off on foot. The time it took for me to exit my patrol car and run around the building was enough time for Evil to vanish.

There was a good bit of blood in the stairwell Evil ran from. I was able to follow the blood trail about sixty feet or so from the stairwell, but after that there was no more trail to follow. Instead of following my own advice and starting to search to the right, I thought that logically, Evil would have followed the path of least resistance, which just so happened to be to the left. (The entire complex was relatively well lit, so that was not an issue.) By that time, the primary officer had turned the victim over to the paramedics and had responded to my call for assistance on the foot chase. I orchestrated a careful search of the entire complex to the left of where I had last seen Evil.

Just as we were about to give up our search, radio told us that they had received a call stating that Evil had just been seen back on the other side of the apartment complex near his own apartment. As it turned out, he had remained true to the principles that I so cavalierly disregarded. He circled right, and went back to his starting point.

We caught up to him a few minutes later and though he gave us a good run, the primary officer and a third unit had him in custody about thirty seconds before I caught up to them all.

"Missed it by that much."

#4.6 Pitfalls

My next story demonstrates one of the many dangers potentially inherent within foot chases. It started simply enough with a call on a shoplifter. The responding unit arrived and made contact with the alleged perpetrator. A foot pursuit followed soon after.

Several units joined in the pursuit and were hot on the trail of Evil. One of our larger, less fit officers was "bringing up the rear" when he announced over the radio that all units should use caution approaching Evil because he had recovered Evil's handgun at the foot of a fence that Evil had jumped over.

Before long, we had captured Evil and informed him that we found his pistol and would be levying the appropriate charges. As Evil often does, he protested the weapons charge declaring emphatically that he had no weapon. We knew better and charged him anyway.

With Evil successfully apprehended, charged and transported to the jail, the primary unit on the call took the pistol and entered it into evidence. It was secured in an evidence locker and the officers all returned to service.

A few hours later, one of the officers involved in the pursuit called the reporting officer and asked the following:

"What type of pistol did you enter into evidence?"

"It was a stainless steel, Smith and Wesson .38 caliber revolver," replied the reporting officer.

After asking a few more pointed questions, the officer realized that the pistol locked in the evidence locker was actually his own backup weapon that had fallen out of his ankle holster.

There was a lot of explaining to be done, paperwork to file, and a charge or two to be withdrawn from Evil before the whole mess was straightened out. This was just another example proving that things are not always as they seem.

Though this particular instance had a humorous ending, that pistol could have been picked up by anyone including a circling perpetrator. Things turned out OK that time but the potential for disaster was there.

There are several other factors to consider when pursuing Evil on foot that may help to make foot pursuits a little safer. Realize that human beings are "sight hunters". Our natural instincts when chasing something lead us to focus on our prey and pursue it with the conscious goal of grabbing it, subduing it and controlling it. When you couple our instinctive response of "chasing to catch" with the influences of the fight or flight response, some dangerous patterns begin to emerge.

Officers often act without thinking and without a plan and they tend to disregard the fact that if someone is running from you, they are by definition resisting arrest. There may be something causing them to want to resist arrest that the pursuing officer may not be aware of. Perhaps there is an outstanding felony warrant or probation or parole issue that is causing Evil to flee rather than the misdemeanor shoplifting charge that initiated the pursuit.

Also, officers tend to forget what we call the "killing zone". The killing zone is the area that is within a ten-foot radius of the offender where the offender can lash out against the officer without warning. That distance can be increased if Evil has any type weapon.

Officers also lose sight of potential dangers, like where it is that Evil might be running. Evil may be running back to his own home or to where he may have Evil friends that can assault an unsuspecting officer. There may be traps intentionally set by Evil prior to the pursuit with the sole goal of injuring the pursuing officer.

There may natural barriers and pitfalls such as holes, walls, water, mud, barbed wire or any number of other things that can be dangerous or even lethal if the officer is not careful. It is a difficult urge to resist, but sometimes, it is better to try to contain Evil until backup arrives rather than rushing in to apprehend.

Lastly, the pursuing officer must consider the possibility that when he or she catches Evil, Evil might just be the one that wins the fight.

Chapter 5

Through Cop-colored Glasses

While I was working a retail job during my high school years, an Asian man came into the store and asked for directions. He had a very thick accent from his native language and we had extreme difficulty communicating with him. With considerable effort from all of the parties involved, we were finally able to resolve his dilemma sufficiently. He thanked us and gave the following parting words, "I guess you can tell - I no from aroun' here." We all smiled and nodded but were thinking facetiously, "Really, you don't say." After a short pause he continued with, "I from Saint Rouis." (St. Louis, MO)

The biggest mistake that we all make as humans is one that is completely natural. We tend to view our interactions with others based on our own life experiences and our own perspectives. How else could we look at things? We, as people, and especially as police, owe it to ourselves and to those with whom we come into contact, to educate ourselves on other peoples' experiences and to try to look at things from more than one perspective. This can allow us to evaluate our interactions with a basis in our own paradigms but also with a temper of the paradigms of others. I'm sure that right about now a lot of you are thinking, "Huh?"

What I'm saying is simple. The way you view the world is tinted by your experiences and your training and any number of other things. Police officers tend to view the world through "cop-colored" glasses. We often view everyone from the police perspective to keep ourselves safe and to catch Evil. Often times our actions are misunderstood and often times we misunderstand the actions of others that we contact.

For example, certain cultures in the world are highly oppressive of their people. The police in many countries are the violent arm of these oppressive governments. Rape, murder and torture are some of their tools. What is likely to happen when a citizen of a country of this type has his first encounter with American police on your traffic stop? To you it may be just another stop for some innocuous little violation, but to that driver, it is the terror of a lifetime.

When you approach the vehicle, the driver gives you all the signs you've been taught to look for, that indicate criminal behavior. The driver is nervous and shaking. He won't make eye contact with you. He is stuttering and stammering if he speaks English at all. You, the police officer, are on high alert and begin investigating further to find out what heinous offense this driver is attempting to conceal. The more you investigate, the more horrified your driver becomes. You are reacting to his behavior and he is reacting to your behavior reacting to his behavior and so on…

People who are scared, especially for their lives or their safety, often do very irrational things. A good police officer must control any situation and keep it from getting out of hand. Control is not always best effected by physical force. Words can be as powerful as a baton at causing an altercation or preventing one. Unfortunately, the best implement of control is often not known until after the interaction is over. We must do the best we can with what we have, realizing and accepting the fact that we may not always be right.

Not long ago in New York City, undercover detectives working a "high crime" area approached a man who matched the description of a perpetrator they were looking for. I do not know the particulars of the case but I do know that the man they approached, a Haitian immigrant named Diallo, got scared and ran. The officers ran after him. The foot pursuit ended in the poorly lit doorway of a building where Mr. Diallo reached into his back pocket for his wallet. He probably thought he was being robbed. The police thought he was reaching for a gun. They shot him. That's really all that matters. One bullet or fifty, dead is dead. At that one split second in time, police did what police do. They responded to a set of perceived circumstances whose outcome cannot be awaited to decide the proper course of action. We cannot wait to be killed to justify a deadly response. In real life, there are no do-overs. Sometimes things just go horribly wrong. It's no one's fault, it just happens.

One night while I was on patrol, I spotted a car with an expired tag so I pulled it over. My initial check of the interior of the car saw no cause for alarm. When I asked the young black male for a driver's license and insurance, the red flags went up. The driver had a heavy West African accent but spoke and understood English.

He was visibly nervous, sweaty, and shaking. He would not make eye contact except for quick glances and was reaching all over the car. He would reach for the glove compartment, and then stop before opening it as if he remembered at the last moment that there was something in there that he did not want me to see. He would reach for the center console and door panel and then underneath his seat. He was making me real nervous. I kept telling him to relax and keep his hands where I could see him but that only made him more nervous.

He reached for the gearshift and I thought he was trying to drive off, so I yelled for him to put his hands back up where I could see them. He got scared and his foot came off the brake so the car started to roll. I told him to stop the car. He slammed the brake pedal and went to reach for the emergency brake. His hands went out of sight again. I barked at him, "Put your hands where I can see them." He jerked his hands back up but then reached towards the floor again.

I had had enough of this. I spoke to him *forcefully, slowly, clearly and deliberately* and told him to put the car in park. (Your tone of voice often sets the tone of an encounter. If you are screaming and yelling and panicking, then those around you are likely to follow your lead.) Once he had done that, I told him to turn off the ignition. Once he had done that, I told him to exit the vehicle slowly, and put his hands behind his back. Several times, I had to repeat instructions but eventually he complied. Once I had him cuffed (no violence necessary), I placed him in my patrol car and the scene was under control. I went to look through the car to see what he had been reaching for. There was a lone beer bottle on the front floorboard, full and unopened. Since the car was on a slight incline, it kept rolling out from under the seat and hitting his feet. I assume that was what he was reaching for.

He was visiting a family member who had just bought the car and had the paperwork in the apartment fifty feet from our traffic stop (the owner has up to thirty days to update the registration). He also had left his international drivers license in the same apartment. He thought all these things were illegal. His license, the paperwork on the car, and the beer under the seat were all things that he thought would cause me to arrest him. The jails and the Police in his country are far different from those in ours, but how would he know that? Add to that the fact that he was dealing with a big, bald, white police officer and you begin to get a glimpse of why he was acting the way that he was.

I took a little extra time to investigate and found out that the whole incident was a misunderstanding. He misunderstood me and I misunderstood him. After I had figured everything out, I let him go with my apologies and an explanation of my behavior. I also explained to him a few things that would make his next police encounter (if there were one) much more pleasant for all involved.

I have found that good communication with people can go a long way. In the "heat of the moment" you may not have the time, ability or desire to explain things to those whom you encounter. But take a few minutes later, after everything has calmed down, and you can restore the dignity a person may feel that they lost in your encounter. Explain to them why you do certain things for your own safety and the safety of those with whom you come into contact and they will often times leave the encounter with a positive feeling about you (and subsequently a positive feeling about police in general) instead of a markedly negative one. A few simple words can make a lifetime of difference. But no matter what you do, never let your guard down.

I know officers who if given the same situation, would likely have ended up in a fistfight and a jail run with that same subject. Those officers would have thought themselves justified and a court would perhaps have agreed. That's not the point. The point is that he was not a criminal (at least not when I encountered him) and should not have gone to jail.

Oh yeah, one more thing. My driver's last name was also Diallo.

#5.2 Things Are Not Always as They Seem

As a civilian you should realize that the majority of police officers in America are good people. Sometimes police officers come across as being unfriendly or downright rude. Bear in mind that the officer who stops you for speeding on the roadway, may have been in a life or death struggle moments earlier or could have come from any number of highly stressful encounters from which he might not yet have fully recovered. He might even have had his donut break interrupted, God forbid!

You must also realize that the officer also does not know you. You may know that you are a nice person but the officer does not. How could he? He must treat you the same way that he treats any criminal. He must always be aware and cautious because our profession is inherently and persistently dangerous. We must constantly be on guard for assaults or we risk not going home that day. Sometimes this hyperawareness or near paranoia can be misinterpreted by the average citizen.

Officers should also keep in mind that most civilians are not murderers and understand why some people are offended by our approach. Things are not always as they seem and we all owe it to each other to at least be cordial and professional until the situation dictates otherwise. We do not have to let our guard down to be polite.

It is not at all uncommon for lone females, driving late at night on unpopulated roadways, to be wary of pulling over for a police car. I tell my wife and will tell my daughter when she is of age that before pulling over, find a safe and well-lit, populated area to stop. Unfortunately, there are officers out there who take personal offense when a car does not immediately stop when signaled to do so. The farther the car goes without pulling over the more enraged the officer becomes. When the car finally stops, the officer runs up to the car and commits battery against the driver before taking him (or her) to jail for his (or her) insolence.

While a refusal to stop can often mean that Evil is afoot, it is not always the case. Before you take drastic measures, make sure that they are warranted. If any of the females in my family were ever treated badly for doing something that makes complete sense, rest assured that I would seek proper recourse against the offender.

To illustrate my point I will relay an incident that occurred one night as I was searching for Evil on the main highway that ran through my beat. I saw a car with only one taillight. The driver also made a right turn out of the left lane so I decided that a traffic stop was in order.

I activated my emergency equipment as the vehicle entered the Interstate. The vehicle neither sped up nor slowed down and continued along its original course. I called radio and advised that I had a vehicle that was failing to stop.

49

A number of units responded with heightened stress in their voices to say that they were on the way to me. A supervisor chimed in telling me to cancel the pursuit. I calmly replied that there was no pursuit and that I had a car occupied by what appeared to be a single, solitary female and that we were traveling below the speed limit.

The supervisor retorted more sternly that I was to discontinue my pursuit. Short of pulling off the roadway and coming to a complete stop, there really wasn't any way for me not to follow her.

Another unit pulled up next to us and we both turned on all of our equipment. The lady slowly pulled off at the exit and stopped. The other unit started to run up to the car but I called him back. We cautiously but calmly approached the vehicle and discovered that the driver was an international tourist who spoke little English and didn't know what the funny lights were on our cars or what she was supposed to do when she saw them.

I recommended a chauffeur for the remainder of her stay. No harm, no foul.

#5.3 In One Ear …

We have an individual who works our area who quite likely holds the dubious distinction of having been arrested by me more times than anyone else in history. He is a homeless drug addict who chooses not to work. Instead he cons someone into allowing him to use their car and then he pretends to be broken down on the side of the road in high-class neighborhoods. He usually "breaks down" at intersections so that people will have to stop for traffic lights or stop signs right next to him. Then he gives them a sob story about running out of gas with no money etc. and needing to get to the hospital where his wife is having a baby (or something similar). Miraculously, whenever police approach him, his car problems heal and he is able to drive away.

He usually dresses well and does not look like a homeless drug addict and he makes a good bit of money with his little scam. On good days he can net several hundred dollars. He also fools most police officers. I happened to have two trainees riding with me when a call on a suspicious person at an intersection came out. It was an intersection that our Evil was known to work quite regularly and I was confident that it was he.

I told my trainees all about the drug-using con man while we were on the way to the call. I told them that he had a revoked driver's license and that he was often wanted, had drugs in his possession and occasionally occupied a stolen car. I told them that if it was him, I would stay in the car where Evil could not see me and let them investigate and make the appropriate charges.

When we arrived at the location, it was indeed the aforementioned Evil. I sent my trainees out the door and wished them luck. They spent a few minutes talking to the man before coming back to the patrol car empty handed. The next thing I knew Evil was driving away. I asked the trainees what had happened and they told me that the man's car had just overheated and he had waited long enough for it to cool down so they let him go. Obviously what I had told the trainees had gone in one ear and out the other. They had not yet gotten their cop glasses and believed everything that the man told them. I made a traffic stop on Evil shortly thereafter and ended up arresting Evil myself. Both trainees earned a failing grade and hopefully learned a valuable lesson.

I have one particular rule that goes with my cop glasses. I assume that everyone I talk to is lying. I investigate in an attempt to prove that they are lying and if I can't prove it, then they must be telling the truth. Many people are just the opposite. They assume that everyone is telling the truth and only investigate when they see evidence of a lie or an inconsistency. That is why so much Evil slips through the hands of some officers.

#5.4 Mine's Bigger

I had my donut break rudely interrupted one night by an officer who pulled out on a suspicious tractor-trailer that was parked on a quiet residential street in a neighborhood on my beat. I had seen the truck earlier and knew that he was waiting until the home construction site was open so that he could off-load the building materials that he was carrying. Many times, truck drivers will arrive at a site early and use the remaining time to sleep in their cabs.

I was a bit confused when the officer put out a 63 (officer down/needs help) moments later and rushed to the scene to see what was the matter. The officer had been looking in the cab of the truck with his flashlight and obviously startled the sleeping driver inside. The driver, not knowing that it was the police looking in his truck, yelled out, "I've got a gun." He thought that the police officer was someone trying to break into his truck. The police officer backed off thinking that he had just had his life threatened by Evil that knew he was the police.

The fiasco escalated and the officer ended up executing a felony stop procedure on the truck driver. He called the truck driver out of the truck over the P.A. and proned him out on the ground. The officer handcuffed him and then searched the truck and found no gun. Neither the officer nor the truck driver would holster their egos long enough to work out the problem in a civil manner so the truck driver ended up in jail and the truck got impounded. Needless to say, the case was thrown out and I was surprised that nothing else came of the matter. The point is that a lot of energy was wasted and a man went to jail needlessly, even though he was a jerk. Thankfully, being a jerk is not illegal or we would all go to jail at least once in our lives.

Chapter 6

Helloooo Radio!

I have the privilege of having a father who has a marvelous sense of humor. In some cases my humor mirrors his distinctly and in others it represents a stark departure. Once when I was very young, he told me a joke that left me quite perplexed. I will repeat it here.

Once upon a time, there were two polar bears frolicking in the snow and ice of the Arctic Circle. The polar bears unknowingly ventured a little too far out onto the ice and all of a sudden, the ice that they were standing on detached from the shore. The polar bears floated away from shore on the ice. Without warning the ice broke once again. The second break in the ice separated the polar bears and they began floating away from each other. Both polar bears were very sad that they were alone and didn't know how they were going to get back home. They floated and floated wondering if they were ever going to see each other again. Little did they know that while one of them was floating to the East, the other was floating to the West. Since they were so close to the North Pole, it didn't take long for them both to float essentially half way around the world. As the polar bears began floating toward each other on the ice they both realized what was happening. They were overjoyed that they would soon be re-united. As soon as they were within shouting distance of each other one polar bear began waving frantically to the other and shouted out, "Helloooooo radio!!"

After my father told the joke, he and anyone else in the room would laugh hysterically while I just sat with a bewildered look on my face much like the one I assume you have on your face right now. Of course, he waited quite a long while before telling me that the reason the joke was funny, was that it wasn't funny. Everyone in the room was told to laugh ahead of time so that I would think that I missed something and that was what was funny.

He later explained to me that when he was in grammar school (during medieval times) that type of joke was somewhat popular and was lumped into a little known genre of humor called the "Shaggy

Dog" story. According to Webster's New Collegiate Dictionary (1977, G. & C. Merriam) indicates that a shaggy dog story is "...a long-drawn-out circumstantial story concerning an inconsequential happening that impresses the teller as humorous but the hearer as boring and pointless; also: a similar humorous story whose humor lies in the pointlessness or irrelevance of the punch line".

At the time I thought it was pretty stupid. I even tried it out on some of my friends and they thought it was stupid too. Years would go by before that joke would find new relevance.

In police work, the term "Radio" can mean several things. It can refer to the actual electronic radio that we use to communicate with one another. The portable radio is the unit that officers carry on their person, while the mobile radio is the unit mounted in the officer's car (also referred to as the car radio). "Radio" can also refer to the communications room or to the dispatcher specifically (depending on context). Lastly, "Radio" can be a verb that refers to calling someone on the radio. It sounds confusing but it really isn't.

I am constantly preaching to other officers that not only should they not expect radio to listen, they should not rely too heavily upon their dispatchers or upon any of the information that comes from radio. I remember playing that grade school game where you whisper something to a classmate who in turn whispers it to another classmate and so on all the way around the room. The starting phrase was "Mary had a little lamb". By the time it got all the way around the room, the phrase became something like, "The monster has a big green hand." This is a rudimentary exercise that demonstrates how unreliable information can be when it is transmitted by mouth. The more mouths it goes through, the less reliable it is.

Police officers should take any information that they get over the radio with the proverbial grain of salt. That information might be true, it might not. If the information comes directly from another officer then, in my opinion, it is inherently more reliable than from any other source, but the information is still not infallible.

Radio operators sometimes fall asleep at the helm or suffer from their own stress responses when a "hot" call comes out. It is not uncommon for a radio operator to freeze and become unresponsive when officers get involved in a high stress situation.

Another caution that I endeavor to impress upon officers is that the radio is not magical. The radio cannot save your life except in those rare instances where it may be used as an impact weapon. The radio is just a way to talk to people, and dispatchers are just glorified messengers, nothing more.

I have noticed in recent years that as a result of some unknown external influence, many new officers are afraid to do anything that might be even remotely dangerous. The standard answer to the "What would you do if..." question is "I would wait for backup." Instead of reaching for the necessary tool to complete the task at hand, officers sometimes reach for the radio instead as if broadcasting your predicament somehow gives you power or validity.

While waiting for backup is not necessarily bad, sometimes you may have to act when there is no backup available. If you have no plan besides waiting for backup or talking on the radio, then you cannot act when action may be the only thing that prevents Evil from causing property damage, bodily harm or death.

Also, when under the influence of the fight or flight response, it is difficult for anyone to consciously do more than one thing at a time. If the one thing that you choose to do is reach for your radio, then you may not be able to take the appropriate action to protect yourself or others. When the excrement strikes the rotating air motivator, you had better ignore that radio and concentrate on the threats at hand. When the situation has been controlled or de-escalated, then you can return to the radio to give any vital information that you were unable to give prior to the adrenaline dump.

With these few broad concepts so precariously placed, I will use the following anecdotal evidence to support and hopefully further explain what I am trying to say. My first story is an example of sheer incompetence on the part of our radio room. You may read this account and think that it is an aberration or a fluke but I assure you that similar instances occur with frightening regularity.

Because I grew up in the area where I have been policing my entire career, I occasionally run across old friends during the course of performing my duties. Such was the case one afternoon when right out of roll-call, I was dispatched to a signal 2 (silent alarm). Alarm calls have a low priority for the simple reason that we receive so many of them and the majority of them turn out to be false alarms. The first year my department kept statistics on those types of things, I saw the printout. Out of over 60,000 alarms in a given year, less than

75 of them were the result of a crime being committed. For that reason, my dispatcher should have sent me to the 54 (suspicious person) call first.

My dispatcher didn't, and I unknowingly passed right by the address where a high school friend had called police in reference to a suspicious person. After I checked the false alarm call, I was finally given the 54 call and went straight to it. I arrived to find my old friend visibly and understandably shaken.

She had been out in the back yard of her middle class suburban home working in the garden. She decided to come inside for a glass of water and when she walked into her living room, she saw a strange man sitting on her couch and pilfering through her jewelry box, which was normally kept in the master bedroom.

She confronted the man and demanded to know what he was doing in her house. He was also visibly shaken and the only reply he could muster was, "I'm just lookin' for some food."

Exercising her characteristic quick wit, she walked over to the freezer and pulled out a blueberry waffle. She threw the waffle at the interloper and said, "There you go, now you can leave."

As the burglar went out the front door, she slammed and locked it behind him and immediately picked up the phone and dialed 911. She told the operator that she had found a burglar in her house trying to steal her jewelry and that he was in the process of getting into a red car in her driveway that was driven by another man. She told the operator that the car was a two-door and that it had a horse emblem on the front grill. She told the operator that the car was backing down her long steep driveway. She told the operator that the car had driven off the driveway and was stuck in her front yard. She watched for twenty minutes while the two burglars worked to get the car unstuck. Then she watched as the burglars drove away, never to be seen or heard from again.

I was given the call as, "…a 54, two subjects in a red car. No further information available." This may seem unbelievable but it happens with such startling consistency in my department, that it no longer even fazes most of us. I admonished my friend to file a complaint. She did and, as usual, nothing was done.

#6.2 Good Job Radio

In the same general neighborhood some time later, my shift was in the process of catching up on all the calls that had come in during a brief thunderstorm. Radio had advised that the last holding call had been handled, so when I came upon a tree that was partially blocking the roadway I transmitted the following, "Radio, I will be out with a small tree that is partially blocking the roadway," and I gave my location. I said, "I will be available to answer any calls that come in."

I sat for twenty minutes while the radio was silent. My dispatcher broke that silence by raising my supervisor to notify him that she was holding a call on a signal 68 (person screaming) at an address not three blocks from my location. I told radio that I would handle the call and started in the appropriate direction.

When I arrived I was a bit surprised to discover the following:

The complainant was at home in his study when two masked men threw a piece of patio furniture through the sliding glass door that was less than ten feet from his desk. They burst into the room like participants in a one-minute, all you can grab shopping spree or general-admission concert goers rushing to see "The Who" in Cincinnati. One perp duct-taped the man's hands while the other ransacked the room looking for valuables.

When Evil became preoccupied, our victim jumped up and ran out the broken door and into the street in front of his house where he began screaming for help. At that point, several residents in the relatively small, upper class neighborhood called 911 to report the incident and went outside to help their neighbor. When I arrived, one of the residents was still talking to the 911 operator.

That call was held for 22 minutes and was given to me as a "68, man screaming…no further information available."

#6.3 It's Just a Radio

My next story is a bit disturbing. It is one that happened in a jurisdiction near mine and is one of the few in this book that did not involve me directly. The lesson to be learned is profound and needs to be told.

Two officers were approached by a citizen in reference to a fight that was going on in a nearby apartment complex. The officers gave their dispatcher the location and proceeded to investigate. As they got within a few yards of the offending apartment, a man ran out the front door carrying a high-powered rifle. He immediately fired at the closest officer and killed him instantly. The other officer turned to run and was knocked down by the non-lethal impact of a bullet from the same rifle.

The wounded officer, now lying on the ground with gun still in holster, reached for the radio to frantically call for help. While the officer gurgled and screamed unintelligible traffic into the shoulder-mounted radio, Evil slowly and methodically walked to within a few feet of the officer. Evil carefully raised the rifle and took his time aiming at the officer's head. The officer had plenty of time to shoot but was still trying to transmit on the radio. Evil pulled the trigger and, for all intents and purposes, that officer should have died and very nearly did. It took more than a year for the officer to recover and the officer has no recollection of the event.

This is a response that I see far too often in today's police officers. While in the midst of a potentially life threatening event, officers will take time out to talk on the damn radio. Or, while in a winnable fistfight with Evil, the officer takes one hand out of the fight, to send a message over the wireless. Evil seizes the opportunity and turns the tables on the officer. If the officer would take two extra seconds to finish the fight, then Evil would be contained.

Officers sometime become far too dependent on others to solve their problems rather than acting for themselves. Perhaps they are merely mirroring the conditions in our society. That is the action of a sheep, not a sheepdog.

If you can only do one thing at a time under extreme stress, please let that one thing be violence rather than inane chatter. It may save your life.

#6.4 We'll Have Someone There Right Away

There is another consequence to an incompetent communications center that receives very little attention in proportion to its severity. The following two stories are an example.

A man was on the way out to dinner with his wife. They were leaving their apartment and walking toward their car when the man began having chest pains. He fell to the ground as his wife called 911 on a cell phone and frantically asked for help. She told the operator that her husband was having a heart attack.

The call taker gave the call to a dispatcher who gave the call to the police and not to emergency medical personnel. Since it was shift change and not necessarily a police matter, the police supervisor on duty asked radio to hold the call for the next shift and have the paramedics advise if police were needed.

About forty minutes later, the officer arrived at the scene of the man who suffered at least twenty minutes of agony before making the transition to the hereafter.

Medical personnel were never dispatched and a man lost his life for no reason. Nothing was ever done.

A few years later, a man was having dinner in a restaurant and began choking. Several people called 911 requesting emergency medical personnel. For some reason, the communications center held the call for some 13 minutes, which gave the man just enough time to die in the crowded restaurant. He was less than three hundred yards from the fire station where the paramedics were stationed.

Aside from holding calls, giving bad information, withholding information and sometimes just making up information, radio dispatchers have been known to go to sleep on duty. The radio system can crash or your dispatchers can panic when something "exciting" happens. All these factors mean one simple thing; the reliability of your radio is limited.

I won't beat the dead radio horse here anymore because I think that I have made my point. The communications room regularly screws up, it is a fact of life. In their defense, their information is only as good as the information given to them by frantic callers. Keep your guard up and never assume.

If you are calling 911 for emergency help, make sure that you stay on the phone with the call taker and do not allow them to hang up on you. It is vital to maintain that link to give responding officers current information and to help you regain a sense of calm and control.

Chapter 7

Oh Crap!
What Did I Just Step In?

My intent in writing these next few anecdotes is to attempt to illustrate a point. That point is that being prepared is always important. Having plenty of tools in your mental toolbox will enable you to deal with virtually anything that those nasty ole perps, or even just life in general, happen to throw your way.

In the following stories, you will see some very interesting stress responses. No one really knows how they will handle extreme stress until it strikes but I sincerely believe that being prepared helps one to cope with the effects of stress much more effectively. I always tell my trainees that performing mental exercises while on patrol and "debriefing" even the most insignificant encounter helps to fill that mental toolbox.

As you drive by that convenience store, apartment complex, school, bank or movie theater etc., ask yourself what you would do if you had to respond to a crime in progress or some other crisis situation. How would you approach? What are the potential avenues of escape, not just for the perps, but also for victims, witnesses or even yourself? What is the best avenue of approach for your backup officers? How would you instruct responding units to set up a perimeter? Where should you direct EMS if they are needed? And the list goes on and on.

The only way you can know the answers to these and any other potential questions is by experience. Practical experience is always best but your mental experience isn't bad either. You would be surprised at what you can think of when you have time. Real life happens in a heartbeat. If you wait until the excrement strikes the rotating air motivator, you may not have time to think of even the most basic response.

My first few stories will deal with officers who were not prepared. Part of the intended exercise here is not just to entertain yourself with my cop stories, rather, put yourself into these situations and ask, "What would I do if that happened to me?" Most importantly, answer honestly…

One night, while working the evening watch, I was preparing to head for the precinct at the close of my shift. The day had been mundane and perfunctory and I was ready to go have a beer. As luck would have it, I had just passed a large retail shopping center when the dispatcher yelled out over the radio, "Any unit in the area, start for a signal 36 at [the movie theater]." The address she gave was the shopping center I had just passed. I answered radio and advised that I would be at the location in a few seconds. The events that were about to unfold would confirm, in a peculiar way, the second law of thermodynamics, which states that "In a closed system, entropy increases and complexity decreases." Or to put it more simply, all things tend towards greater disorder.

To bring the reader up to speed, I will do my best to describe the incident location. The shopping center in question shares an entire block with another smaller shopping center. The block is square, with the main street running along the front of the shopping center, and the other three sides are bordered by smaller surface streets. The shopping center faces east, with one driveway on the front and one driveway on the south. These two driveways lead to the upper portion of the shopping center. The lower portion of the shopping center is in the rear. There is one driveway on the south edge of the lower parking lot and two on the far West side. There are no entrances on the North side of the complex but there is an internal driveway that connects the upper and lower portions of the shopping center. The movie theater in question takes up the majority of the rear section of the shopping center.

When facing the theater, the ticket booth is positioned in the front and center. Immediately to either side of the ticket booth are two glass double doors. Next to those doors is a wall where the movie advertisements hang. Continuing down each wall past the advertisements there is a set of solid double doors leading from the lobby that are "exit only". There are stairs across the entire front of the theater and on each side is a wheelchair ramp that runs parallel to the front wall of the building.

As a matter of expedience or perhaps of reflex and as a result of my location, I chose to take the side street to the North of the complex and enter from one of the rear driveways. As is customary in responding to crimes in progress at night, I extinguished my headlights. However, the moment I entered the driveway, I realized that if there was a lookout posted, I would have been seen as soon as I entered the parking lot. "Oh well, too late now." I was committed.

I parked my patrol car as far to the northern edge of the theater and as close to the building as I could and exited the vehicle. The parking lot was full but there were no people in sight. There was no one visible in the glass enclosed ticket booth that sits in the center of the front of the theater. That was not at all unusual because the last movie of the day had already started and the employees generally locked the front doors at that time and retreated to the manager's office to count the day's receipts.

I began to do a standard geometric progression across the first set of glass double doors to see what I could see. The lobby was empty. I did the same to the ticket booth and to the glass double doors on the other side. Still I saw no one.

Up to that point, I had no idea if there was any radio traffic because I was concentrating 100 % on what I was doing. I took up a position on the southwest corner of the theater and was about fifteen feet from the exit door and at the top of the wheelchair ramp. Simultaneously, I noticed that my first back-up unit was arriving. My plan was to wait outside until the bad guys came out and hopefully take them by surprise. My plan was soon to be disrupted when my back-up unit drove right up to the center of the stairs in front of the ticket booth. To my amazement, the officer parked his car with the headlights on. He left the car running, exited the vehicle and stood next to it, right out in the open. There's an old axiom that says, "No plan survives contact with the enemy." Sometimes it doesn't survive contact with friendlies either.

Before I had a chance to say anything, the dispatcher yelled out, "Complainant advises all three suspects are heading for the exit." One milli-micro-nano-second after that transmission, the door right in front of me crashed open. The first of three perpetrators was looking behind him and running straight for me. I challenged him with my pistol and the requisite expletives that we all have come to cherish, causing him to face forward and turn his attention to me.

If he had been a cartoon I would have heard skidding sounds as he struggled to reverse his forward momentum in an effort to avoid me. In his face I saw a level of amazement that would be hard to match and in his hand I saw a dark duffel bag and a MAC 11 (high capacity 9mm pistol). As he back-pedaled, Evil number one reversed direction and threw his duffel bag and weapon straight at me. He and his next closest partner in crime ran around a large support column and down the stairs to the parking lot.

One perp ran on each side of my back-up unit so close to him that if he had stuck out either arm he could have close-lined one of them. The third suspect ran back inside the theater. I made the decision to go after the two that I could see. I ran through the parking lot and stayed pretty close to the perpetrators until they hit the woods on the opposite side of the street.

There was a steep embankment leading down to a small creek and then a steep embankment going up again on the other side. As I started down my embankment, I saw one of the perps stop on the top of the other side. He turned and looked right at me. At that point, like a lightning bolt from the blue, I was struck by the realization that there were two of them and probably at least one more gun. I might be heading for an ambush!

I stopped and directed my energy back towards the radio. It was then that I discovered a unique response to stress. My back-up officer, (who happened to be a native of a non-English speaking country) was speaking what sounded to me like his native language on the radio. He wasn't too far behind me so I ran back to him and told him to be quiet so I could direct responding units to set up a perimeter.

He gave me somewhat of a bewildered look and relinquished the precious air-time. We were actually at an advantage at this point. Being very familiar with the area, I knew that Evil was, at least for the next few minutes, contained in a one square block area that was all residential and mostly wooded. I was able to direct one patrol unit to each side of the block that Evil was hiding in, and it wasn't long before we had a search team go in and locate our two misguided youths. They were taken into custody without incident.

"But what about perp number three?" you ask. As far as we knew he was still in the theater. By that time, we had most of the evening watch officers on scene (probably eight or so) and several of the morning watch officers. It was the decision of our leadership to maintain a perimeter around the theater and check each individual who exited the theater as the movies let out.

When all the patrons and employees had been evacuated, we would send a SWAT team inside to clear the building and search for the perpetrator. Anyone matching the perps description would be detained. As luck would have it, very few (if any) movie patrons matched our suspect's description. Among those exiting the movies, however, were one of our off-duty officers and a local sports hero. I was glad to see that at least the off-duty officer was armed.

We now move to another curious stress response. My initial back-up officer was the officer who was assigned to the call since the call was on his beat. That meant that he would be responsible for taking the initial offense report. While we were maintaining the perimeter, our shift supervisor noticed that the officer in question was nowhere in sight. He asked if any of us knew where that officer was. We all responded in the negative.

Our supervisor then raised the officer on the radio and asked him his location. The officer replied that he was inside the theater taking the report. Our supervisor reminded him that he was ordered to remain outside of the business until SWAT arrived. The officer apologized and came outside the building to join the perimeter team.

Several minutes passed with more patrons exiting the building and the supervisor noticed that the aforementioned officer was again nowhere to be found. He again raised him on the radio and asked his position. The officer stated that he was inside the business working on the report. Obviously a bit frustrated, the supervisor ordered the officer back outside and gave him a standard ass-chewing and told him not to move from the perimeter. The officer apologized and agreed that he would stay put.

Several more minutes went by and, you guessed it, our illustrious officer was missing again! (I'm not making this up.) The supervisor once again raised the officer on the radio and inquired as to his location. The officer responded that he was inside the business, taking the report. Our supervisor ordered him out a third time, gave him a huge ass-chewing and then ordered him to go home. With tail between legs he complied.

We waited. All the patrons and employees were eventually removed from the building. SWAT arrived and cleared the building but found nothing. Evil apparently made it out a rear exit before anyone arrived to cover it. The two perps we had in custody were taken to the precinct for interrogation and all the officers left the scene.

Not long after that, the theater manager called to ask what the police report number was. Since the reporting officer had been sent home, no one had taken a report and all of our witnesses and victims were gone - but that's another story. I'll add that the next shift had to send an officer to start the report from the beginning.

It's not over folks. Our two misguided youths were actually some pretty experienced perps for being in their late teens or early twenties. They started complaining of injuries, which meant that according to our departmental policy, we had to take them by the public hospital for treatment prior to taking them to the jail. Since I wasn't there, I will refrain from speculating as to what transpired but I will say that often times, doctors can be a bit naive. They tend to view all people the same (which is not necessarily bad, just sometimes foolish) and consequently are not good at spotting Evil. Many times doctors will request that restraints be removed from prisoners so that they can be treated like humans rather than animals. (The primary fallacy here being that some humans are indeed animals.) Some time while being treated at the hospital under police guard, both perps got up and ran away. Good detective work recaptured them some time later.

As one final insult, the next day we received a call to the movie theater. Apparently, on his way out the back door, Evil number three (who I am not sure was ever caught) dropped his jacket and his pistol in the middle of the stairs. They were found by a movie patron and turned over to police.

The lessons to be learned here are potentially infinite...

#7.2 Help?

It was another typical day working the evening watch. We were all busy answering calls and backup units were few and far between. A call was dispatched to my beat partner on a signal 55 (trouble unknown) at a rather run down apartment complex. Maintaining their usual standard of excellence, the call takers had gotten no further information or if they did, the dispatcher neglected to pass it on.

Before I had time to advise dispatch that I would be responding as backup on the call, I was dispatched to a signal 24 (demented person) at an address that I knew shared a parking lot with the complex where the previous call had originated. It was then not much of a stretch to think that the calls might be related. Another point of interest is that in that particular area, our department's twenty million dollar radio system rarely worked for whatever reason makes radios not transmit from a given location (like sun spots or something).

The first unit arrived on scene quickly and was about a minute ahead of me. A few moments after advising radio that he was on scene he put out a signal 63. For those who are not familiar, the signal 63 is a sacred and thankfully relatively seldom heard signal that indicates that an officer is down and needs help. It also implies that someone will at least be going to the hospital and possibly to the morgue. It is not uncommon for officers to start from neighboring jurisdictions, or when they are off duty in their personal cars, or when they are thirty miles away or more. It's serious. Within seconds I was there but could not get on the radio due to the fact that all the other units felt it necessary to get on the radio and say that they were on the way. (A peculiar and somewhat universal problem with police is that they never seem to know when to shut up.)

The proper procedure of course would have been for everyone to hold their traffic until a unit at the scene could advise on the situation. As long as you respond to the 63, does it really matter if you tell dispatch? (no duh)

Anyway, as I drove down the long straight driveway into the complex, passing the small, run down, two story buildings that are cookie-cutter copies of each other, I came to the last building and cautiously drove up to it since I knew ahead of time that it was where the "officer down" had last been located.

My angle of approach put me right at the base of an outside staircase on the far end of the building. At the base of the stairs was a body. I could tell that it was not wearing a uniform. I was a bit relieved yet worried at the same time.

Approaching the body I saw blood. There was lots of it on the stairs and smeared down the wall from the second floor to where the body was lying (not laying – learn the difference). My first thoughts were that whoever had assaulted this man must be the one who was assaulting the other officer. I began scanning the area for Evil.

It just so happened that Evil was right next to me occupying the body that was lying on the staircase. When I got within ten feet from what I thought was an unconscious and possibly dead male in his late twenties, he suddenly sprang to life and lunged at me.

He was covered in fresh, wet, sticky, gooey blood and had a look in his eye that only a crazy person can get. He began flailing his arms wildly in the air, screaming and jumping up and down. I was doing my best to put distance between us without turning my back to him, and I thought for sure there was about to be a killin'.

After his first few steps, he stopped heading for me and began random gyrations and gestures. He also began screaming some rather severe racial epithets directed at those who comprised the bulk of the resident population for that particular area - a group to which he did not belong.

I was faced with three dilemmas. The first was the welfare of the officer who had put out the help call. The second was with the crazy bloody guy who might try to harm me, someone else, or even himself. The last was a growing crowd of curious, if not angry, residents might try to harm me and/or the crazy bloody guy.

Crazy bloody guy, hereafter referred to as Evil, began walking away from me. He continued spewing his vitriolic venom at the crowd, adding that he wanted to kill everyone. Then, without warning, as suddenly as he had leapt up from the staircase, he collapsed to the ground.

I spoke a few conciliatory words to the surrounding audience and cautiously approached Evil. I tried to take advantage of the momentary calm to transmit the particulars of my predicament, but like so many times before and since, the radio would not broadcast. I resolved myself to the fact that at least for the time being, I was on my own.

Just as I got within arms reach of Evil, he burst back to life and picked up right where he had left off, only this time he added a rather unique dance that he performed on the top of someone's car. Then, as if on cue, he again fell unconscious and collapsed all the way from the top of the car, to the trunk of the car, to the unforgiving pavement that lay beneath us.

I was a bit quicker to seize the moment that time and was about to handcuff him when closer inspection revealed that the blood was apparently coming from huge gashes in both of his wrists and forearms.

I improvised. Instead of cuffing him, I stood on top of him with one foot between his shoulder blades supporting the bulk of my weight and the other foot on his head. He again burst to life but when he tried to move, my weight was just enough to keep him down (Thank you, Lord).

Amidst this melee, the officer who had put in the help call miraculously emerged unscathed from parts unknown. He said that he had been looking for the guy I had pinned to the ground. I said, "I found him." He began trying to transmit but his radio wouldn't get out either.

I tried to ask the officer what happened and he just turned and walked away. His unexpected stress response left me alone, without explanation, to deal with Evil and the encroaching mob. Needless to say I was a bit confused but I was also a bit preoccupied. My questions would have to wait. It wasn't long before the proverbial cavalry arrived to relieve me. Emergency medical personnel attended to Evil while everyone asked, "What happened?"

I replied, "I really don't know" and we all set out in search of officer 63. We followed the blood trail and it led back to a second floor apartment. It is truly amazing how much blood the human body can lose without dying. At any rate, the officer we were seeking was poking around in the apartment as if nothing were wrong. Different people deal with stress in different ways I guess, but this guy was down right dangerous.

Obviously a bit annoyed, I asked him what was going on (only not quite so nicely). He said that Evil had apparently gotten hold of some bad drugs and ran through his own plate glass sliding door. There was no reason whatsoever for the implementation of the sacred 63. So I clarified my interrogative by asking in no uncertain terms, why he had felt that it was necessary to declare a signal 63.

His response was, "Because I saw all that blood. "

I was too infuriated to counsel him on his transgression and relegated the job to any of the umpteen officers who had since arrived.

#7.3 Epiphany

Our next encounter is one that revolves around a trainee that I had in his first two weeks as a police officer. He was fresh out of college and wanted to be a police officer like his father. He was a good size man, built like a football player, and as far as I knew he was smart, strong and in pretty good shape. I believe in the concept of "total immersion" when it comes to training recruits and this officer would be no exception. Though the first two weeks of training are supposed to be for the recruit to "observe", I had him working hard right away.

We concentrated our efforts in large part on making traffic stops since that is one of the easiest and most productive ways to combat Evil. While I don't think that traffic violations are that important in the grand scheme of things and do issue far more warnings than tickets, traffic stops do allow the officer unprecedented accidental access to Evil and its fruits. It's like playing perp-lotto and hoping for a winning ticket. However, when playing perp-lotto, the odds of winning are much better than in a standard lottery. In both, however, "you can't win if you don't play".

The young officer and I had just finished conducting an investigative stop on a suspicious vehicle that was parked in the entrance to an apartment complex. The recruit was driving and I was in the passenger seat. I also had assumed the duties of operating the in-car computer that allows us to run computer checks on license plates, individual people, and virtually anything with a serial number.

As my "chauffeur" was returning to the driver's seat after completing the interaction with the suspicious person, a vehicle entered the apartment complex and drove by the patrol car. I could see the license plate clearly so I typed it into the computer and pressed "enter". By the time my recruit had sat down in the patrol car, the computer had returned information that the vehicle which had just driven by us had been reported stolen.

Often times when a stressful situation arises while training a recruit, I will try to raise the level of stress felt by the recruit further by talking fast, turning up the radio volume or shouting at the recruit. I don't do this to be mean, I do it because I think it is a valuable tool for helping me and especially the recruit, see how he or she reacts under pressure and thereby learn to cope with it more efficiently.

Consequently, I first told the recruit that the vehicle just ahead of us was reported stolen and that he needed to go arrest the Evil inside. He was visibly rattled at this revelation but managed to put the car in gear and drive forward. I could tell the dump of adrenaline he was having had given him tunnel vision because he drove right by the stolen car as it made a left turn into a side parking lot and positioned itself to back in to a parking space.

I was yelling commands and questions rapidly at the recruit and could see that it was having an effect on him. He managed to put the car into reverse and get back to the stolen car just as the driver was getting out of the car. Since most of what we had practiced up to that point were "routine" traffic stops, I was not surprised that when he got out of the patrol car, the first thing that the recruit said was, "Uhhhh, I need to see your drivers license and proof of insurance, sir."

Then the perpetrator did what I call a textbook avoidance technique. He began hurriedly walking away while engaging the officer in conversation. He said that his license was in his apartment and he would go get it. I knew immediately that Evil was paving the way for an escape. Evil kept looking at the officer (to see what he was doing and where he was) and then away from the officer (to find an acceptable escape route), then back at the officer and away again. This particular behavior is very common amongst the disciples of Evil. It's almost like they are waiting until they cross some magical line that is their starter-pistol-like signal to begin their escape. I told the recruit to close the gap between himself and the perp because Evil was getting ready to run.

My recruit was having obvious difficulty dealing with the sensory overload he was experiencing and was very slow to react to my command. I shouted my commands two more times with increasing volume each time before the recruit's brain finally processed the information and directed his muscles to move toward Evil. By then it was too late. My prediction came true and Evil broke into a sprint.

At this point I was almost giddy thinking about my front row seat to a foot chase with a felon, where for once the officer had the upper hand. Evil was in his late forties/early fifties and was overweight and slow. My recruit was young, tall and fast. The chase proceeded around the far side of the first apartment building and I took a short cut around the other side to evaluate and referee. Also, during this particular encounter, I would play the role of "cover" officer while the recruit was designated the "contact" officer.

As Evil came around the building, I fully expected to see my recruit hot on his trail and preparing to make a tackle. Evil came around the building and there was no officer. Shortly thereafter, the recruit appeared but was walking, not running. He looked confused.

I screamed at him, asking what the problem was and telling him to go lay the smackdown on Evil. He said he didn't want to chase Evil anymore because he had dropped his radio and was afraid to continue without it. I told him to forget about his stupid radio, that if any transmissions needed to be made, I would make them. I then pointed across the parking lot to where the perp was staring at us. Exhaustion was beginning to set in and he had slowed to nearly a walk.

After my brief and forceful pep talk, the recruit went back in pursuit of Evil and I thought for sure that the tackle I was anticipating was but moments away. Once again, I moved to a vantage point that would give me full and unobstructed view of the impending confrontation. I watched as the aging thief slowly came around the corner of a building and into view. I waited patiently for the recruit to appear. I watched as Evil got farther and farther away and then finally disappeared, and still there was no recruit. At that point I think that I was the one who was in shock because a car thief had literally just walked away from me.

Still stunned with disbelief, I turned to look for the trainee and found him walking back towards me from the side of another building. I administered my career's most serious ass-chewing and in the process, woke up half the residents of the apartment complex. When I was done, I asked my visibly shaken and remorseful counterpart if he had any explanation for his dismal performance. He could not have been more correct when he responded with shaking hands as he wiped off his glasses, "I think I had a panic attack."

I seriously doubted his ability to succeed in his chosen profession from that point forward and after a little more yelling (the most I have ever done on duty) I calmed down and we searched the area to no avail.

Evil was kind enough to leave his drivers license in the stolen car he had just evacuated, along with his current address, which just happened to be the apartment building adjacent to where he had parked. I had a few stern words with his wife that evening and though it took a few days, Evil and his lawyer arrived at the precinct for the appropriate charges to be made.

I can only assume what must have gone through the first time police officer's mind that night and in the days to follow.

Two nights later we had another foot chase with another car thief. This one got away too but he was far younger and far faster than the first. I yelled less and actually felt sorry for the recruit because the second brush with Evil was handled reasonably well. I could see after the second escape that he was visibly bothered and was having his own crisis. I did not want to make things any worse for him. I did, however, let him think that he had screwed up again, hoping it would cause him to do the necessary soul searching to decide if he had what it took to be real pO-lice.

Within two weeks, he redeemed himself many times over, when after a brief vehicle chase with two armed robbery perpetrators, he single-handedly chased one of them down in an apartment complex and took him into custody with a justifiable smackdown. Whatever epiphany he had must have been a good one. Though he had to remain in training the requisite two additional months, he in fact graduated that night. I was proud to be part of the process.

#7.4 Like a Chicken With His Head Cut Off

One of the first, really curious stress responses I ever had the privilege to witness first hand occurred when I was working the evening shift. I was sitting with another on-duty unit and an off-duty unit when radio shouted out that we had a signal 50 and 4 (person shot with ambulance dispatched) at an apartment complex about four blocks away from where the three of us were sitting.

By the time we had a chance to notify radio that we were responding to the call, the other on-duty unit and I were already entering the apartment complex in question. As we entered the complex, the other unit was in the lead and I was following. The dispatcher had told us that the call originated in the clubhouse, so naturally that's where we headed.

As we pulled up in front of the clubhouse, I immediately noticed that there was a large party going on and that no one was outside the building as you might expect if someone had been shot. The unit in front of me drove straight by the clubhouse at a high rate of speed. I assumed that he was driving around to the other side (good tactical maneuver) but as soon as I notified radio that we were on scene, I heard the unmistakable sound of screeching tires.

Almost immediately, the lead patrol car came around the corner in front of me, traveling in reverse and still squealing the tires. By that time, I was out of my patrol car and thought I might have to take evasive action to avoid becoming a victim of his excessive, erratic driving. As the other unit came to a stop, I returned my attention to the clubhouse and began assessing the situation. I try to make it a habit not to run into anything blindly, and try to see everything that I can before approaching a potentially hazardous situation.

I was walking cautiously toward the side of the clubhouse where there was a gate in a roughly six-foot tall privacy fence when my fellow officer came running past me. I was about twenty feet from the aforementioned gate when the other officer collided with it at full force. He was a large man whose weight was not what you would call "muscle weight" and when he hit the gate, a whole section of fence recoiled with the impact. After he struck the gate with his full body mass, he bounced backward and the gate swung open (towards us) about twelve inches. The officer proceeded to regain his balance and once again ran full force into the now closing gate. The gate slammed closed on impact. The fence rocked forward and the aging boards crackled from the force of the strike. The officer fell backward again and again the gate swung open – towards us. The officer was getting up in preparation for a third assault on the stubborn gate when I reached out with one finger and pulled it toward me. Magically, the gate opened exposing the once concealed swimming pool and rear yard of the clubhouse.

Without missing a beat, the officer charged through the unobstructed gateway like a bull rushing to meet the matador. I quietly and cautiously entered behind him. The yard was not large and the swimming pool occupied most of it. The other officer ran around the pool and back out the gate toward the patrol cars. I looked up at the clubhouse and saw a crowd of people drinking and dancing. No one seemed interested by my presence.

A man stepped out of the clubhouse to ask if there was a problem and I told him about the call the call that had brought us there. He said that he was sure there was no one inside who was injured and went back to his party. I began walking around the pool, looking for anything that seemed out of place.

When I got about half way around the swimming pool, I heard the other patrol unit advise radio that we would be back in service code 2 (meaning that the call was unfounded). Just then I heard a whistle. I stopped and listened and heard the whistle again. The second time, the whistle was followed by a person yelling, but I could not make out what they said.

I looked in the direction that the sound had come from. About forty yards away, at the bottom of a staircase that wound through a small, wooded area, I could see a person waving at me. I made my way down the stairs and found two females. They were attending to a man who was lying down on the last couple of stairs. He was bleeding profusely from the back of his head.

I told radio to disregard the code 2, that I had found the subject and I gave my location. As radio was responding to my traffic I heard the unmistakable sound of squealing tires once again. The next thing I knew, my backup unit was sliding sideways through the parking lot coming to my rescue.

Before he got to me, I was able to determine that the injured man, who incidentally was quite intoxicated, had simply fallen down the stone stairway and hit his head. As that information was broadcast to radio, my faithful assistant (who had not gotten out of his car yet) just drove away.

The frightening thing about extreme stress responses is that they are so unpredictable and that usually, the person affected does not remember his or her aberrant behavior. Different things affect people in different ways and you will never know how you handle stress until it hits. If and when it does, always debrief with others who were there and ask them what you did to see if you remember things the same way. That will be your best clue as to how you handle stress.

#7.5 By The Grace of God

An officer should try to avoid approaching potential Evil while still inside of a patrol car. Ideally, the officer should exit the patrol car before making personal contact with a suspect. It is too easy for Evil to hurt you if you are stuck sitting in an automobile while he has the free range of motion afforded a person on foot.

A case in point is an officer who responded to an armed robbery at a restaurant. The perps were known to be on foot in the general vicinity. The officer at first exercised good tactics by not going to the scene of the crime and by beginning his search a few blocks away, along a possible escape route.

He spied a suspicious male walking through a parking lot and for reasons unknown, the officer decided to drive right up to the individual to investigate. I would postulate that the officer was not expecting to find Evil and therefore approached the suspect under the assumption that he was not the target of the search. The officer was wrong. When searching for Evil, expecting to find it is a prerequisite.

As soon as the officer was within twenty or so feet of Evil, Evil produced a small semi-auto pistol, pointed at the officer and began firing while simultaneously walking closer and closer to the patrol car. The officer froze. He did not drive away and he did not draw his pistol to return fire. He simply sat until Evil quit shooting. By the grace of some guardian angel or other higher power, bullets struck all around the officer and riddled his car with holes, but did not hit him. When all ammo was expended, Evil fled the scene.

I asked the officer some time later why he didn't do anything. He told me that he tried to get his pistol but couldn't get it out of the holster while sitting in the patrol car. He apparently had no plan B. Ever since I became a firearms instructor, I have recommended to my students that they practice drawing their pistol from the seated position…and any other position that they are likely to be caught in by Evil.

The funny thing about Evil is that he rarely makes a concerted effort to emulate the conditions under which we train.

#7.6 Thanks for the Mammaries

Some people are not meant to be police officers. The warrior mindset is so far removed from their paradigms that they are just not psychologically capable of dealing with the dangers of police work. One of my trainees discovered that he fit that description and he promptly made the proper decision to end his law enforcement career after a relatively innocuous and mildly humorous encounter.

We were dispatched to a disturbance call in a neighborhood bar. When we got there, we spoke to the manager who pointed out a half naked woman who was intoxicated and behaving obnoxiously and irrationally. He wanted her removed from the premises so naturally, I sent the trainee to make "contact" while I assumed my "cover" position. I could tell that he was nervous and flustered about confronting the topless, jiggly Evil. In fact, as he approached her, his gaze was fixed upon her mammaries. While he stammered and stuttered trying to tell the woman to leave, he did not see her wind up for a substantial right cross that took him totally by surprise. He was so shocked when she hit him square in the face that he just froze. She was about to nail him again when I stepped in and contained her with minimal effort. He quit the force two days later.

#7.7 Improv

I repeat ad nauseum throughout this writing that having a backup plan or the ability to improvise is a must for any police officer. Often the best course of action is not known until after a given confrontation has concluded. It is too late at that point to implement that plan. Consequently, we often have to live with inferior plans concocted at the spur of the moment. The one thing we must keep in mind, therefore, is that any plan that works is, by definition, a good plan. That plan may not be the best plan, but if it works, it certainly wasn't the worst plan.

Take for instance an officer that responded to a call on a burglar in a house (signal 6). The officer had one backup unit. The officer in question went to the rear of the apartment that the burglar was supposed to be in and the other officer went to the front. Evil saw the officer coming to the front door so he headed for the back door.

Evil had no weapon but was considerably larger than the officer that was covering the back door. When Evil stormed out of the residence toward the officer, the officer did what most police do. She drew her revolver, pointed it at Evil, and ordered him to stop. Evil kept on going and ran right up to the officer and tackled her. Evil then began trying to wrestle her gun from her hand.

The officer did not have a backup plan when she went to that call. She improvised. While Evil tried to wrestle her gun away, she squeezed the trigger. Once, twice, three times and on until all six rounds in her magnum were fired. Evil successfully wrenched the pistol from her hand after the last round was discharged.

The second officer at the scene made it to the rear of the building just in time to see Evil pointing the officer's gun at the officer's face and pulling the trigger. Thank God the gun was empty.

We would never teach that tactic in cop school. What if the stray bullets fired by the officer had injured or killed someone else? What if the officer only had time to fire five rounds before losing her weapon? What if the officer had never unholstered her weapon? The "what ifs" can go on forever but only one thing really matters. The officer lived through the encounter. She improvised a plan and it worked. Since the plan worked, it was a good plan. There may never be another situation where that same plan will work again. Whether because of fate, divine intervention, or mindless synchronicity, it worked that one time and it kept that officer alive.

Chapter 8

Hey Scumbag!…Got Change for a .40?

On one particular night, I was assigned to the morning watch and had the fortune of having a beat partner that I both knew and worked with quite well. Such alliances are rare and valuable and usually short lived. I don't remember the exact time, but it was near the beginning of the shift, probably just after midnight. We received a call on a suspicious person outside an apartment on the second floor of a two-story apartment building. Nothing alarming, and by all indicators just another "routine" call.

The apartment was located in what you would call a high crime area. Being familiar with the complex, we both knew exactly where to go. This particular apartment complex had three driveways, all of which fronted on the same roadway, which was oriented in a line running East and West. The western-most driveway led to a separate part of the complex that was not accessible by vehicle to the part of the complex served by the other two driveways.

We entered simultaneously into the center driveway. The building we were looking for was right in front of us. It is a rectangular building situated perpendicular to the roadway with apartments on the front and the back. It has two levels, which are accessed by open staircases at either end. The building is situated in such a way that when we pulled into the parking lot, we were facing the windowless, south end of the building. No one in the building could see us unless they were outside of an apartment on the common walkway.

As soon as we exited our patrol cars, a resident in the building next to our cars came outside and pointed to an apartment on the rear of the second floor of the building to which we were dispatched. This particular community was predominantly Mexican at the time and few residents spoke English. Often though, sign language seems to be universal.

I headed for the staircase on the opposite end of the building. My beat partner, of course, headed for the nearer staircase and we climbed to the second floor in concert. Tactically speaking, it is usually a good idea to allocate manpower in such a way as to cover the maximum amount of area with the minimum amount of officers. Just be conscious of potential cross-fire situations. If you are on one end of a walkway and your partner is on the other and you start shooting at someone in between…well, you get the idea. As we reached the second floor walkway, we both noticed that about midway down the corridor, there was what appeared to be a window screen lying on the concrete floor. I motioned for my beat partner to cover me while I approached the apartment in question.

As I got closer to the apartment, I was able to see broken glass scattered around the mangled window screen. Closer inspection suggested that the damage was recent. I could make out a broken windowpane in one of the windows that was right next to the only door in or out of the apartment.

I used a geometric progression to look in through the broken window. The aluminum mini-blinds were dispersed around the broken pane. As my vantage point improved, I saw a figure standing inside the well-lit apartment. He was wearing a mask. At that point, relying on my finely honed, keen cop senses, I made a dangerous leap of faith and assumed that he was Evil. I also saw a pistol in his hand and what looked like people lying face down on the floor of the apartment.

The masked man appeared to be looking around for something and as I watched, he was joined by two other masked men (also Evil). Those two men moved from one room, across my field of view and into another room that I could not see. I could hear someone saying something inside that sounded angry but could not make out what they said.

I slowly and quietly backed away from the apartment and moved back to my end of the corridor at the top of the stairs. Confident that I was out of earshot of anyone in the apartment, I raised radio and gave the following broadcast, "120, we have a confirmed signal 36 (holdup in progress). There are at least three masked perpetrators 69 (armed) with handguns. We have several possible victims face down on the floor of the apartment. Hold traffic and advise units enroute to enter through the middle driveway. Our patrol cars will be parked directly beside the building. We are on the second floor of that building in the rear."

Richard A. Nable

So we sat and waited for what seemed like minutes but was probably only seconds. Three units announced via radio that that they had arrived at our location. I felt a bit relieved because while my partner and I had the two ends of the corridor covered, Evil could still jump over the railing and avoid our trap. I expected to see additional officers any second but instead heard one of the units that was supposed to be on scene, call out on the radio. "Radio can you raise 120 for TAC?"

I remember thinking to myself, "Oh my god you can't be serious. Okay, I'll play your silly game." I clicked my radio to the tactical channel and said, "120 go ahead."

The unit responded by saying, "We are in the complex but are having difficulty locating you."

Obviously a bit irritated, I responded as clearly as I could, "Enter the complex through the middle driveway. You will see our patrol cars directly in front of you. Park there. We are on the second floor of that building in the rear. I will be returning to main channel now."

Shortly thereafter, we no longer had to worry about our backup units. Not because they found us, but because the first perpetrator came out of the apartment. I heard footsteps running toward the other end of the walkway, so I knew my partner was going to make "first contact". I remained crouched at the top of the stairs on my end, so as not to give away my position until absolutely necessary. I heard my partner begin yelling those cherished expletives and an uncontrolled grin came over my face.

Shortly thereafter, those footsteps that initially went to the other end of the hall were suddenly coming my way. This is what we call an "oh shit" moment. When it sounded like the footsteps were getting close, I jumped up from my hiding place pointing my pistol, and fired my expletives. Even through the masks worn by the two perps I was now facing, I could see that their "oh shit" moment was having a much greater effect on them than mine was on me. They both immediately threw up their hands and their weapons hit the floor in front of me. They began back-pedaling and I began advancing. I remember tucking my pistol in close to my body and knocking one of them down with my non-weapon hand, and with that they both went face down on the floor.

80

I took a step back to assess the situation. I could see that at the other end of the hall, my partner had the first perp in much the same position as I had the second and third. I then yelled for him to cover me as I holstered my weapon and secured my two (always carry at least two handcuffs). When my two bad guys were secured and given a quick pat for weapons, I stood up and took a cover position for my partner to do the same with his bad guy.

So there we were with three bad guys contained and an unchecked apartment with who knows what inside…and oh yeah, still no backup units! I looked at my partner and asked, "Where is everybody?" He just looked at me and shrugged. Not too long after that, our shift commander came boppin' up the stairs on my partner's end. He looked at the bad guy on his end. Then he looked at the two bad guys on my end. Then he asked, "Where is everybody?" We both shrugged again and one of us asked the shift commander if he could watch over the Evil while we cleared the apartment to make sure there were no more perps or injured parties. He did. We cleared the apartment. No more Evil and the victims were fine.

We took the bad guys down to the patrol car and as we were putting them inside, there came all three backup units. As it turned out, the first unit went into the complex across the street and the other two followed. They kept driving around in circles until one of them had the bright idea to check elsewhere. Better late than never …I guess.

As a side note, while interviewing the victims, they told us that $6000.00 in cash had been taken. In and of itself that is not out of the ordinary. Many of the Mexican immigrants in that area are hard workers who don't trust our banks, so they keep lots of cash on hand. That makes them good targets for home invaders. And since many don't trust the police either, many such crimes go unreported. We did recover $6000.00 from one of the evildoers. I then decided to make a cursory search of the area around the building to make sure I didn't miss anything. On the far end of the building I found a duffel bag. In the duffel bag was eight pounds of marijuana. That duffel bag wasn't there ten minutes before, so I asked the male head of household at the apartment if he knew anything about the duffel bag.

He said, "No," and that he had never seen it before.

I asked if he was sure. He said, "Yes."

Then I asked, "Then why does it have your name on it?"

Remember, things are not always as they seem. Evil is everywhere! Both victim and perpetrator were arrested.

#8.2 Crimes Against Children Are The Worst

My next story is again from my days working the evening watch. If I recall correctly, I had been on the force for about two years. I responded to a call on a signal 56 (missing person) at the local Office Depot, which, at the time, shared a building with another large discount store. Even with only two years of service, I was at times plagued by complacency. I immediately went into report takin' mode and casually drove up to the front of the store and stepped out of my patrol car with clipboard in hand.

I was met by a frantic mother and father who also happened to be the co-managers of the Office Depot. They explained to me how their five-year-old son regularly accompanied them to work. He normally played around the front of the store and the employees treated him like family. He always stayed close by and it was not like him to wander off. He had been gone about 15 minutes and the mother was sure that something bad had happened. The father was trying to be strong and reassuring to his distraught wife but I could see that he was worried too.

I started taking down the pertinent information and gave a description (signal 78) of the missing five year old over the radio for units in the area. At that particular point in our department's history, we were changing over from the old UHF radios to new and more sophisticated 800 MHZ radios. They were a little larger but they did a lot more than the old radios. They also didn't come with shoulder microphones so when you wanted to talk, you had to take the radio off your belt and hold it in front of your face. Needless to say, talking on the radio put us at a distinct tactical disadvantage because that meant at least one hand was occupied. In this particular case, my other hand was busy juggling my clipboard and pen.

As luck would have it, while I was sending the boy's description over the radio, his mother shrieked and pointed to the far end of the shopping center. "That's my baby!" she screamed.

The only child I could see in the direction she was pointing was riding on the shoulders of a man who was walking around the end of the building about seventy-five yards away. The father and I looked at each other in disbelief for a moment. Then I took off on foot.

A curious thing about stress: your muscles become tense and I discovered that day that anything you hold in your hand when the adrenaline dump happens, gets gripped that much harder. It wasn't until I came running around the corner at the end of the building and saw the kidnapper that this fact came so strikingly clear. I went to reach for my pistol and discovered that my clipboard was in the way. I used a few precious moments to consciously discard the cumbersome equipment and drew my magnum.

In retrospect, I'm not sure what I hoped to accomplish by unleashing my stainless steel partner but hey, that's what cops are conditioned to do. We point our guns at Evil and expect it to do what we tell it to do. The only problem is that in real life, Evil rarely complies. In this particular case, the man who was on his second week of parole after serving just two years of a life sentence for aggravated child molestation and kidnapping (among other things), dropped his would be victim and ran like the wind.

That particular moment was the closest I had ever come to firing my pistol at anyone. I felt the pressure of my trigger finger increasing and in the back of my mind knew that the hammer was drawing closer to its ultimate, un-retractable conclusion. At the shooting range, I hadn't yet shot below 100% and I knew I could hit him. I can't tell you the myriad of emotions and things that leapt through my mind in the split second that it took me to holster my weapon. I guess all that matters is that I holstered.

The little boy's mother had time to scoop up her little angel, who undoubtedly had no idea of the narrowly averted tragedy that would have changed his life forever, or might even have brought it to an abrupt end.

I had also dropped my radio when I dropped my clipboard, so in the eternity that it took to holster my weapon and pick up my radio, Evil got a good head start. I remember calling out on the foot chase over the radio, but just as I began talking, a civilian drove up next to me and yelled, "Get in!" I looked and saw that he was wearing an Office Depot shirt and decided that his suggestion was a good one since my patrol car was at the other end of the parking lot. I jumped into his car and directed him to the side streets behind the shopping center. That neighborhood was a good one for setting up a perimeter. I knew it like the back of my hand and I wasn't about to let that Evil get away.

Moments later I was jumping out of the civilian car on the residential street behind the shopping center. I was on a ridge that was roughly even with the elevation of the shopping center I had just left, and Evil was in the valley between the two. As I made my way between the houses, I could see the embankment directly behind the shopping center. At the top of the embankment, working their way down, there were about ten people. All of them were wearing those bright red Office Depot shirts. I knew Evil was about to lose. I felt good.

Sure enough, within minutes we had our bad guy in custody. He sustained only a few contusions that wouldn't be visible for a few more days. Once surrounded, he offered little resistance. All the time we were taking statements, attempting to interrogate him and finally taking him on the thirty or so minute ride to our jail, he never said a word.

That day offered me a lot of lessons. I learned that "justice system" is a misnomer and have since called it a "legal system". I also learned that doing Good is it's own reward - it has to be. As far as I know, neither the little boy nor his parents ever thanked me or anyone else involved in the recovery of their son or the apprehension of his kidnapper and would-be molester. I thought I was a shoo-in for Officer of the Year, but instead it went to an officer who publicly cried when he found a missing three-year-old girl. That little girl wasn't so lucky. She wandered away from home when her mother passed out drunk. Hours later the mother woke up and called police when she couldn't find her daughter. The swimming pool the little girl drowned in is now a parking lot. If that's what it took to make Officer of the Year that year, I was glad that it wasn't me. Crimes against children are by far the worst.

#8.3 Good Job – Good Attitude

While stopped at a red light one night early in my morning watch shift, I was suddenly startled by someone banging on my car window. I am usually very observant and make it a point not to let anyone sneak up on me, but this guy truly took me by surprise. He was a Mexican male who spoke little or no English, but I could tell from the way that he was frantically jumping up and down, holding his hand with thumb up, index finger extended and other three fingers curled that something was amiss. Oh yeah, I did hear him say "pistola" as he pointed to the shadows of a building behind me and on my left.

My years of training and experience coupled with my razor sharp instincts told me that Evil might just be nearby.

As I turned to look in the direction the frightened man was pointing, what to my wondering eyes would appear but Evil dressed all in black and wearing a sneer...and carrying a big black gun. As our eyes met it was truly magic. He took off running and I took off after him.

I was smart enough at least to begin the pursuit with my car but he was smart enough (or lucky enough) to run quickly to a place where my car could not follow, so I was forced to continue on foot.

I was initially unable to get onto the radio because of some inane chatter, but before long, I noticed a conspicuous lack of noise in the speaker that sits perched on my left shoulder. I seized the opportunity to give a burst of speech from my already overtaxed lungs.

It is important when in a foot chase to spend as much energy on the chase as possible and as little on anything else as is practical. The police officer is automatically at a disadvantage because even on the off chance that the officer is in good shape, he or she is carrying some twenty pounds of extra gear and is often far less motivated to catch Evil than Evil is motivated not to be caught.

I mentioned earlier that my philosophy on foot chases is that if you don't catch the perp in the first 100 yards, then the goal is to slow down but keep him in sight and begin directing responding units on how to effectively establish a perimeter to contain the fleeing Evil. When the perp sees that the police are no longer near, then he usually slows down also. If he thinks he is out of sight, 99 % of the time he will take the opportunity to hide rather than continue running. Once a perimeter is established, a careful search may be conducted starting from the last place the perp was seen and he will usually be caught shortly thereafter.

I managed to blurt out on the radio, "122, foot chase, 5920 Roswell Rd. West through the upper lot." Perhaps that's not an exact quote but it's darn close. For once (and to my utter amazement) the dispatcher said very little and so did responding units, leaving the air clear for me to continue my blurted and strained announcements.

Shortly thereafter, the 100-yard window had been reached and I began slowing. I was transitioning from pursuit mode to stalking mode. Just then I saw Evil come to an abrupt stop and turn my way. I stopped and drew my pistol because I knew he had a pistol also and thought that he might be getting ready to take a shot at me. Instead he seemed not to know I was there as he deposited his weapon under a bush and covered it with pine straw before continuing his flight.

I would like to take a moment to add that any police officer who engages in a foot chase with his pistol in his hand has perhaps not thoroughly considered the tactical implications of such an action.

I re-holstered and continued my mobile surveillance. I was still a bit stressed but was recovering from the anaerobic energy burst required for an impromptu foot chase and advised radio that Evil had just jumped a wall and was running along an adjacent side street. I heard one or two units say, "Clear" on the radio and nothing else. I was proud of my people.

I noticed that a civilian car had been driving through the parking lot in the same direction as we were running and I even remember thinking that there should have been an off duty officer working an extra job in that particular shopping center, but did not immediately connect the two.

Just as I was traversing the aforementioned wall, I saw the civilian car out of the corner of my left eye. It was accelerating towards Evil. The driver of the vehicle honked the horn, slammed on the brakes and jumped out of the car yelling. When Evil turned to look, he just happened to be crossing the driveway of the shopping center and tripped over the curb.

Evil fell flat on his stupid little face and gave us both just enough time to jump right on top of him. The civilian car had in fact been occupied by the uniformed, off duty officer working his extra job. He also happened to be an officer I had trained not long before.

The first words out of Evil's mouth were an all too typical, "I didn't do nothin'." After securing the bad guy in the first arriving patrol car, I immediately went to retrieve the pistol. Upon returning with the weapon, I found my original complainant standing by the patrol car. The officer who searched the prisoner had found the complainant's wallet in Evil's back pocket.

A translator later verified that Evil had robbed the young man of his wallet, but to the victim's credit, the hard working, young immigrant managed to retain his dignity and fortitude. He was the primary reason that this Evil was captured. I left him with one of my signature phrases…"Good job – Good attitude."

#8.4 I Always Run From The Police

There is a curious phenomenon that rears its ugly head from time to time, usually in the more urban areas. That phenomenon is the desire to run from the police, whether in a vehicle or on foot, just to see if the police will run after you. I don't really understand it but it does happen. One example in particular occurred one night when, during shift change from evening watch to morning watch, (a time when my jurisdiction is for all intents and purposes devoid of police, thanks to the bizarre method of shift construction used by our administrators) a pedestrian was robbed in one of our local "high crime" areas.

Several evening and morning watch officers responded to the scene in a rather untimely manner and began half-heartedly canvassing the area for anyone who even remotely matched the description that had been given of the perpetrator. Before long there was a very large police presence in the immediate vicinity and wouldn't you know it, someone spotted someone matching the description of Evil.

The officer gave his location and promptly followed his transmission with a winded burst of, "He's runnin'!"

We were all certain that this must be our man so we began to set up a perimeter and closed in. The foot chase headed for a creek in the rear of an apartment complex. I knew the area all too well and knew that the perp could follow the creek bed through two more complexes before coming out on a side street. I went to the intersection of that side street and creek and hid and waited.

It wasn't long before my strategy proved fruitful and I saw a man matching our perp's description walking toward me on the sidewalk of an apartment building adjacent to the creek. I let radio know that I had him in sight and began trying to close the distance between us as stealthily as possible. Evil saw me and made an about-face.

I ran on the other side of the building but parallel to him, hoping to meet him on the other side. When I got to the other side, all I found was more police. We sat bewildered for a moment trying to figure out where Evil had gone. Someone mentioned hearing a door slam. Making use of our acute powers of deductive reasoning, we collectively concluded that Evil must have gone into an apartment.

By logical deduction we narrowed down the possible apartments to two. I knocked on the door of one and a mute female answered the door with quite a strange and wild look in her eye. I asked her if anyone had just run into her apartment and she gave a subtle but somewhat panicked, jerky nod in the affirmative.

My next question was, "Is he still here?".

Again the jerky little nod.

My next question, "Does he live here?"

Again a jerky nod but this time in the negative.

I then asked, "Do you know him?"

Jerky negative nod.

" Can we come in and get him?"

With that she stepped aside and flung the door open, pointing to the rear of the apartment.

We began a slow and deliberate search of the apartment with a man standing guard outside. The first room was clear, then the second, which was the bedroom. All that was left was a hallway and the bathroom to which it led.

The hallway was clear as was the closet in the hallway, which meant he had to be in the bathroom. We jerked open the shower curtain and the fight was on. It didn't take long to subdue the individual and we took him, handcuffed, to a waiting patrol car. As usual, Evil said, "I didn't do nothin'."

Just before reaching the car, Evil broke the grip of the escorting officer (who happened to be me) and again attempted to flee. Even the most adept runners find it difficult to escape when cuffed. This one made it exemplary thirty or so feet before I gave a gentle push between his shoulder blades and down he went without the benefit of arms to break his fall.

When it was all over, we had the victim come to identify the perp. It took only a second for the victim to declare adamantly that the man we had in custody was not the person who had robbed him.

The next logical question was, "Why did you run from the police?" (Which, incidentally, is illegal in Georgia under some circumstances.)

He said, "Cuz I always run from the police. "

How can you argue with that?

#8.5 Evil-sicle

For several days, there was an old, 1960's era Chevrolet with a "For Sale" sign in the window, parked next to the roadway in a shopping center parking lot. The car had been decked out with the latest metallic spray paint technology and had some chrome rims that were more suited for yard art than a platform for a motor vehicle. Nevertheless, if something stays in one place long enough, someone will eventually try to steal it.

That axiom proved true and it just happened to be coming to fruition as an officer drove by. He noticed that the car we had all passed countless times was now on blocks. Ducked down, behind and beside the vehicle was Evil number one in the process of removing the last wheel.

The officer pulled out on the radio as he turned around to investigate. Unbelievably, when the officer drove up to Evil, Evil ran away…even though the officer told him to stop.

The foot pursuit had commenced and, as is typical of the morning watch, within seconds there were half a dozen officers on scene. The pursuit went as many do, with Evil running and hiding, officers searching and finding, and Evil running and hiding again.

By the time I made it to the scene, there was a good perimeter set, and we knew Evil was inside. I picked up two officers that were on foot in the area and I dropped one of them off in a subdivision behind where Evil was last seen. I deposited the other officer at a strategic point in the perimeter and went to join the search.

As I approached the point where the primary officer had last seen Evil, officers called out that they had him in sight and that he was running in my direction. I pulled into a parking lot and got out on foot, headed for the wood line to meet Evil.

Instead, I met other officers who swore they had chased him right to me. I knew for a fact he hadn't come past me, so he had to be somewhere else. The officers knew he hadn't come back toward them, so that meant that Evil must have found a nice little hole to crawl into.

We searched intently for a minute or two before the process of elimination assured us that Evil had gone into a 3-foot wide drainage pipe that ran underneath the parking lot where I had parked. We positioned one officer on the end of the pipe where Evil went in. I proceeded to the other end of the parking lot to see where the pipe came out.

On the other side of the parking lot was dense vegetation including some briars that Br'er Rabbit would be happy to call home. On that side of the parking lot, the drainpipe continued its course in the form of a small creek that was at the bottom of about an 8-foot ditch. The dense vegetation grew all around the banks of the creek but I could see straight down into the water.

I must add here that the temperature that night was about 20 degrees and those of us who weren't in the water were freezing badly enough. I knew, when I looked into the creek and saw a tennis shoe that appeared to be attached to a foot, that I was looking at one cold Evil.

I announced quietly over the radio that I had located Evil in the creek and that officers needed to position themselves around the creek to contain him when he inevitably ran, as he was sure to do if his hypothermic limbs would allow. I had my beat partner go down the creek about 50 yards and wait. He advised over the radio that he was in position at which time I illuminated Evil's foot and yelled some of my cherished expletives.

Evil was slow in responding but as expected, got up to run. He ran straight down the creek bed to the waiting officer. As I was trying to forge my way through the briars with limited success, I heard some muffled yelling in the distance and then a few thuds and some splashing. When I made my way to the apprehension site, most other officers were already there and Evil was face down in the creek, gurgling and getting handcuffed.

We dragged his nearly frostbitten body up the slippery, ivy-covered bank while the steam billowed from his person as if he were a hot iron just placed in cool water.

We all performed the "high-fives", praises and exaltations that customarily accompany a victory against Evil. We turned our Evil-sicle over to the initiating officer and everyone left.

I got about a block away before I came to the startling realization that we had not recovered the stolen wheels. I raised the initiating officer on the radio and asked if he had seen them. He said that he had not. Most of the other officers had left the vicinity when I advised radio that I would be checking the area for accomplices and the stolen rims.

The best place to start a search is where the item you are searching for was last seen. In my particular case, that place was in the parking lot where the car was parked. As I drove into the parking lot, I noticed that there were three or four cars parked on the side of a bank building next to the parking lot where Evil had been caught stealing.

I parked out of sight and snuck up on those four cars. Outside and behind one of the cars (which was backed into a parking space) I saw what looked like the missing wheels. As I got closer, I saw that Evil number two was in that car. I got even closer and realized that Evil number two was sound asleep.

I went back to my patrol car and quietly moved it to a strategic position in front of Evil's car to block any vehicular escape attempts. I told radio that I had located Evil number two and gave my location. Then I calmly approached Evil's car and aimed my 75,000 candlepower flashlight (which replaced my older, less powerful unit) directly in Evil's eyes while simultaneously knocking on the window with my Glock. The combination of sensory inputs was enough to startle him back to the land of the living and I once again had the opportunity to use my cherished expletives.

By the time all of my backup came screaming into the parking lot, I had Evil in cuffs and was beginning to inventory all the potentially stolen items that filled Evil's stolen car. The lesson learned is, no matter what you're searching for, if you find one...there is always a chance that there are more. Be careful and have fun.

#8.6 Something Wicked This Way Comes

I enjoy many of the tools of the police trade. We have so many neat little gadgets available to help us do our jobs better. We have little tiny flashlights that are brighter than car headlights were when I was growing up. We have cloth that stops bullets. We have computers that give us instant access to information from all over the nation. We have guns with plastic frames and metal that doesn't rust. We have passive infrared detectors that can see a heat source three hundred yards away in the dark. We have fast cars and cool bikes and all sorts of neat toys that just had to be back-engineered from downed alien spacecraft. (Just kidding about the alien thing.)

One of my personal favorites is my night vision. In the early 1990's, the price of light amplification devices came down considerably and they are at the point now where some of the low-end units are available at the local discount store. I got my second-generation night vision monocular in 1995 and was truly amazed. I could go outside in the complete darkness and see everything as clear as if it were daytime (except it's green). I could see stars and animals that you would never know were there; but most important of all, I could use it to find Evil.

That device came in quite handy on one particular occasion when one of our officers located a car in a parking lot next to a very dark neighborhood. The officer recognized the car as one that he had linked (through superior investigative work) to a perpetrator who had been stealing from cars in the general area.

We had the advantage at that point because we knew Evil was in the neighborhood and, in all likelihood, Evil did not know we were there. We had ample time to position about seven units in the area of the parking lot. The majority of us were on foot trying to find a place to hide so that we could pounce on Evil when he returned to his car with the evening's cache of stolen goods.

I had my trusty night vision and was trying to decide the best and most strategic place to position myself. I came to the conclusion that our forces were amassed too heavily to one side and decided to head for the side of the street opposite the parking lot where everyone else was hiding and waiting. The only problem was that we didn't know exactly where Evil was and there was a large open area I would have to traverse to get to my destination. The other tactical problem was that from Evil's suspected vantage point, my form would be backlit by a distant streetlight.

I turned on my night vision unit and checked the entire area that I could see. I saw no Evil so I quickly moved to a position near the entrance to the parking lot and behind an enormous pine tree. The initiating officer followed me. I whispered that I was going to use the night vision to check down the roadway into the neighborhood before making the final move to the other side of the street.

I glanced from behind the pine tree and saw through the night vision what looked like a man. I studied the image for a second and determined that it was indeed a man and that the man was jogging up the street right toward us. I carefully laid my night vision on the ground at the base of the pine tree and turned to the other officer that was with me and said softly, "He's running right at us."

I had whispered so quietly that the officer did not understand me and asked me to repeat. I whispered and pointed, "He's right there."

The other officer said, "What?"

I said, "Just follow me."

I could tell by the sound of his footsteps that the man was very near the tree where we were hiding so I jumped out from behind it and hit him in the eyes with the beam of my high-powered flashlight. He was disoriented by the sensory overload caused by my blinding light and the dissident chords of several, randomly screaming officers. Everyone else's attention also turned to Evil as a result of my unexpected illumination. He was surrounded instantly and though he started to "bow-up", I think common sense got the best of him. We pounced on him and took him into custody without injury to any of the parties involved. He was a huge man and I am glad we avoided a fight. He had broken into two cars in the neighborhood and was still clutching his "take" for the night when we took him down.

#8.7 Polly Wanna Perpetrator?

I was sitting in the parking lot of a drug store doing paperwork when my attention turned to some indiscernible yelling coming from my surrounding environment. I looked up in time to see a man running across the parking lot being chased by two other men. Once again, my acute and finely honed instincts suggested to me that at least one of the three men was likely Evil.

I began this particular foot chase in the most desirable position, which was inside of my patrol car. I drove alongside of the two men who were doing the chasing and they began pointing at the man ahead of us. At that point I made the leap of faith that perhaps Evil was the man being pursued. I called out on the radio with my location and direction of travel and closed the gap between Evil and me.

When Evil darted off the roadway into the yard between two houses I figured it was about time to join him on foot. He ran and scaled an eight-foot, wooden privacy fence and dropped his brown leather jacket in the process. I was not at all confident in my ability to scale the aforementioned fence with the same agility and cat-like prowess as my prey, so I went around it.

My chosen path strategically landed me directly behind Evil once again. Surprisingly, Evil ignored my direct orders to "stop right there" etc., and we continued running through the backyards of the World War II era neighborhood. Each yard was separated by smaller, roughly four-foot tall, chain link and welded wire fences that I was able to hurdle with minimal difficulty.

Evil stayed true to foot chase principles and circled back to his original starting point by making consecutive right turns. He had gained on me by the time he got back to the drug store parking lot and jumped into his gold, late 1980's model, four-door Chevy. The last thing I saw before he drove out of sight, was the manager of the 24-hour breakfast joint that shared a parking lot with drug store, running up to the driver's window of the Chevy pointing a Government model .45 caliber semi-auto pistol and yelling something.

Thankfully, the man had the wisdom not to fire on the driver as he screeched out of the parking lot. I thanked him for his help and told him to be careful with the weapon. I then went in search of my extemporaneous, tag-team relay-race partners.

As it turns out, they were the manager and an employee of a pet store that was about a block away. They had been having trouble with the theft of exotic birds and the man they were chasing was their likely suspect. I asked if he had stolen anything and they said that they were not sure. I told them that Evil had dropped his jacket during the chase, that I was going to retrieve it, and that I would meet them back at their store.

I returned to the privacy fence where Evil dropped his jacket, and thankfully it was still there. I picked up the jacket and immediately noticed that it was a good bit heavier than expected. Further investigation revealed that there was an adult cock-a-too imprisoned in one of the sleeves of the jacket. (A cock-a-too is a large, white, exotic, Australian bird like the one made famous in the TV show "Baretta".) The bird was valued at $2500.

Despite his harrowing adventure, the little avian was safely returned to his keepers, none the worse for wear. Besides the bird, Evil left some other interesting things in his jacket - like a Western Union receipt with his name, address, and phone number on it.

While I was in the parking lot taking down the necessary information for my report, a citizen pulled up and said that he had followed Evil's car down the street to a grocery store, where Evil had parked and fled the scene on foot. Since the grocery store was across jurisdictional boundaries, when the citizen had called 911 from the grocery store, he got the runaround from the call-takers so he decided just to come back to the scene to get me.

I was able to impound the car and get an arrest warrant for Evil, who just happened to reside on the beat adjacent to mine. When I went to arrest the budding young ornithologist in his run down, ramshackle apartment, the only things that he had in his home were a mattress, a pregnant girlfriend and about twenty untraceable and most probably purloined, exotic birds.

#8.8 I'll Take You Out…And I Don't Mean Dinner And A Show

I responded to a fight call one afternoon in one of our target rich environments. As was common in those days there was no backup available. I entered the small apartment complex cautiously since the fight was supposed to be in the parking lot. I did not have to look long to find it. Just inside the complex there was a group of thirty or more people all gathered in front of one of the buildings. They all seemed to be looking at something and did not see me pull in.

I exited my patrol car quietly, about twenty yards from the crowd and approached on foot. There was some yelling but I couldn't understand what was being said. When I got to about halfway between my car and the crowd, someone charged out from the building toward the crowd, and the crowd moved en masse away from the charger. It did not take long to see why. The person charging the crowd like a bull in the streets of Pomplona, was wielding a very large butcher knife.

I decided to make my presence known and pointed my magnum at the perceived Evil. I yelled, "Drop the knife or I'll drop you." Everyone's attention seemed to turn to me at that point and Evil started walking toward me with the knife. I yelled something else at Evil (like "I'll take you out and I don't mean dinner and a show") and, realizing the gravity the situation, it calmly laid the knife on the ground. I secured the knife and Evil, and then tried to decipher the events that had brought me there.

I asked for a spokesperson from the now docile crowd. A man stepped forward to explain to me that the person who was wielding the knife had been seen behind one of the buildings performing an act of sodomy on another individual. Residents were understandably upset at that development and since there were children in the neighborhood who could have seen the act, they were doubly incensed. Instead of calling police, some of the residents were about to take matters into their own hands and deliver unto Evil a punishment they thought was appropriate.

I then interviewed Evil, which at first glance appeared to be a very large and very homely woman who was wearing a bad skirt and an even worse wig. I soon discovered that a major reason for the ire of the local townsfolk was that Evil was not a woman but was a mid-transgender individual named Towana (nothing else, just Towana). To be more specific, Evil was a man who had undergone breast implant surgery and was undergoing hormone therapy as a precursor to the operation needed to turn him into a woman. (That particular operation is called a dickectomy. It is soon followed by an addavagtome. The opposite operation, for turning a woman into a man, is called an addadicktome.)

I was able to defuse the situation and leveled the appropriate charges. The preliminary court hearing was interesting because in an effort to confuse the judge, I would alternately refer to Towana as he and then she. After all, it could go either way. About half way through the testimony, the judge became obviously frustrated and confused and said, "I don't mean to be rude, but what exactly are you?"

#8.9 Honest Chief, It Wasn't Me!

The last few stories in this chapter come with a disclaimer. The activities discussed are not necessarily presented as sound tactics and they may represent a stark departure from current accepted behavior and departmental policies. I personally would never condone such activity and certainly would not participate in it. The following accounts are of the activities of officers who will remain nameless and will be written in the first person solely for the sake of convenience.

Often when cars break down or are for other reasons left on the shoulder of the highway, Evil comes along and steals things from them. Anything is fair game. Evil will steal tags, tires, batteries, stereos, fenders, air bags and anything else it thinks it can sell for more than a dollar. Evil will also occasionally park on the Interstate and walk through the woods to perpetrate a particular crime and then run back to the Interstate for a quick getaway. For that reason, most good police officers will spend some time patrolling the highway looking for things other than just traffic violators.

One night in particular, I was driving down the Interstate for about the twelfth time and had already made a mental note of all the vehicles parked along the side of the roadway. Across the median of the divided highway, I saw one of the cars that had been parked on the side of the road for several days and there was another car parked right next to it with its lights off. That meant one of two things; either another car had broken down in exactly the same spot or Evil was there.

I sped down to the next exit to turn around since the median was not crossable at that location. By the time I made it back to the car in question, the other car I had seen was gone. I didn't need to get out to see if Evil had been there, the freshly broken glass on the ground and the absence of the second car were enough to confirm my suspicions. I told dispatch what I had and sped down the Interstate to check the next abandoned car for Evil.

As I came around the corner approaching the location of the next abandoned car, I saw another car parked right next to it with its lights off. I was sure that I had found Evil, so I quickly pulled in front of Evil's car and got out. I shone my flashlight in through Evil's windshield, momentarily blinding the two young occupants who had just finished breaking into the umpteenth car of the evening. I pointed my pistol at the driver and ordered him not to move.

He froze for a second or two and then put the car in gear and began to drive around my makeshift roadblock. Instinctively, I fired two rounds at the front left tire as it squealed by, narrowly missing my feet. (It's important to note that contrary to the Hollywood perception, most vehicle tires deflate quite slowly when struck by handgun rounds, assuming that the rounds penetrate the tire at all. The rubber in the tire usually has a tendency to seal over once the bullet passes through and only lets out a small amount of air.) I ran back to my patrol car and jumped in simultaneously telling dispatch that I was in a pursuit. The little Japanese car had gotten a head start, but in no time I was gaining fast. As we approached an exit ramp a mile or two down the road, I could see sparks as they started to peel off of the wheel I had shot at. The car began swaying from side to side and with each over-correction, the juvenile driver lost more control of the vehicle.

It wasn't long before he lost control completely. He spun around several times before his crippled vehicle came to rest, harmlessly blocking the right hand lane of the highway. Both occupants vacated the vehicle with remarkable speed and agility so common to individuals under twenty years of age. The passenger ran towards the exit ramp and the driver chose to run down the shoulder of the roadway.

If possible, I always try to go after the driver. That's what I did here. I drove up onto the grass behind Evil and was preparing to smack him with my front bumper. He was running as fast as his little legs could take him and as he turned to see where his pursuer was, I was so close to him that I could see the shock and amazement in his eyes at the impending doom barreling down upon him in the form of a Ford police interceptor.

It was at that point that I realized two important things simultaneously. Evil couldn't have been more than fifteen years old and that we were fast approaching a natural barrier that would destroy my car. The thought of all the paperwork involved in making a juvenile arrest that generally only nets the functional equivalent of a wrist slap, made me slam on the brakes just as Evil went flopping and rolling down the steep, kudzu covered embankment and into the creek below. I almost got out to run after him but then thought that in the grand scheme of things, perhaps it would be better to let him get away…so I did. That way there was only one account of what had just transpired.

An officer responding to the scene said, "Any idea what made them crash?"

I casually responded, "I'm really not sure. Must've been something in the road," and I left to police up my brass.

#8.10 Two Out Of Three Ain't Bad

Most of the common, everyday, run of the mill varieties of Evil are stupid. They commit crimes because they cannot or will not get jobs. They spend their lives living off of taxpayers in two ways. They commonly are the recipients of any number of government entitlement programs and to supplement their socialist income, they often resort to stealing from honest people who work for a living. I am glad that they are usually stupid, because otherwise they would be much more difficult to catch.

Evil struck one of our all night convenient stores in the form of three young men brandishing pistols and demanding money. The clerk complied with their demands and as they jumped into the car that was backed in directly in front of the front doors of the business, the clerk called 911 and gave a complete description of Evil, its car and even its tag number.

Then, Evil proceeded directly down the main road heading South toward the city, as Evil often does. Within a mile or so, Evil was spotted by officers responding to the scene of the crime, since they too were driving up the main road. Surprisingly, Evil did not pull over as officers requested and a short vehicle chase ensued.

For whatever reason Evil does stupid stuff, Evil decided to pull off of the main road and try running on foot. As they headed down a dead-end side street, they slowed to an acceptable speed and leapt from the still moving car. The driver zigged when he should have zagged and was struck by the closest pursuing police car. One perp and one sheepdog were out of the race.

The other two representatives of Evil continued their flight into the woods and the residential neighborhoods nearby. As units converged, the next piece of Evil was found relatively shortly thereafter, pummeled and taken into custody.

The third and final Evil was a bit more slippery. Our entire shift was devoted to capturing the remaining perp. Several units were on foot and several more circling in vehicles. He defied the rules of foot chases by continuing to run non-stop for an impressive amount of time. The pursuit progressed over literally several miles, with officers finding, chasing, losing and finding again, the object of our pursuit.

We thought we finally had him cornered in a square block of a residential neighborhood and were moving in to spring a trap. One officer (who shall remain nameless) surprised Evil, and Evil took off on foot again. Evil was still faster than the frustrated and worn-out officer and in a common expression of desperation, the officer ripped off a few rounds in the general direction of Evil. Officers in the vicinity froze and called out to each other by voice rather than over the radio.

Several more reports came from the pistols of pursuing officers. Rather than having the desired effect of scaring Evil into submission, they had the often seen, and reverse effect of instilling greater motivation into the heart and limbs of Evil. That is the main reason we don't use warning shots (in addition to the fact that we don't want stray bullets just flying around willie-nillie). Residents began calling 911 to report the sound of gunfire in their backyards. Our supervisor took over the radio and said, "That's negative on signal 25s (shots fired) radio, I'm in the area and it sounded like a car backfire."

The supervisor decided rather prudently at that point to put an end to the pursuit and had all units go back in service. To borrow a phrase from the rock star "Meatloaf", two out of three ain't bad.

#8.11 Maybe, Maybe Not

My last story for this chapter is a short one. It revolves around a chase that was coming into our county from a neighboring county. The alleged Evil was driving a full size, Ford Bronco and was running down the left lane of the Interstate at whatever its maximum speed was.

As luck would have it, I was very close to the Interstate when radio advised of the approaching pursuit. When I got to the highway interchange, I could see down the Interstate for a relatively good distance in either direction. I saw the blue lights and highbeams that signaled the location of the rapidly approaching pursuit. I timed my entry to the highway so that I would be near the front of the pack as the chase went by.

This was one of those rare times when everything worked almost as planned. The chase was going a little more slowly than I suspected and before I knew it, I was actually in a position to be ahead of the bad guy. In a moment of what I believe to be divine inspiration, I drew my backup gun. I rolled down my window and assumed the lane to the right of Evil. As he was passing me, I briefly matched his speed and fired one round toward the right front wheel.

To avoid any unnecessary entanglements, I merged quickly and smoothly to my right to where there was a very well placed exit ramp of which I took full advantage. The pursuit went screaming by and I went about my business. I later learned that shortly after leaving our county, the pursuit ended when Evil had a single car accident that was apparently precipitated by a mysteriously flattened, front tire.

Chapter 9

The Devil is in the Details

Regardless of whether I am teaching a class or training an individual recruit, my comments will inevitably turn to the old adage that "The Devil is in the Details." In my opinion, there are a lot of good police officers in the world, but relatively speaking there are only a few exceptional police officers. One thing that the exceptional police officers have in common with each other is that they pay attention to the details. Consequently they catch things that ordinary police officers miss.

My first example is from an experience I had when my brother and I were actually assigned to the same shift (morning watch) and were working together one night. He had stopped a black Chevrolet Caprice four door with expired Alabama plates. I was operating one of the only cars that had a working computer and, as was often the case, I would use it to help other officers avoid relying on our dispatchers for information.

I started to my brother's location to see if perhaps I and my trusty computer could be of assistance. While I was on the way to his location, radio advised that the tag he ran was registered to a 1990 Chevrolet Caprice, black in color, to the individual that was driving the car and that the tag was expired. (Incidentally, Caprice is pronounced kuh-PREES and means a sudden or impulsive change in the way one thinks or acts. It is not a Capri - pronounced kuh-PREE - which just so happens to be an Island near Naples, Italy, a very thin cigarette, and a car made by Mercury.)

The driver and sole occupant of the vehicle had presented my brother with a traffic ticket that he had received that same day for driving that same vehicle with an expired tag. (In Georgia, by law you can only receive an expired tag ticket for the same car one time per calendar day). The ticket was written by one of our department's traffic enforcement officers (a.k.a. "ticket writin' officers"). The ticket indicated that the driver had an Alabama driver's license as well.

When I arrived on the scene of the traffic stop, I immediately noticed the first detail that led to the eventual arrest of the driver. The black Chevrolet Caprice that my brother had stopped was the kind that had the round edges and resembles a "bubble". That particular model represented a stark design departure from the "square" body style that was used on the Caprice for over 10 years up to the year 1991. In other words, the tag was registered to a 1990 Caprice but we were looking at a 1992 or later model. Perhaps it was a clerical error at the tag office but a good police officer should investigate, not assume.

The insurance and registration paperwork that so many officers take for granted, had the same vehicle identification number as the 1990 Caprice on the tag registration. Now the likelihood of something nefarious being afoot increased sharply. We now had three different documents asserting that a 1992 Caprice was a 1990 Caprice.

The next step, which should be automatic for a police officer, was to check the vehicle identification number on the dashboard of the vehicle. Surprise, surprise, surprise, the VIN on the car did not match the rest of the paperwork. A computer check of the VIN on the car revealed that the vehicle was reported stolen.

Also, a computer check of the driver's license number through Alabama showed that he had a valid driver's license and was not wanted. However, when we checked him not by his license number but by his name and date of birth, we discovered that he had a revoked Georgia driver's license and several outstanding warrants.

When we asked Evil why he didn't try to run from my brother when he initiated the traffic stop, Evil said, "Because that other officer was too stupid to figure it out, I figured you would be too." I couldn't wait to tell that to the officer who had written the first ticket.

To explain the last few paragraphs for those who may not be familiar, simply put, each state has its own "crime information center" which in Georgia is called GCIC (GA Crime Information Center). There is also a National Crime Information Center (NCIC). NCIC networks all the state computers so that they can talk to each other. This enables people hooked by computer to GCIC to get information on people from out of state. The system is not intelligent. It is just a computer that operates on the "garbage in - garbage out" principle. It cannot think. It gives us what we ask for.

When a judge issues a warrant for someone's arrest, the warrant is issued for a person with a name (except in extreme circumstance that won't be covered here). That warrant must then be entered by a human into the appropriate crime information center computer. That human may choose also to enter the warrant by the wanted person's OLN (operator's license number) but that is not often the case. Either way, the only way the warrant may be retrieved is if the person is checked by the information that was entered into the computer.

When you check an OLN, the number must be entered exactly as it appears on the license and checked through the specific state where it is used as a license number or no match will be found in the data files (Social security numbers are not accessible unless they are used as OLNs).

Here's where it gets tricky. A name and date of birth check is a grossly different animal. The crime information computers are preprogrammed to search for similar sounding names and dates of birth when a query is entered using those criteria. As a result, when you run a check by name and date of birth you access files for the name that you entered **and** for any similar names with similar dates of birth as well as any aliases that have been linked to those names.

Other information that you can get by running a name and date of birth check, which does not come back with an OLN check, is information from criminally deported alien files, probation information, parole information or the recently added domestic violence and sex offender database information.

The crime information computers cannot cross-check a name to see if it has an associated OLN in each of the 50 states. Neither can it create a name/OLN association that it has not been given specifically by data entry personnel. Hopefully this very brief and general description has been helpful but if it only served to confuse, just remember, a good police officer ALWAYS CHECKS NAME AND DATE OF BIRTH FIRST!

Now for a descriptive analogy. Imagine that a man moves to Florida from Wisconsin and gets a Florida driver's license and establishes residency there, but maintains a second residency in Wisconsin without telling anyone. This may be illegal, but you know sometimes criminals do actually break the law on purpose. The individual commits a crime in Florida and superior detective work takes no time at all to identify him as the perpetrator.

Warrants are issued in Florida for the man and entered on the computer by detectives. These detectives are smart. They check him by the name and date of birth that they have and find out that he has a valid Florida driver's license, so they enter the license number into the crime information computer along with his name and DOB to show that he is wanted.

Our perpetrator is out driving one day and, for whatever reason, gets stopped by the police. He provides the officer with his Wisconsin driver's license and the officer checks that OLN. The computer return will show that he is not wanted and has a valid drivers license. That officer just allowed Evil to slip through his fingers. It happens every single day. The report takin' and ticket writin' officers just don't have time to be bothered with checking someone by name and DOB. They just want to go get those reports and tickets written.

#9.2 Send in the Clones

This section could easily have been entitled "Clone Wars" but someone said that title had already been used. Nonetheless, the subject of this section is what I call a cloned vehicle. There are some crafty little disciples of Evil out there who have devised many ways to cover up a stolen car.

One of those ways is to go to a junkyard and look for a wrecked car that is the same make and model as one that Evil has stolen or is going to steal. Evil can then buy the junked car and register it in his name and take all the paperwork from the junk car and apply it to the stolen car. Then all Evil has to do is take the VIN plate from the junked car and use it to replace the VIN on the stolen car. At that point, for all intents and purposes the car is his. That is relatively simple and most police officers will not catch even a moderately well replaced VIN plate as long as there is supporting documentation. Since the car would appear to be legally owned, insurance and tag and title etc. would be easy to get.

A variation on that same theme is when Evil steals a car, strips it and then makes sure that it is recovered by law enforcement. Then he goes to the auto auction and buys the stripped-out hull of the vehicle at a very low price. Since he legally owns the car, he takes it back to the chop shop and puts all the parts that he took off, back on. Voila! A nice new car, legally owned and operated, for next to no money.

Another similar way is to fabricate a whole new identity for the car. Evil can again go to a junkyard (or any number of other sources where the missing tag would not likely be reported stolen) and take a tag off of a vehicle that is similar to one that he has stolen. A good forger with a good computer can make false documents of virtually any kind. Vehicle registrations and insurance cards are not difficult to forge in a reasonably convincing manner. As long as the forged paperwork matches the tag information, a cursory investigation would likely not uncover the deceit. The only problem with this method is that the information that is created by the forger will not be in any of the crime information computer databases. That in and of itself is not necessarily a problem since occasionally, legitimate vehicles are "not on file". But if a curious officer investigates well, the deceit will be uncovered.

I uncovered one such forgery by accident when I came up behind a dark blue Chevy Tahoe at about 0230 hours (2:30 A.M.). One red flag on late night patrol is when you come up behind a suspicious vehicle and it immediately turns off the roadway. The more attentive criminals look out for police and when they see one, they try to subtly get away from him to lessen the likelihood of being noticed.

As a countermeasure, whenever I have a vehicle that makes an abrupt turn as I approach it, I continue on my way as if nothing is out of the ordinary. I go down the road a block or two and I hide. If the vehicle was in fact turning to avoid me, then it will inevitably return to its original course. That is exactly what happened in this instance.

As I snuck up behind Evil to regain my position of advantage, I ran the tag on my in-car computer. Evil made this one easy for me since the license plate had been reported stolen. I notified my beat partners of our location and direction of travel and we orchestrated our ambush. By the time we made it to the next major intersection, there were police cars poised to pounce from every direction. As luck would have it, the light turned red and Evil was the first car in line to stop.

On cue, we moved in. Evil was so startled and so quickly surrounded that when I appeared at his window with my Glock 22, he threw his hands up and complied with all my orders. He was taken into custody without incident. He had in his vehicle, a State of Georgia registration form and a valid insurance card for the vehicle that he was driving. All the paperwork showed that the vehicle was his.

I asked him why he had a stolen tag on his truck and he said that he just couldn't afford the Georgia ad valorem taxes for such an expensive vehicle. That sounded like a reasonable excuse to me so I did not think much more about it. I did ask one of the officers on scene to go confirm that the VIN on the truck was the same as the VIN on the registration papers. The officer returned stating that there was a match.

I was a little suspicious when I ran the VIN through GCIC and it came back "not on file". VINs are almost always on file on any car that is older than a year or so. I asked the other officer to double check that we had the correct VIN and he did with the same answer as before.

I took the young man to jail and on the way became more and more suspicious of my "not on file" VIN. Something just wasn't right. I went back to the truck and looked at the VIN again, this time in person rather than vicariously through some other officer. The VIN didn't look right. I really can't explain what didn't look right because it was a very good forgery, but it looked odd. I began looking through the car for another VIN.

For those of you who are not aware, the VIN is placed on a number of additional places on a car to make it easier to recover if it is stolen. I found one of those other places and as expected it showed a different VIN. The VIN that I found came back to a vehicle that had been stolen a year and a half earlier. Evil had likely been driving it that long. He had manufactured everything he needed to convince anyone that the truck was his. The only thing he couldn't do was make a fake plate, so he stole one. If the tag had not been reported stolen, he might not have been caught. When I confronted him with the new information, he admitted to forging all the items in question. He said that he learned it from a network of friends who all drive cars acquired in the same manner.

#9.3 The Tell

Another cloned vehicle came to my attention while on regular patrol. When there is not a lot of traffic on the road, Evil is easy to spot when it's there. I was driving down a long, straight, multilane road with a trainee riding silently in the passenger seat. There was only one other car on the roadway and he was approaching me from the opposite direction. I watched in the rear view mirror as he drove past me.

I immediately noticed that for no traffic related reason whatsoever he had applied his brakes. While it is not uncommon for people to hit the brakes briefly when they see a police car, this guy kept the brakes on without slowing down.

What this behavior normally means is that the driver of the vehicle is watching you (or something) in his rear view mirror. It is a common maneuver when you shift your gaze from the road ahead to your mirror that your foot instinctively leaves the accelerator and depresses the brake pedal. Most times, the weight on the brake pedal is light and does not slow down the car, but it is sufficient to activate the brake lights. Usually the driver will not even be aware that he is doing it. It is the same type of subconscious behavior that poker players call a "tell".

I watched this car's brake lights stay on for a long, long time. I knew he was up to something and only needed to figure out what it was. I made a u-turn and caught up to the vehicle quickly. His late model but excessively dirty Volvo had an Alabama tag on it (I'm not picking on Alabama, it just seems to come up a lot). Again, Evil was going to make this one easy because that tag was expired.

I activated my emergency equipment to stop the car and with a little apparent hesitation, he pulled off into a long, dark private driveway. My spider senses were tingling and I was more than ready for him if he were to try anything. Instead, everything went smoothly. He provided me with the registration and insurance information and his driver's license. Everything checked out except the car allegedly belonged to "a friend".

I was also struck by the fact that a relatively new and moderately expensive car was so dirty. I asked my trainee to check all the paperwork against the VIN on the dashboard and he came back informing me that everything was a match.

I couldn't shake the idea that something was wrong so I went to recheck everything myself. The VIN plate on the dash immediately caught my attention. It looked real but also looked like it wasn't very well attached to the dash. I opened my pocketknife and slid the blade under the VIN plate. Surprise, surprise, surprise…the VIN plate popped right up. Underneath it was the real VIN, which when checked showed that the car was stolen.

I showed my trainee that he almost let Evil go with his inattention to detail. As we were impounding the car, I found in the glove box three traffic tickets. Each ticket was written by a different officer in a different jurisdiction. All of the tickets were written to the Evil I had in my patrol car. All of the tickets were written while he was driving that same stolen car. As a result of one of those tickets, he had been taken to jail and the stolen car was impounded. The police department that impounded it returned it to him when he got out of jail. No wonder he wasn't worried about getting caught.

#9.4 Always Check Name And DOB

One of our officers, shortly after being released to police on his own, was dispatched to work a hit and run accident. When he arrived at the scene, he found a small car that had severe damage to the back end. There were skid marks leading up to the wrecked car and debris on the roadway. The driver told the officer that he had been stopped in the roadway waiting to turn left when another car came up behind him, hit him, and then drove away.

The driver provided the officer with his Texas driver's license and all the other necessary paperwork. The officer proceeded to ask dispatch to run a Texas OLN. The dispatcher advised that the OLN was valid and that there were no warrants for that OLN. I immediately called him on the cell phone to chastise him for not checking a name and date of birth. He whined that it was only a 43 call (hit and run traffic accident) and he didn't feel like spending all that extra energy to do a name and DOB check.

I made him feel guilty and the next thing you know, he was running a name and date of birth check. The dispatcher ran the requested query and within seconds told the officer that the person he had (with valid OLN, etc.) was now showing three outstanding Federal warrants with nationwide extradition orders.

What our Texas Evil did for a living was buy wrecked cars and then stage fake hit and run accidents to get insurance money. How many other officers had let this guy go in the past by not doing something as simple as a computer check? No one will ever know. I don't think that officer has run an OLN since.

#9.5 Just A Simple Traffic Stop

Often times, simple traffic stops for seemingly innocuous infractions can lead to good felony arrests. Most police officers of any merit know this axiom all too well, and many of us use traffic stops for no other purpose. I made such a stop on a young man who ran a red light in the middle of the night. Normally, provided the person does so "safely", I will not write a ticket for running a red light when there are no other cars on the road. I will simply issue a warning. However, many times there is more to the driver than the simple running of a red light. That was the case on this particular stop.

The well-spoken and well-dressed young man did not have his driver's license with him but provided me with the information necessary to run him by name and date of birth. The computer check showed that he was not on file. It is very rare for an individual born and raised in the U.S. not to be on file after reaching the driving age. I was suspicious and investigated further.

When I made a second approach to the vehicle, I noticed that the keys in the ignition were on a key chain that looked like it would belong to a woman. It had some frilly, foofy stuff on it and was not the type of thing that you expect a teenage boy to carry. I asked him to confirm his information and asked to whom the car belonged.

He said that the car was his mother's, which might explain the key chain, and then he repeated his name, giving me a slightly different birthday.

It is not uncommon for people to use names of friends or relatives to avoid being caught for whatever their particular crime may be. That is what I suspected here.

I placed young Evil into my patrol car and began looking. I found nothing incriminating inside the car so I turned my attention to the registered owner. He said it was his mother so I asked for a phone number. He gave me a number where there was no answer. I then asked my dispatcher to look up the phone number of the registered owner in the phone book. Surprise, surprise, surprise…it was a different number.

I called the number in the phone book and spoke to the registered owner of the car. She confirmed that the car was hers, that she did not have a son and that the car was supposed to be in her driveway. Needless to say, it wasn't. I made my felony arrest and the victim came to retrieve her car. I pointed out before she left that it might be a good idea not to leave her keys in her car anymore.

#9.6 Car-Kabob

Attention to detail, or rather the lack of it, very nearly caused me to allow Evil to escape and quite easily could have cost me my life. While no one person can be expected to perform flawlessly all the time that doesn't mean we should not try. Many of us are alive only because no one has been determined enough to kill us. One of my most memorable brushes with Evil began with a call to work a vehicle accident.

I got the call very near the end of my shift and was a little irritated that my plans to get off on time had been thwarted. The dispatcher told me that the complainant on my call had "heard" an accident on the roadway near his apartment but had not seen anything. I was hoping there would be nothing to it but wasn't counting on it.

The area of roadway that I was going to was shaped like a horseshoe, with either end intersecting with the same, larger roadway about a half mile apart. I chose to check for the accident starting from the eastern end of the horseshoe around to the western end.

As I approached the East intersection, I looked down the main roadway (which runs East to West) and made note of a person that I saw off in the distance walking away from me. He was a little over a tenth of a mile away and I could barely see him through the fog. He was walking east and I was heading north, into the horseshoe.

I continued around the horseshoe and just before reaching the West intersection, I found the object of my search. It was a late 1970's era Oldsmobile four door. Apparently, it was traveling down the steep grade and for whatever reason had not been able to make the sharp left curve and went straight off the roadway to the right. The car was traveling so fast that when it impacted with the end of the guardrail, the guardrail went straight through the engine compartment (just to the passenger side of the engine block), through the firewall, through the glove compartment, through the front seat (which is how I knew there wasn't a front seat passenger), through the back seat, through the trunk and out the back of the car. I guess you could say that it was "car-kabob".

The ignition was still on and the keys were in it. On the floorboard were a few empty beer cans and I began to suspect that perhaps I had a drunk driver staggering around in the area and that it might have been the person I had seen walking on the main road.

I gave dispatch the location of the car and broadcast that my driver had left the scene. I also said that I was going to check the individual that I had seen earlier, walking east down the main road.

I sped off in the direction of the suspected Evil and before long had located the man in question. He was a little farther east and did not appear to be bothered by my presence. I asked who he was and what he was doing. I also asked for identification. He provided me with a Florida I.D. card and perfunctory answers to my standard interrogatives. He said that he had been hitchhiking and was let out of the car down the road a ways, and that he had nothing to do with the accident that I was investigating.

I asked if he had heard anything that sounded like a car wreck and he said that he hadn't. I thought that was a bit peculiar because at the speed he was walking and using the time frame he had given me, he should have been very near the accident site at the time it happened. I asked him if he would accompany me back to the site and if my investigation showed that he was not involved, I would gladly give him a ride to his destination.

He agreed. I told him that it was departmental procedure for me to pat down anyone who got into my car. He said, "No problem." I patted him down through his heavy layers of winter clothes and found nothing suspicious, so off we went.

When we returned to the wrecked car, I again asked him if he had anything to do with it. He nonchalantly replied that he had not. He showed none of the common signs of deceit and he was very calm, cool, and collected. In a standard interrogation, it is a common practice to ask the same question several times and in several different ways to see if the answers are consistent. It is difficult to keep up with lies and most criminals often slip up when answering questions. The more they talk, the more they lose track of their lies. Also, it is a good practice not to let the person you are questioning know what you know. Ask some questions that you know the answers to and use them to gauge the honesty of the answerer.

I checked the car's tag and it came back "not stolen" and registered to a man who lived a few counties away. Items in the car also had the registered owners name on them and there was nothing in the car that connected the man I had to the wrecked vehicle.

I thought that something just wasn't right but was at a loss to find any evidence. My last effort was to ask radio to get me a phone number for the registered owner. (As a side note, make sure that all investigating is done away from Evil. The more you know that he doesn't know, the more likely you are to catch him in a lie or take him by surprise if you have to.)

While standing outside of the car, I phoned the registered owner of the Oldsmobile. The woman who answered the phone sounded as if she were middle-aged. I identified myself and asked if the registered owner of the car was at home. She said, with a noticeable degree of apprehension in her voice, that he was not there at the moment.

I asked if anyone else should be in the car and described the man whom I had in my back seat. It was then that the woman gave me a bit of information that struck me like a baseball bat to the teeth. She told me that her husband, the registered owner of the car, had phoned her from the Gwinnett County police station a few minutes earlier. He told her that he had picked up a hitchhiker. She said that her husband told her that the hitchhiker produced a very large revolver and forced him to drive into some woods. The hitchhiker took his wallet and kicked the man out of his own car and left the scene in that car.

I asked if her husband had told her what the hitchhiker looked like. She said that he was a young man with very long hair and she proceeded to describe the young man who was in my back seat.

That meant that somewhere nearby there was a probably very large revolver. I backed away from my patrol car as I called for another car. Moments later my backup arrived and I told him what had transpired. I told the officer to cover Evil while I took him out of the car to search him again.

I opened the back door and ordered Evil out. He complied, still showing none of the "red flags" we grow accustomed to seeing displayed by Evil. I immediately handcuffed him and passed him to the cover officer. I lifted up the removable back seat of the patrol car and there was a wallet. In the wallet was the I.D. of the registered owner of the car.

I informed Evil that he was in deep dookey and that I knew what he had done. I asked him where the gun was and he said there wasn't one. We searched his heavy winter clothes and didn't find it. We looked everywhere to no avail. I was certain that there was a gun somewhere and as a last resort, I unsnapped his pants, opened them up and pulled them down.

Somehow we had missed a .357 magnum revolver not once, but twice. It was loaded and ready to fire. I asked him why he didn't shoot me when he had the chance.

He didn't say, "Because I didn't want to."

He didn't say, "Because I'm not a killer."

He said, "Because I didn't think you'd figure it out."

You can never be too thorough and you can never let your guard down.

#9.7 Neon Breon

Whether it was a stroke of luck, a feat of pure cop genius, or a mixture of the two, we will perhaps never know for sure, but one night in particular while working the morning watch, Evil was thwarted once again by attention to detail.

During roll call that night before my tour of duty, my shift commander told me that the previous night, Evil had once again reared its ugly head on my beat in the form of a burglar who had struck a car rental agency. According to the report, someone had made entry through the roof of the business and once inside had taken over twenty sets of car keys to cars that were parked in the parking lot of the rental agency.

Under the cover of darkness, Evil then proceeded to remove nearly a dozen of the rental agency's automobiles and transport them to parts unknown. The preceding shift had recovered a few of the cars thanks to the manager of the store. He had driven around to apartment complexes in the area and had located some of his cars parked randomly throughout the neighborhood. Each time he located a car that had been stolen from his company, he called 911 and had an officer meet him to make a recovery report.

It just so happened that he had found another car right before I came on duty. My shift commander sent me to meet with him to write the latest recovery report. I met the man in a nearby parking lot where he had located two of his stolen cars parked next to each other. I wrote the reports and asked for descriptions of the remaining missing vehicles.

In the next hour or so, we managed to recover all but two of the stolen cars. The manager told me that he did not have tag numbers for the last two cars because the cars were so new that they had not yet had tags assigned to them. All he could tell me was that he was missing a white Dodge Neon and a blue Ford Explorer.

He thanked me for my efforts in locating the other stolen cars and we parted company. I went back on patrol.

A few hours further into the uneventful night, I was driving south on Highway 400 trying to find some type of violator to stop. I was having absolutely no luck whatsoever. I exited the highway and was about halfway down the exit ramp approaching a red light when I saw two cars go by, crossing the intersection in front of me.

It took about three seconds for me to realize that the first car that had crossed my path was a white Dodge Neon and that it was being followed by a blue Ford Explorer. I hesitated at first, thinking that it was too good to be true and that it must just be a coincidence. However, I decided to go check it out. As I turned left to catch up to the two cars, I saw that they both had gotten onto Highway 400 going north.

Neither vehicle was traveling very rapidly, but they were driving erratically and staying very close to each other, even though they were the only cars on the road. I remember thinking that they were behaving as if they were following one another and were either intoxicated or horse playing behind the wheel.

As I got close enough to read the license plates, I could see that neither vehicle had a plate. I was in no hurry and was becoming more convinced with each passing moment that these vehicles were chock full o' Evil.

I called my beat partner on the cell phone to ask where he was and of course he didn't answer the phone. I then raised him on the radio and found out that he was in the middle of a donut break. I told him what I had and asked him to hurry.

Meanwhile, we continued Northbound and went several miles before my backup was even close. We had just crossed the jurisdictional boundaries into a city that is incorporated inside of our county when I decided to tell my dispatcher that my beat partner and I were going to attempt to stop two suspicious vehicles.

I decided to take the first car (the Neon) and delegated my beat partner to the task of attempting a stop on the Explorer. We activated our blue lights simultaneously and the cars kept driving. I wasn't surprised and at that point was convinced that we had our Evil. Our speed gradually increased as we continued up the highway.

I think the driver of the Neon wanted to go faster but the little car he was driving would not oblige. We gradually accelerated to about 90 mph and then the driver of the Neon decided to exit the highway. He barely slowed down as he made a wide, almost fatal, right turn onto the secondary roadway. As I checked my rear view mirror I saw the Explorer behind me followed by the other patrol car.

It wasn't long before the Explorer got up enough speed to pass me so that he could get in behind his Evil mentor. Thus we began our accelerated following (MVI) as the less than competent drivers led us down an increasingly narrow roadway at increasingly higher speeds.

For safety's sake, I had allowed the distance between the fleeing vehicles and me to increase. I knew that a crash was imminent and did not care to take part in it. I did, however, want to be close enough to witness it, because after all…you can't buy that kind of entertainment.

We continued down the now two-lane road at blistering speeds toward what I knew was a dead end. The drivers were obviously not very experienced and I was betting that they were unaware that their flight was heading for an abrupt end.

As they crossed the last intersection into a closed subdivision, the Neon lost control, slid sideways, flipped over once or twice and came to rest upside down. It took mere seconds for the two occupants to exit the vehicle and flee on foot. The Explorer continued past the wrecked Neon and over a hillcrest into an upper class residential neighborhood that had no other exit.

I did not actually see the occupants exit the vehicle so as I pulled up to the crash site, I stopped to see if anyone was still in the vehicle or if there were any bodies close by. I directed my assisting unit to continue into the subdivision to locate the second vehicle.

Just as I had determined that Evil must have hit the ground running, I heard the unmistakable sound of a high revving engine and the sound of a man yelling that I was sure was my beat partner.

I was then struck by the realization that Evil was coming back my way and might very likely try to run me down. The Explorer crested the hill that was less than 30 yards from me. I had drawn my pistol and was determined to fire if he tried to run me over. I have heard people argue that shooting the driver of a car that is trying to run you over serves no purpose because the bullet can't stop the car. That may be true, but if you hit the driver, you have at least damaged the missile's guidance system, and that's better than nothing. Evil made a good choice. Instead of heading at me, he drove over the landscaped median and back toward the only viable exit.

I was proud to see the police car in hot pursuit once again. He was on his own now as I began searching for evidence and perpetrators. As I recovered the remaining ten to twelve sets of keys that had been taken from the rental agency and were now strewn about the roadway, the Explorer was retracing his path, heading back to the highway.

Within minutes, the driver of the Explorer took a corner too fast and met with the same fate as the driver of the Neon. Before long we had all three suspects in custody.

The driver of the Neon was a 15-year-old man. I call him a man because even though he was young and small, he had taken it upon himself to make adult decisions regarding life and death and to commit adult crimes. In my book, that makes him a man, not a boy, and warrants that he be punished as such. He had been out of juvenile detention in South Georgia for about a week. He had been arrested for burglarizing a car rental agency and for stealing cars.

His passenger was a 14-year-old woman whose 17-year-old brother happened to be driving the Explorer. The driver of the Neon turned out to be a surprisingly polite, intelligent and well-spoken individual – not your typical perpetrator. He was prosecuted once again as a juvenile and within a month or so had been released. He then proceeded unremorsefully to commit countless other crimes that cost the honest citizens of our society many thousands of dollars. He led police on several other high-speed chases, during the last of which he felt the need to carry a .45 caliber semi auto handgun that he had stolen in a burglary. He also tried to murder a police officer with the stolen car he was driving. The last I saw him he was being carted off to serve at least a whole year in jail for his crimes.

The driver of the Neon had an unusual first name. His name was Breon. In all of our subsequent encounters with this individual (and there were many), his moniker was of course, Neon Breon.

#9.8 If Ifs And Buts Were Candy And Nuts, We'd All Have A Wonderful Christmas

I was directing traffic one night around a tractor-trailer rig that had stalled in the roadway not far from our precinct. The rest of the officers on my shift were busy handling calls. An acquaintance of mine who managed a local pizza restaurant drove up to tell me that he had just come from a bank that was about a block away where he had gone to make a night deposit. He saw what he thought was a very suspicious male loitering near the bank and thought I would be able to send someone to check him out.

Since there were no other units available to handle the call and since I was so close, I decided to leave the tractor-trailer for a few minutes and go to investigate the suspicious person. I quickly drove up the street to the bank in question and turned into the parking lot. As soon as I rounded the corner of the bank that led to the rear parking area, I saw the target of my search. He was right where the complainant said he would be and as soon as I saw him, he saw me. He jumped up from where he was sitting on top of a stone wall directly underneath a streetlight and began walking toward me.

All the little bells and whistles were going off in my head telling me that something wasn't right. I quickly stopped my patrol car and exited so as to meet the man near the front of my car. (Any time you approach someone who is on foot, I recommend getting out of your car. Sitting in the patrol car you are a sitting duck.) I told him to put his hands where I could see them and patted him down for weapons. He was very friendly and agreeable and even had his driver's license ready for me to check.

He said that he had been in an argument with his mother who lived in an apartment complex within walking distance of our location. That same address was on his driver's license. He said that he was just out walking around trying to cool off. I explained to him how suspicious he looked and he said that he understood and would go back home. I ran a computer check of the man and nothing out of the ordinary came back.

I still felt that something wasn't right with the man and talked to him for a few more minutes trying to figure out what it was. I could not find anything wrong so I reluctantly let him go. As he was walking away, I thought about how eagerly he got up off the wall to come to meet me. I thought then that perhaps he left something over by the wall that he did not want me to see. I went to look and once again found nothing.

Three days later the manager of a pizza restaurant (not the same as the restaurant where my acquaintance worked) was shot in the head and killed after closing. The pizza place was one block from the bank and used that same bank to make night deposits. I was watching the evening news while they covered the story and I instantly thought of the man I had encountered. I called the detective in charge of the case immediately and told him what had happened. He in turn told me that the man I had stopped was a disgruntled ex-employee of the pizza place in question and that he was the prime suspect.

He was later arrested and eventually confessed. He probably even had to serve a year or two in jail for his crime. Though I am relatively certain, I will never know for sure if the night I met him he was planning his homicide. I feel certain that somewhere in the vicinity of that bank parking lot was his murder weapon but I did not find it. I will always wonder if I had found it, if it would have made a difference, or if he was so determined to perpetrate his particular Evil that he would have done it eventually, no matter what. It never pays to second-guess yourself but it does pay to learn from your mistakes.

I'm not sure that I could have handled our encounter any better, but I know for sure I will never forget it.

#9.9 Cap-Scum?

Right around 1990, our department issued and we subsequently began carrying a new weapon in our patrol arsenal. That weapon was a chemical irritant called Cap Stun. Cap Stun is a trade name for what is now commonly known as pepper spray. For those who are not familiar, the substance is basically a can full of concentrated pepper particles with an aerosol propellant. When sprayed onto an individual, it hurts really bad. When sprayed into the eyes, nose, mouth, respiratory tract or open wounds etc., it hurts really, really, really, really, bad.

I will admit that I was a bit skeptical about this new weapon's ability to assist me in the performance of my duties but since it was required, I carried it anyway. I went to one of the first training classes that was required before we could carry the pepper spray. When I completed the course, I was issued my little can of Cap Stun but since it was so new, we hadn't yet gotten any holders for the cans so I had to carry it in my back pocket.

I carried it that way for a few days and really forgot that I even had the stuff. Then came the domestic violence call at a hotel on my beat. When I arrived at the scene, a young lady flagged me down in the parking lot. She was a muscular, athletic looking woman in her twenties that was holding her right arm. She began to explain to me that she had been in a fight with her husband and that she thought her arm had been broken.

When the paramedics arrived, they confirmed the lady's suspicion. She was a tough woman and she was very adamant about wanting us to find the little scumbag that had broken her arm. She pointed out the direction he had gone and admonished us to be careful because he was some sort of Army Ranger or special ops something or other.

As I started out across the parking lot in the last known direction of Evil, I heard her yell out behind me, "There he is!"

She was pointing to the trees at the edge of a nearby parking lot. I got my first glimpse of that night's Evil as he took off running down a steep embankment, through the woods, and towards the parking lot of the office complex next door.

I managed to blurt out over the radio that I was in a foot chase and proceeded to do my level best to catch the little dirtbag. The chase went about fifty yards from where he had started running. Since I was about seventy-five yards away from him that made it about a hundred and twenty-five yards for me. Just as I was closing in on the disgrace to our armed forces whose physique was much like that of a fire hydrant, he ran into some very thick woods.

As soon as he was out of sight in the dense growth of scrub brush and briars, I stopped at the edge of the woods and listened. It sounded to me as if he made his way about twenty to twenty-five feet into the tangling vegetation and then, for whatever reason, stopped.

That particular area was very dark and I was pretty sure that he had no idea what my location was. I held my position and stood by for the backup units. Two units arrived and it took them a minute or two to find me since I was standing in the dark and still trying to keep my location secret.

I whispered to the backup units that I was pretty sure of Evil's location and directed one of the units to set up down the road from me along one possible avenue of escape. I then directed the other backup unit to circle around the "briar patch". Once on the other side of Evil, that unit was to make his way slowly into the woods making as much noise and using as much flashlight power as possible. My hope was that Evil would see the other unit coming at him from behind and would run back out of the woods towards my location where he could be taken into custody.

Both the other units performed their assigned tasks well. I was a little surprised (but not much) when the plan worked exactly as expected. Moments later, Evil was clamoring out of the sticker bushes, looking behind him, and running straight toward me. In a physical manifestation of my cop preconceptions, I pointed my magnum at him, yelled a few expletives and expected him to give up. It only took me a second or two to realize that he had no intention of giving up. I could also see that he had nothing in his hands and was wearing only a tight T-shirt and shorts.

Thankfully, I had a plan "B" to move to. I quickly holstered my pistol just in time for the impact of our bodies slamming into one another. One of the worst types of people to have to fight is the little "fireplug". Even though they are small, they are stout. Their short limbs give them good leverage and their dense muscle mass is tough to control. I wrestled around with the little guy, unsuccessful in all my attempts to get him to comply. I started striking him with hammer blows to the body. When my strength was almost sapped, I resorted to elbow strikes, but still could not get him under control.

It was then that I remembered that nifty little can in my back pocket. I disengaged from Evil and I could see that he was preparing for another attack. I gave him a quick squirt of pepper spray to the face, and down he went like a load of bricks.

He was coughing and gagging and whining like a little girl. Snot was pouring from his nose and mouth and he might have even thrown up a little. Needless to say, he was easily subdued at that point and taken to the county jail. The whole battle had taken probably less than two minutes, but for me it seemed like a week. My first backup unit reached me at about the time I let loose with the pepper spray. My other backup unit was still stuck in the sticker bushes.

In compliance with departmental rules and regulations, my backup unit raised our supervisor on the radio to let him know that I had used the pepper spray.

"Nable had to use the Cap-Stun", he said to the supervisor on a secondary channel.

The supervisor paused for a moment before replying with a heightened sense of stress in his voice, "Did you say Nable capped one?"

"No sir. He had to use Cap-Stun on the perpetrator", replied the officer.

The supervisor responded with a noticeable amount of relief, "Cap Scum? What the hell is that?"

The officer explained over the secondary channel that it was the "new" chemical agent that we were transitioning to.

"Doesn't he have to take some kinda class before he can use that?" asked the supervisor.

"Yessir, he took the class last week."

"Oh. Okay then. Just put it in the report."

That was the first deployment of pepper spray in our department and that time it worked flawlessly. It has been used many times since with varied results. People using pepper spray as a tool of self-defense must realize that it is not 100% effective. In the case cited above, it worked very well, but often times Evil is not adequately affected by pepper spray, so there must (as I have said before) be a backup plan.

Also, if you deploy an aerosol chemical agent in a confined area, you are in effect, secondarily using that chemical agent on anyone else in the room, including yourself. If you are not in a confined area, wind may be factor in thwarting your efforts to direct the chemical agent. I can't tell you how many times one officer has been in a fight with Evil when the officer's backup unit arrives and deploys a chemical agent into the fray without warning. That is a very dangerous practice as it has the tendency to incapacitate or at least distract one of the officers in the fight. That gives Evil a potential opportunity to either subdue and/or disarm the officer, or simply to escape.

Chemical agents are like any other tool. They have limits. A good officer learns the limitations of himself and his equipment and develops sound strategies to make proper, effective use of all the tools available. Nothing works 100%, all the time. Different and dynamic situations require different tools. If one doesn't work, move to the next. Most importantly, always have a backup plan.

#9.10 Jackpot

Officers working drug interdiction on our nation's highways perhaps understand better than most, that traffic stops can lead to the discovery of all kinds of felonious infractions. A violation as innocuous as a broken taillight can lead to any number of felony arrests if the officer making the stop pays attention to details and knows the law.

Just before heading for my nightly donut break, I saw a large sport utility vehicle driving down the roadway. This particular sport utility vehicle had white taillights. For reasons known only to those who choose to install these devices on their car, some individuals think that it is OK to replace the factory lights on their cars with bizarre, colored lights. In my state, (and I assume in many other states) the color of lighting equipment on vehicles that are operated on state roadways is governed primarily by code section 40-8-34 which requires all vehicles to conform to the Society of Automotive

Engineers standards as printed in their Ground Vehicle Lighting Standards Manual section J578. I'll dispense with all the technical crap and just say that taillights have to be red. Not only do they have to be red, they have to be a particular shade of red. White, therefore, is not allowed.

With that in mind, I figured that I would have my trainee knock out a quick citation to the driver of the SUV with Alabama plates, before making the donut run. I activated the blinky-blinkies and the vehicle pulled into the empty parking lot of a shopping center. As I often do with trainees that are in their final weeks of training, I stayed in the patrol car while the trainee handled the traffic stop. I could see that there were three individuals in the truck but could tell little else.

I noticed that the trainee was taking a little longer than was normal with the initial contact phase of the stop so I got a little curious. However, I was not curious enough to leave the area by my patrol car where I was talking to another officer who had since pulled up next to us to see what we had.

A minute or two passed when the trainee left the driver's window area of the target vehicle and motioned for me to come to her. She told me that among other things, the occupants of the vehicle were acting very nervous and that there was a strong odor indicative of burned marijuana coming from inside the truck. That is what we in the business call reasonable, articulable suspicion. With reasonable, articulable suspicion we can investigate further and can request that any or all occupants of the vehicle step out to talk with us. (See U.S. Supreme Court cases Pennsylvania vs. Mimms and Maryland vs. Wilson.) So we did.

All three subjects gathered at the rear of the vehicle so that we could interview them. During that interview, one of them dropped a small plastic baggy containing what darn sure looked and smelled like a plant whose mere possession is against the law (in this case that would be marijuana). Since none of the three pillars of the community would admit to dropping the contraband, we had no choice but to charge them all. There was a lot more to this particular case than I care to bore the reader with but let it suffice to say that all three men ended up under arrest and on their merry way to jail.

As a consequence of that action, the police department was charged with taking care of their vehicle. As we looked through the vehicle prior to impounding it, as is our departmental policy, we found a backpack under the driver's side back seat. In the backpack was nearly $30,000 in cash. Most of it was in twenty-dollar bills. As you might guess, all three subjects had different and conflicting stories about the origin of the money and its intended use.

The only thing that really matters is that the money was confiscated and added to the county's "general" fund. The bad guys all went to jail and the SUV was seized as well. To officers that do interdiction work regularly, this would be considered a moderate take. Similar traffic stops have yielded grotesque amounts of money and drugs.

Warrantless search and seizure of motor vehicles is a subject that could take up an entire book on its own. Sheepdogs owe it to themselves and their communities to learn the rules and to follow them and to keep up with the changes in those laws and procedures that are dictated by court rulings. As long as drug dealers exist, they will use motor vehicles to transport their product and their profits. Officers who pay attention to details and know the law will always be the ones who stop them. My trainee that night earned some of the highest marks I have ever given.

#9.11 I Can't Believe They Stopped

There's an interesting phenomenon that often is an element of "reasonable, articulable suspicion". The phenomenon of which I speak is one that I call the "Perp-look". Though it is difficult to describe, it is the way that a guilty person looks at an authority figure. It's the look that screams, "I'm up to something".

I noticed that very same look on the face of a young man that was driving passed me going in the opposite direction. He and I were the only cars on the road and since it was a quiet night, of course I directed my trainee (who was driving) to turn around and follow him. In moments we were behind the late model Honda with no tag. The tag issue was more than enough probable cause for a traffic stop.

I told the trainee to take over and I assumed the role of supervisor. My trainee activated the emergency equipment and the driver of the Honda pulled somewhat reluctantly into the parking lot of a fast-food restaurant. I was glad to see that before even approaching the vehicle, my trainee noticed right away how nervous the driver appeared to be. We both also noticed that there was a passenger in the fully reclined front seat. The passenger had uprighted himself just as my trainee and I exited the patrol car. The passenger was also acting squirrelly.

My trainee made her approach to the driver's window and asked for the standard documentation (license and insurance). The driver immediately stated that he had neither. As the trainee was preparing to remove the driver from the vehicle to a more secure location, the passenger began getting very fidgety. He was reaching all around his seat in a manner that suggested that he was trying his dead level best to keep us from seeing what he was doing. My trainee turned her attention from the driver to the passenger and barked at him to keep his hands where we could see him. That command coupled with the subsequent realization that his concealment efforts were woefully inadequate, made the passenger noticeably more nervous.

His movements became more pronounced and when he reached under the front of his seat, my trainee drew her pistol and began pointing it in his direction while I simultaneously opened the passenger door. I shone my flashlight in the passenger's face as he turned to look at me and I ordered him to put his hands up. He had moved straight past nervous all the way to scared shitless as I snatched him mercilessly from the car and handcuffed him.

I was impressed that my trainee understood that she had become a "cover" officer and waited until I announced that my Evil was secure before we swapped roles. She then removed the driver in much the same fashion that I had removed his cohort.

After both parties were secured, it took about thirty seconds for us to locate the loaded, semi-auto pistol that the passenger had been reaching for and the license plate under the same seat that would confirm that the car had been reported stolen out of our jurisdiction the night before. After congratulating ourselves on a job well done, we took the two fifteen-year-olds to the juvenile detention facility where I am sure they were promptly rehabilitated and are by now well on their way to becoming productive members of society.

Chapter 10

_____

Crackin'

No book that deals with nighttime street police work would be complete without a quick chapter on the crack. In this particular context, crack has nothing to do with a plumber's butt or the cocaine derivative. It is a term that we use to describe the places that we go to rest our eyes. The word "crack" can be a noun (example, "I am going to the crack."), a verb (example, "I am crackin', leave me alone."), or an adjective (example, "I am looking forward to some quality crack time.").

I remember the summer when I was seventeen years old. I had just graduated high school and had used the money I had gotten for a graduation present to rebuild the engine in my 1969 Chevy Chevelle Malibu coupe. I wanted to take new motor out for a spin to see what she could do. I stopped for a red light at about 1:00 AM, and looked all around me to see if there were any witnesses and especially to make sure that there were no cops. When I was supremely confident that I was alone on the roadway, I made a right turn onto a side street and put the hammer down.

Clouds of smoke billowed from my back tires as they screeched across the pavement. The only sound louder than the squalling tires was the roar of my massive new motor as it churned out all the horsepower I had asked for, and then some. I made it a grand total of one block before I saw blue lights in my rear view mirror. Another set of blue lights approached me rapidly from the side street on my left and then yet another from the opposite direction.

I of course pulled over immediately and turned off my car, stunned by the sudden appearance of all those police. I sat quietly while I watched the primary officer approach my car from the rear.

"God dammit! Just what the hell do you think you're doin' you stupid little shit?" the officer said as he jerked open my driver's side door, spun me around and slammed me onto the hood of my own car.

I assumed that the question was rhetorical and kept silent as he torqued the handcuffs down on my wrists, yanked me back to his car and threw me into the back seat. I barely had time to pull my feet inside before he slammed the car door. He proceeded to perform a full cavity search of my entire car that turned up nothing incriminating. He returned to the patrol car to berate me a little more while writing my ticket for laying drag.

I remained polite and apologized for my bad behavior. The officer had time to regain his composure and said that if it weren't for the fact that he needed to get back to the crack, he would have taken "my sorry ass to jail". I had no idea what he meant and wasn't about to ask. I cheerfully accepted my ticket and slowly drove back home. It would be several more years before I grasped the full implications of what he had said.

Constantly looking for Evil can cause severe and undue stress on one's eyes and at times we find it necessary to rest them. On rare occasions, a completely unintended consequence of this action is that the officer may, for a brief time, actually fall asleep. It is just one of the day-to-day hazards that police must deal with and we accept the risk.

Police officers often go to extreme lengths to find remote locations for crackin'. The reason is simple; we don't want to be disturbed. If we park anywhere that a citizen can see us, inevitably some citizen will approach us with questions pertaining to directions, state laws or just to be "cordial". With years of practice, we become quite adept at finding remote and inaccessible locations to crack in. Officers forge their own roads through miles of forest or seek out water and cell phone towers on top of mountains. We become masters of camouflage, finding the darkest alleys, the most secluded fields and parking lots, and we make use of our environment as completely as any military special forces unit or accomplished woodsman or hunter.

On that summer night so long ago, I had apparently chosen as my vehicular testing ground, an intersection within earshot of the three most popular crack spots in the entire jurisdiction.

#10.2 What Kids?

Early one morning, two of my fellow officers had overtaxed their ocular organs intently searching for Evil and required a brief rest before resuming the hunt. I agreed to supervise the event and the location chosen for the execution of the ritual was the inside of a large grocery store building that was under construction.

The three of us strategically positioned our police cruisers in what would become the health and beauty section near aisle five. We sat silently for an indeterminate amount of time. The tomb-like quiet and near total darkness was violently interrupted by one of the other units as he sprang to life, turned on his blinky-blinkies, threw the car into gear and took off like a shot through the doorway of the grocery store and into the parking lot outside.

The patrol car made it about half way through the parking lot before slamming on the brakes. Then the backup lights illuminated and the patrol car came speeding in reverse back to our location. I must admit that I was still bewildered and confused at what had just transpired but apparently not so much as the officer who transpired it.

As soon as his window was even with mine, he stopped and looked at me while pointing to his back seat and said, "What am I gonna do with these kids?"

He paused, looked at the astonished look on my face, looked at his back seat, looked back at me, looked forward and then turned the blue lights off and went back to sleep.

Must've been a good dream.

#10.3 Where Oh Where Has Our Little Cop Gone?

Honing one's crackin' skills involves a considerable amount of trial and error. A case where trial ended in error happened one night when I thought I would be clever and parked on the side of the Interstate, in a curve, over a hillcrest, next to a bridge abutment in the total darkness where I thought I was well hidden. In addition to resting my eyes, I needed to also rest my back. Just as I had stretched out across the bench seat of my Crown Victoria, someone ran up to my car and knocked on my window. Painfully aware that my concealment tactics had failed miserably, I rolled down the window to learn that there had just been a multi-vehicle accident with injuries on the exit ramp behind me.

With incidents like that happening all the time, is it any wonder that an officer (who shall remain nameless) thought he had found the perfect crack spot in the form of a house under construction that had just had a garage door installed. He backed into the garage and closed the door and commenced with his eye resting. Though the end of his shift came and went with little fanfare at the regular time of 0700 hours, the officer did not complete his exercise until the 0900 sun beamed through the garage door onto his face. I'm not sure what's worse, the fact that he was two hours late getting off work or the fact that no one noticed.

#10.4 Scary

On extremely rare occasions, an officer may accidentally fall asleep and miss some vital information dispatched over the radio. Take for instance the officer who one night had crawled into his favorite crack in what he thought was an obscure and out of the way area. The rest of us were in the process of responding to a call for assistance from another jurisdiction that was in a vehicle pursuit with four armed robbers.

Evil was fleeing South on the freeway when they realized that the vehicle they had just stolen did not have the fortitude to engage in a protracted flight from the police. Consequently, they decided to stop and perform their rendition of a Chinese fire drill. All four representatives of Evil evacuated the vehicle and sprinted randomly for parts unknown. One perp was apprehended as he tried to scale a fence behind one of his co-perps. The other three ran toward a building on a street that ran parallel to the highway.

Officers were screaming their location and direction of travel on the radio, when out of the blue, officer Crack-spot chimed in on the radio to ask what was going on. Units re-advised all the information and he acknowledged and said that he was in the area. Within moments, officers on foot and accompanied by a canine officer followed Evil's tracks to right where the officer had been crackin'. According to the tracking dog and the conspicuous footprints in the mud surrounding his patrol vehicle, Evil had run right up to the patrol car, stopped, circled it once or twice, and continued along its original flight path away from sleeping beauty. That's scary.

#10.5 Wake-Up Alarm

Most of us have the habit of letting others know where we are crackin', on the off chance that we might fall asleep or miss a radio call. That way, we have someone who can come get us if need be. I had just left two of our officers in a regular crack spot to go back on patrol, when minutes later one of those officers screamed out over the radio. The two of them had heard an alarm go off near where they were and when they went to investigate, they found a burglary in progress.

One of the officers ran on foot down the large steep hill that led from the crack spot to the strip mall where Evil was trying to pilfer electronics from one of the national electronics chain stores. The other officer took a more circuitous route in his patrol car. The officer on foot confronted Evil and drew his weapon yelling his full repertoire of expletives. Evil piled into the getaway car and tried to run the officer over while speeding out of the parking lot. Someone in the car fired a small caliber handgun at the officer. He fired two rounds back at the car but hit nothing vital. The chase was on.

Evil fled straight down the side street about three blocks before crashing in the midst of a poorly executed evasive maneuver. As one would expect, Evil fled on foot and left the gun and his identification behind in the car. Though they escaped capture on that night, they were eventually hunted down and arrested with vigor.

#10.6 Ooops

The first few months of working the morning watch were very difficult for me. The last few hours of the shift usually found me very tired and ready for bed. On one particular night, I should have taken the opportunity to experience the crack first hand for the first time, but didn't. I was about as tired as I had ever been and I think I actually started hallucinating at one point, but it was nearing the end of the shift so I thought that I could hold out for another hour or so. I tried my best to keep conscious but was fading fast. I finally decided that no one would notice if I went back to the precinct 58 minutes early.

I remember activating my right turn signal in preparation for the final turn into the parking lot of the police station. The next thing I knew, there was a horrible crashing sound and I awoke to find that I was three feet off the ground running about 60 MPH. The first thing I saw was the telephone pole that broke off my driver's side, rear view mirror as I whizzed passed it. Then came the bone-jarring thud as I crash-landed into the dirt embankment. My faced slammed into the airbag as it exploded, causing some nice friction burns and nearly breaking my nose.

I sat for a moment, wheezing in the cloud of airbag propellant and disturbed topsoil, trying to figure out what had just happened. I slowly opened the door and fell out onto the cool grass beneath me. I surveyed my surroundings and realized that I had landed in the front yard of a nursery store that was about a half mile past my precinct. I also realized that my patrol car was nearly broken in half along a line roughly confluent with the roll bar. Later, when it was parked on a flat surface, only two wheels could touch the ground at any given time.

I took a deep breath and broadcast over the radio, "120, can you start a supervisor and a wrecker to [my location]. I just had a 41 involving a county car."

It wasn't long before the shift commander arrived. He got out of his car and slowly walked up to my demolished and half buried police car.

"Well, Goddamn…What Happened?" he said in a somewhat condescending, irritated tone.

"I fell asleep and crashed," I answered with a mixture of shame and embarrassment.

"Mmmm, mm, mm," he grunted as he got back into his car and drove away.

My beat partner showed up moments later and started laughing. He said that he had passed me right before the crash and saw that my turn signal was on. He also said that he thought it was weird the way my head was slouched over against the window.

"It almost looked like you were asleep," he said.

"I was you idiot…and if it hadn't been for that curve in the road I'd probably still be sleepin'."

Chapter 11

Hop Kangaroo Hop

I thought it prudent to include a quick commentary on our court system. During the Clinton administration, our President often boasted about adding 100,000 new COPs to the street. Like most things that spew forth from the mind and mouth of Government, that was a lie. After all was said and done, only about fifteen thousand new officers were added to the roll-call rooms across America. Many of the positions funded by the government were filled with existing police officers and not new ones. Even if we had gotten 100,000 new officers, it would have been a useless and meaningless waste of resources.

The proper way to approach the crime problem is not to add police. We have enough of them already. The proper way to attack the problem is from the opposite end. First, our jails are grossly overcrowded; we need more jails to hold the violent offenders who plague our society. Statistics vary on the matter, but up to 52% of all violent crimes in this country are committed by individuals who are on active parole or probation for the exact same crime. Theoretically, if you had a place to contain that 52% then our violent crime rate would be cut in half practically over night.

More jail space would also allow us to have truth in sentencing. In my county, the average Evil serves approximately one month for every year of his sentence. If he gets twenty years for armed robbery he will be out in less than two years on average. Though I do not have direct knowledge of court and jail systems across the country, I would imagine that many systems are similar to ours. I am reminded of the state of Texas in the 1990s. While the nationwide crime rate was rising at nearly twelve percent per annum, Texas showed a thirty percent decrease. The only thing that Texas did differently in those years was build more jails and increase the time served per sentence ratio. With more jail space, Evil was contained longer and committed less crime.

What we need to do is simultaneously develop, adopt and implement community level programs that help prevent children from growing up to be criminals. (I strongly believe that if you can influence them early enough, children that would otherwise grow up to be Evil, can be turned. I also believe that most adults who are Evil, cannot be turned.) Most politicians shy away from this type of legislation because the benefits are gradual rather than the American requisite of instant total gratification.

We need to segregate the non-violent or non-felonious offenders from the misdemeanor offenders. Not only would the facilities need far less security, you would also lessen the likelihood of prison making a hardened criminal out of a guy arrested for his fourth DUI.

Next we should concentrate on staffing our court systems so that we can process all the people that our adequate number of police officers are arresting. The very last thing we need is more police. If we lower the crime rate, we will need even less.

To illustrate one of my points I will relay an incident that happened to me in the early 1990s. Part of my county's long-standing policy of criminal prosecution is not to sweat the small stuff. While not necessarily a bad idea on its face, our courts can sometimes take it to an obscene extreme. Our courts have a policy that if a person is arrested for a felony, then any of the misdemeanor arrests that accompanied the felony arrest are "small stuff" and often are not prosecuted.

One afternoon in rush hour traffic, witnesses reported that a young woman whose car was stopped at a red light, inhaled a large quantity of white powder in through her nose in a scene reminiscent of Chevy Chase in the movie Modern Problems. She sat for a moment while the chemical worked its way into her bloodstream and her psyche. Then with an almost demonic expression on her face, let out a maniacal yell and stomped on the accelerator.

She ran through the red light and aimed her car at another vehicle that she soon rammed off the roadway. Over the course of the next three miles she ran into roughly six more cars in much the same manner. Witnesses reported that during her rampage she was laughing hysterically and doing her best to cause as much damage as possible. Her one-woman demolition derby came to an end when she drove off the roadway, through a boxwood hedge, over the lawn of an apartment complex and through the brick wall of an apartment into its living room. The vehicle came to rest halfway in and halfway out of the living room.

When I arrived at the scene, the woman was sitting cross-legged on the grass next to her wrecked car and rocking back and forth. She seemed detached from our reality but when I spoke to her she snapped back a little. She smiled and asked, "Oh …Can you take me home? There's something wrong with my car." Then she giggled.

I placed her under arrest for multiple charges of "Leaving an Accident Scene", "Reckless Driving", "DUI", and "Trafficking of Cocaine". Since there were no serious injuries, all of the traffic charges amounted to misdemeanors. The only felony arose from the nearly thirty grams of cocaine still in her purse. When she went to court, all those pesky misdemeanors were dead-docketed (not prosecuted) and the woman only went to trial on the cocaine charge. She pleaded guilty and got community service and probation but no jail time. She also applied for what we call "First Offender Status". As a first offender, after the successful completion of two years probation her arrest record would no longer reflect the felony cocaine charge, and all rights and privileges prohibited to a person with a felony conviction would be reinstated. Within two years of trial she had no criminal record and not a single charge on her drivers license. How's that for justice?

#11.2 Hot Car

A problem that seems to plague every community is the theft of and from motor vehicles. We had been having a rash of thefts from vehicles in a particular commercial area and were patrolling that area heavily. One officer spotted some suspicious characters and began surveillance. Before long his instincts proved true and the suspicious people were seen breaking into some cars in a parking lot. We also determined that the car they were driving to commit their crimes was stolen.

We surrounded the parking lot and pounced on them as they exited. In a less than textbook execution of a felony traffic stop, the initiating officer yanked the driver of the suspect vehicle out through the window and then slammed him on the hood of the patrol car, while the rest of us removed his wife and two young children from the stolen car. With Evil's face jammed into the hood of the patrol car, Evil began yelling and screaming. The officer bellowed, "What's your problem *&%$#@!"

Evil replied still screaming, "It's hot! It's hot!"

The officer gave a genuine retort, "Shut up. We know your car is stolen."

Evil said, "No, the car…it's burning my face!"

The officer picked Evil up off of the scalding hot patrol car hood and secured him in the back seat. A check of the adult members of the family showed an extensive criminal history for vehicle related thefts. During an interview, the man told us that he made his living breaking into cars and was teaching the art to his wife and kids. He also gave us some insight into the court system when he stated that of the over one dozen times in recent years that he had been arrested for felony theft, the only time he spent in jail was from the time he was arrested until the time he posted his own bail. Every time he went to court, he got probation or a fine or community service. To him there was no deterrent. (Stop, or we'll be forced to tell you to stop again.)

While jail probably would not have rehabilitated the man there is one thing that I can say for sure; if he had been in jail, he would not have broken into any cars.

I could go on and on with similar stories that would all make the same point. The bottom line is that jail is not a place designed to fix people. Most adults are not "fixable". Jail is a place designed to punish people and keep them contained for a specific amount of time. If they are Evil, without divine intervention they will stay Evil. Society's interest lies in keeping them contained so that they may not perpetrate their particular form of Evil at least for a certain amount of time. The more severe the Evil, the longer it should be contained.

Chapter 12

_____

Stop!…or I'll Poop

Many of my friends and relatives have asked why I would have a chapter just on stories about "poop". Well, because it's funny. The chapter title comes from this first story (yes, there's more than one) that comes from my time on the evening watch.

The area I was patrolling just happened to be in the neighborhood where I grew up. My parents lived on my beat and as a result, when it came time to go 10-200, I usually picked either the local fire station or my parents' house. On this particular day, I began to feel the urge while on patrol but it didn't seem like anything that would reach emergency status. I was close to the fire station but since I preferred going to my parents' house, I continued onward.

The farther I got from the fire station the more intense that urge became. As bad luck would have it, I found myself stuck on a two-lane road behind a car that was actually going the speed limit (the nerve!). With each passing second the "banging on the back door" increased exponentially. I knew that if I didn't hurry, the expulsion of hazardous materials would require the deployment of emergency pants. So I did what anyone driving a car with blue lights and siren would likely do in a similar situation. I turned them on.

Fully expecting the car in front of me to pull over so I could speed by and get on with my business, imagine my shock when the car in front me began to flee. Before I knew it, we were going close to 100 mph down a winding, two lane, secondary road, in the dark. I began to get a totally new understanding of the term "sphincter factor".

With every hard turn or inescapable downward impact with the roadway after cresting a small hill, I completely reevaluated my position. I didn't even call out to radio that I was in a pursuit because I knew there was no backup close by, I didn't have any charges (other than the fleeing) and I was in a signal 29 with my own intestines.

It wasn't long before I broke off the pursuit to take care of my more immediate problem. I was already prairie-doggin' and I knew if

I didn't find relief fast, there was going to be trouble. I was so far away from any of the approved depositories that there was no way I would make it to either one without need of a new uniform.

I saw a subdivision under construction and figured that it was time to improvise. I sped all the way to the back of the subdivision where, thank God, there was a cul de sac, lots of trees, and no people. I jumped out of the patrol car, slung my gun belt to one side and squatted right in the middle of the roadway. Good thing I always carry napkins in my seat organizer.

#12.2 The Smell Of Fear

My next poop story revolves around one of those slow nights on the morning watch. No radio traffic for up to an hour at a time and everyone who isn't sleeping is dying for something to do. I was patrolling up and down the main commercial thoroughfare in my beat looking for even the smallest of violations. As I passed an old florist shop for the umpteenth time, something caught my eye in the alley on the left side of the building. This particular building is one that is very old and has been haphazardly added to in the years gone by. The rear area is a greenhouse with walls made mostly of corrugated, translucent green fiberglass.

I really couldn't tell what was out of place but I just knew that something was different. So I parked my car in an adjacent parking lot and got out to take a look. I went down the alley and checked the outside of the building first. I initially noticed that there was a hole in the greenhouse wall where it looked like one of the fiberglass panels was missing. Not too strange considering the age and general condition of the building. I went to look into the hole in the wall.

The business was partially lit on the inside because of grow lights and security lights dispersed throughout the interior. As I looked at the hole in the wall, it appeared as though it could have been made recently, but there was nothing concrete to confirm my suspicions. I decided to go ahead and call for another unit just in case.

I called radio and asked for one additional unit. I told him to park away from the business and to meet me on the side. I sat tight and waited and listened. It wasn't long before the car I had requested arrived. He met me in the alley and I briefed him on what I had. I then asked him to stay by the hole while I checked the rest of the building.

I went around the opposite side and found a sliding glass door standing part way open, with no signs of forced entry. I stayed in the shadows and looked into the business for a minute or two. Then I saw a person's head. The head was moving past the other side of a two-way mirror that was in a wall between us. I assumed that the area the head was in was some sort of office.

I watched for a minute and there was the head again. I decided to go ahead and call for some more cars just in case. Since it was a slow night, most of them were already there and I just didn't know it. I asked for a few units to meet me on my side of the building and requested the rest to secure the perimeter. Two other officers and I just sat by the open door and watched.

The head inside turned into full-grown Evil and we could see that he had something on his hands and was rummaging through the entire office area. Our shift commander asked us to stand by until he arrived.

It wasn't long before he got there and we all gathered around the open door and watched for a second. I said, "since we're all here now and I'm reasonably confident that there's only one perp (since we had watched him for so long) let's go get him." I started in the door and my supervisor called me back. I was worried that he might have blown our cover but when I reluctantly returned to my surveillance position it was clear that he had not. The supervisor decided that we would just wait for him to come to us. Fair enough.

Three officers and one supervisor sat and waited outside the open door hidden from anyone who might be inside. Then our hapless perp meandered toward the open door with his sock covered hands full of change from the petty cash drawer and a take-out box of leftover pasta that he had stolen from the refrigerator inside.

As soon as he broke the plane of the doorway we all revealed ourselves simultaneously and shouted our cherished expletives. Evil froze for a moment, staring in disbelief, and was then promptly tackled by the nearest officer. As he hit the ground I heard the unmistakable sound that we all equate with the expulsion of noxious gases from the rectum (wrecked 'em hell, he damn near killed him). Only in this case, as we confirmed shortly thereafter, the noxious gasses were accompanied by their host, solid material. I guess it was a good thing that he was wearing sweat pants with tight elastic cuffs.

#12.3 Oooh Oooh That Smell

While on routine patrol one night, one of my fellow officers happened to see a car full of suspicious characters driving down the roadway and initiated a traffic stop. All three occupants of the vehicle were acting quite nervous and the red flags were going up everywhere. The officer soon called for backup and decided to have the passengers exit the vehicle for safety reasons. (Police are allowed to order the driver and all passengers out of the vehicle, pending the completion of the traffic stop, according to the US Supreme Court decision in Maryland vs Wilson decided February 19, 1997.)

When the front seat passenger was asked to exit the vehicle, he did. He got out of the car and kept on going. Several officers immediately gave chase and tackled the subject not far from the car. The subject was wearing nylon running shorts and a t-shirt. When he was tackled by officers, the exceptionally large perpetrator underwent a complete bowel evacuation. As he continued to resist, the officers continued to subdue and after a short wrestling match, three officers emerged who were literally covered in crap. I distinctly remember laughing my proverbial rear-end off at the scene (since I was not one of those officers upon whom the poop had been deposited) and then again as I returned to the precinct some time later and was struck in my olfactory organ by that all too familiar scent that had by then permeated the entire building while the officers completed their paperwork. Ever since then I've kept a complete emergency uniform in my locker – just in case.

#12.4 Which One Is The Turd?

One of our DUI enforcement units was working my beat when he tried to stop a car going the wrong way on a one way street. The intoxicated driver mistakenly hit his accelerator rather than his brake pedal (I'm sure) when signaled by the officer to stop, and as a result, the officer thought that the car was trying to run from him.

The small, bottom of the line BMW, was a good bit quicker than the patrol car and given the long straight road that led out of the county, he was gone in a flash. The only problem for Evil was that he was going so fast when he finally met a curve in the roadway that he lost control of his car and it flipped over a time or two before coming to rest upside down.

As is normally the case with drunk idiots, he emerged from the twisted, mangled metal without a scratch just as the DUI unit was pulling up to the scene of the accident. The DUI unit yelled at him and it was either that or the high speed flipping and crashing that caused Evil to make an unscheduled deposit of solid waste material into his cotton briefs.

As I stood by as backup in case he decided to resume his flight, the DUI unit asked Evil if he would mind submitting to a few voluntary field sobriety evaluations. Evil said that he would but that he had to do something first. The DUI unit asked what it was that he had to do. With that, Evil hiked his leg a little and tugged on the fabric of his nylon running shorts. Out dropped a nice, neat, little turd.

"I'm ready now," said Evil.

#12.5 No Shame

My last, short, poop story also revolves around a DUI suspect. This particular female was heavily intoxicated and was in the process of failing her sobriety evaluations with flying colors when she asked the arresting officer if she could use the bathroom. He told her to hold it for just a few minutes and they would be done.

She repeated her request, punctuating it with the urgency of an impending containment failure. The officer, assuming that she was going to urinate in the bushes as many drunks are known to do, said, "All right. Go ahead."

With that, the seriousness of her situation was fully displayed (as were her private parts) as she hiked up her skirt and squatted on the center yellow line of the roadway. Illuminated in all her glory by the patrol car headlights, she let loose her hideous intestinal sculpture.

It was gross then but it's funny now.

Chapter 13

_____

Make the Bad Man Stop!

Domestic violence is a curious thing. People who profess their undying love for each other and then brutally beat, torture, and/or murder the object of that love, will forever perplex me. Neither can I get my mind around the concept that "If I can't have you, no one will." But just because I don't understand it, doesn't mean it's not there. The thought has never occurred to me to raise my hand against my wife. I would sooner cut it off. I personally believe that violence should only be used in self-defense or defense of others (and occasionally in the defense of property). Having been immersed in a vast number of domestic disputes has convinced me of one thing. People rarely change and violent behavior unchecked becomes more violent.

The first few years I was a police officer, my state had no laws defining "domestic violence". The only person who could prosecute any offense was the victim. Since then, we have seen the passage of laws that require police to prosecute domestic violence whether the victim wants to or not. Sometimes it's a good thing, but sometimes it's not.

One of the quirks in the current law is the way that it is interpreted by some enforcement officers. The Georgia Family Violence law reads as follows:

"…family violence means the occurrence of one or more of the following acts between past or present spouses, persons who are parents of the same child, parents and children, stepparents and stepchildren, foster parents and foster children, or other persons living or formerly living in the same household:

Any felony: or

Commission of offenses of battery, simple battery, simple assault, assault, stalking, criminal damage to property, unlawful restraint, or criminal trespass…"

What this law does **not** do is change the definition of those crimes enumerated. It also does not say that a person's emotional state is a determining factor in whether or not something that person does is illegal. There is a reason why I am going to such great pains to make a point. That point is that if your wife locks you out of your house for whatever reason and you come home and cannot get in, you are perfectly free to break into your own house. Since it is your house, you are allowed to damage it. Providing that you do not endanger anyone's life or safety in the process, breaking your own stuff is not illegal. It is not illegal if I am happy and it is not illegal if I am mad at my wife. Yet every day officers are arresting people for similar reasons.

A good litmus test for those type of situations is a rule I call the "break it or take it" rule. Very simply, if you cannot be arrested for taking it, you cannot be arrested for breaking it. If I cannot arrest the woman of the household for driving the family car to her mother's house, then I cannot arrest her if she takes a baseball bat and destroys it. As long as she does not endanger someone else's life or property (which would constitute a separate crime anyway), she has done nothing illegal.

Tools are only as good as the craftsman using them and the same goes for law enforcement. I have seen officers with obvious "issues" go to a domestic dispute convinced that no matter what, the male is the primary aggressor and will go to jail. From that point, they just look for some incriminating testimony or some slight hint to take the man's freedom. That's bad.

If a person knows that all they have to do is call police and say, "He pushed me," and the accused goes to jail, then many people will have their freedom unlawfully taken away by a jealous or angry spouse. The police then become criminals and the tools of vengeance for the complainant. I have a simple rule. I will not deprive someone of their freedom based solely on the unsupported testimony of someone with whom they are emotionally involved. That being said, I believe that I have a few good stories to tell.

In the case of a particular woman, domestic violence laws might have helped. We will never know for sure. In my first year on the force, I had the pleasure of meeting this quiet young woman with a three-year-old daughter. I responded to a call to her apartment in reference to a fight she had had with her boyfriend, whom I believe was also the girl's father. He had pushed her around the apartment and caused minor injuries to her face. Like most cowards that beat up women, he ran away before I got there.

She didn't want him to go to jail. In an all too familiar scenario, she just wanted him to stop hurting her. Since he was gone, there was nothing for me to do. I tried to tell her that she should prosecute, because violent behavior almost always gets worse as time goes by. She thanked me for the extra time I spent trying to help but thought for sure things would get better.

Over the next few weeks, things did not get better. As predicted, they got worse. She sought help from her pastor when she decided to end the relationship with her boyfriend. The pastor and his family allowed her to move into their apartment until she could get on her feet again.

Her boyfriend, whom I'll just call Evil (not his real name), somehow found out where she was staying and came to visit. The pastor would not open the door so Evil kicked it and knocked it completely off its hinges. Evil then proceeded to beat on the woman in front of her child and her pastor. The pastor called police but before I arrived, Evil had run away again. The pastor and I counseled her and tried to get her to prosecute. She thought that prosecuting might make things worse and since he was gone, she declined.

Not long after that, the woman had a good job and her daughter had turned four years old. She had just picked her daughter up from daycare and was on the way to her new apartment when she looked in the rear view mirror and saw Evil right behind her. She called 911 on her cell phone and reported that she was being followed by her ex-boyfriend. She told the operator that he had beaten her in the past and that she had had enough. She wanted directions to the police station so she could file a report and have him prosecuted. She also wanted the operator to stay on the line in case he tried anything.

The 911 operator dispatched the call and gave us the pertinent information. We were to be on the lookout for her car and someone was to meet her at the precinct. At about the same time, I had been dispatched to a fight call with the only other unit that was in service. The other unit arrived first and advised via the radio that we had a barricaded gunman (again as a result of a domestic dispute).

The call the woman made on her cell phone had been placed on hold due to the higher priority call of the barricaded gunman. Before long, a lot of police officers had formed a perimeter and had the gunman contained awaiting the arrival of a special unit. The woman was still on the phone and was now exiting the freeway about a mile from where we were amassed awaiting the outcome of the other drama.

Radio then asked if one of us could clear to respond to the woman's call because Evil had since displayed a handgun and tried to run her off the roadway. When the call came out, I had no way of knowing that the caller was the same woman I had dealt with several times in the past. I would find that out soon enough.

There were plenty of officers on the aforementioned perimeter and since I was close, I responded to the freeway exit that the woman said she was approaching. Then radio advised me that the call had been upgraded to a signal 50/4 (person shot/ambulance enroute). I was only seconds away.

As I pulled up to the intersection, I could see Evil walking away from a small red car holding a very large pistol. I was preparing myself to take cover and start shooting but before I could even stop the car, Evil, holding the blue steel 44 magnum revolver in his right hand, pressed the gun against his right side and pulled the trigger. As the bullet ripped through his thoracic cavity, destroying several vital organs in its path before exiting the body and falling harmlessly to the ground, Evil collapsed and went into what we call the death shivers.

I ran up to him and grabbed the gun to make sure it was secure. People were frantically pointing at a car stopped in traffic almost right next to me. I hadn't noticed it because I was so focused on Evil and his really big gun. With the weapon now secured, I turned to see what everyone was yelling about.

What I saw was a red Pontiac Fiero, three cars from the red traffic light that forced the cars to stop moments earlier. When it had turned red, that same traffic light afforded Evil the opportunity it had so desperately sought by trapping the woman in traffic with nowhere to go.

According to witnesses, Evil casually approached the Fiero and without hesitation fired through the windshield. I saw that the Fiero had three large holes in the windshield. When I looked inside the car I immediately recognized the corpse of the woman with three corresponding holes in her torso.

Her four-year-old daughter was in the seat next to her and was silent and shaking. Physically the little girl was fine. I have no idea what toll Evil exacted on her in the years to come as a result of those three pulls of the trigger, but I'm sure that it was great.

As for Evil, that little piece of it died there in a bloody puddle in the roadway. Ironically, I am confident that in his attempt to elude responsibility for his heinous deed, Evil only expedited his judgment at the hands of the Almighty. For that I am truly grateful.

#13.2 Veggie Tale

I was contacted one evening around donut time by a young professional woman (I believe that she was a nurse) in reference to her missing sister. The woman told me that she and her sister lived together in an apartment on my beat. She went into great detail explaining how responsible her sister was and how something had to be wrong. The woman also told me about her sister's boyfriend and how much she disliked him.

The final and most important detail the woman told me was that the door to her sister's bedroom had been locked since her sister was last seen about two days prior. She showed me to the door in question and I immediately detected a hint of an odor that any police officer recognizes as rotten meat.

I radioed for an additional unit and asked the woman to wait in the hall. I think she must have realized that I had realized something. Her concern began to noticeably turn into panic.

When my backup unit arrived, I quietly explained to him what was going on and that I fully expected to find the woman's sister behind the locked door. I also let my supervisor know what was going on and he came out to the scene.

Most interior door locks are easily defeated and this one was no exception. With a small screwdriver and a few seconds, I had the door unlocked. We opened the door and the three of us stepped in.

The room was dark and cluttered and the smell we had detected on the outside of the room was much stronger on the inside. The reason for that was abundantly clear once we entered. At the foot of the bed that was in the center of the right hand wall, was a man wearing boxer shorts. He was lying on his back and had a small pool of blood under his head that was dried and black. The odd thing was that he appeared to be breathing. Closer inspection confirmed that he was so we called for paramedics.

My boss ordered me to secure the man even though he appeared unconscious and I complied. With that task accomplished, my focus turned to the bed. On it lay the woman's sister. She was partially clothed and wrapped carefully in a clean white sheet. Her body was positioned like a crucifix. Her head was sunken into and subsequently concealed by a large down pillow. The reason for that was that when her boyfriend shot her three times in the head at close range with a small caliber pistol, her blood pooled up in the pillow and nearly encased her entire head.

She was dead all right, just as we had suspected, and had been for at least two days. Her boyfriend, likely despondent over the hideousness he had just perpetrated, turned his little weapon on himself. The head wound he inflicted on himself was not fatal. It was, however, serious enough to turn him into a veritable vegetable and confine him to a state facility for lord only knows how many years to come.

The woman's feelings about her sister's boyfriend were right on target. The sister was going to break up with him and he couldn't stand the thought of not having her. I hope he is happy.

#13.3 I Love You To Death

The reason that we have domestic violence laws is because some people are incapable of breaking away from an abusive partner without assistance. There are those who would prefer to stay in a violent relationship to the point of risking their life rather than end the relationship and risk being alone. Some people are simply afraid of change and, like the stoic dog, have to be dragged into it kicking and screaming. Our domestic violence laws are designed to help those who cannot or who will not help themselves.

One family that had a long history of interactions with the police in my jurisdiction was a prime example of this aberrant mentality. There was a father, who seemed to be the most stable of the bunch. There was the mother who was an alcoholic and a petty thief. And there were the two daughters who represented the least stable of the clan.

This story revolves around the oldest daughter. She was a chronic alcoholic who moved from one abusive relationship to the next. The police were called to violent, knock-down, drag-out fights between her and each of her consecutive love interests. Most of her boyfriends were as unstable as she was and none of them were strangers at the county jail.

This woman was in and out of treatment programs. Some of them she entered voluntarily while some were ordered by various courts. It was in one of those treatment programs that she met her final significant other. He was a large man, 6'08'' or so, and had been some type of soldier at one point. He had an alcohol addiction and an extreme proclivity towards violence. All she knew was that he was the love of her life. She didn't even care that he had been diagnosed with HIV and she freely engaged in unprotected sex with the man. It was her way of professing her undying love for him and was also the thing that eventually ended her life before she turned 35.

The woman's mother called police one night. I was the one who responded. She knew me by name because of all the times I had encountered each and every one of her family members in a cornucopia of police related actions. She explained that she had been on the phone with her daughter minutes before and that there was some type of fight going on in the apartment where the daughter had recently moved in with her abusive boyfriend. Mom was afraid for her daughter and wanted us to go and check on her.

I went to the ground floor apartment and had a backup unit with me. It is my policy when responding to fight calls to check around the exterior of the dwelling and peek in all the access points to attempt to determine a threat level and formulate a strategy for the encounter. This particular time I got an eye full.

I could hear screaming through the brick walls of the apartment building. It sounded like it was coming from a back bedroom. While my partner knocked on the door, I went to the window of the back bedroom to try to look inside. I was able to see through the sheer curtains into the well-lit and poorly kept bedroom. I was just in time to see the woman scurry into the bedroom as if she were a little girl running from an impending bout of corporal punishment from a not so loving father.

She was naked from the waist down. She turned to see her attacker/lover just as he was entering the room. He rushed up to her, grabbed her by the throat with his left hand and with his closed fist, nailed her in the left cheek with a right hook that would have taken out a man twice her size. She immediately went down and with her figure out of my way, I could see that the man was naked as well and was "sporting a tremendous woody".

All that transpired in a matter of seconds. I ran back around to where my partner was and beat on the door with my nightstick. There was no response from inside so I gave the door a swift kick. I could hear the crack of the doorframe as the door almost gave way under the pressure of the impact. I was about to give a second kick when the naked man opened the door and looked like he was ready to fight.

Not only was he stark naked, but his body was covered with open sores and there was fluid dripping from his still turgid, Clintonian statement of manhood. I knew that he was HIV positive and I wasn't about to let him pass the favor. I drew my pistol and pointed it directly at his head while taking a few steps backward. I made it quite clear that if he did not follow my subsequent commands to the letter, his death would not be the direct result of a viral infection, it would be from lead poisoning as the result of the impact of a full magazine of 9mm ammunition.

He obsequiously relented and both his ego and his turgid member deflated. I told him to turn around and put his hands behind his back. I then carefully put handcuffs on him like I was performing heart surgery on my own mother. I transported him to the county jail where I promptly soaked everything I could in bleach and threw away my handcuffs.

The man's arrest changed nothing in the lives of the two lovers. He in fact died of his infection within a year and she followed suit soon after. I have no doubt in my mind that had he not complied with my orders, his demise would have been much swifter and much less painful. Would I have been justified? A post encounter, cost/benefit analysis, led me to the conclusion that the question itself was irrelevant.

#13.4 It's The Principle

Some domestic violence calls are the result of the irrationality and sheer stupidity of the involved parties. Take for instance a call I responded to recently after the implementation of our state's domestic violence statute. The female of the house, who was a large, burly, obstinate woman who was perfectly capable of taking care of herself, had called because her husband had just come home. In and of itself that would not be cause for alarm but he had just gotten out of jail after being confined for three months for allegedly assaulting her.

He just wanted to come home and go to bed and she did not want him there. During the three months he was incarcerated, she had plenty of time to get any number of court orders that would have prevented his return. She also had plenty of time to move if she had wanted to do so. But since she did neither, we had no legal means of removing him from the apartment.

She kept saying that if he didn't leave, there would be a fight. She felt the need to impress upon us that he had sores on his penis and that somehow validated her argument. She said that if she left the apartment, he would "win" and that was not acceptable. We kept telling her that they needed to separate or someone would end up hurt or dead and the other would end up in jail. She had plenty of relatives nearby that she could stay with but refused to leave because of "principle". He had nowhere to go and just wanted to go to sleep.

We left and within two hours, she had struck him in the head with a cast iron skillet and stabbed him with a kitchen knife while he slept harmlessly on the couch. She nearly killed him and as we predicted, she landed in jail to serve a much longer sentence than he had.

#13.5 Weed Bagger

In addition to the standard arrests that arise from domestic violence calls, sometimes they lead to much more. As I said before, I make a habit of doing a little "recon" on certain calls to maintain a tactical edge. I did that very thing when responding to a report of a fight at a neighbor's apartment from a complainant who wished to remain anonymous.

Before knocking on the front door, I looked into the partially open kitchen window to see if there were signs of a disturbance. I saw nothing that indicated that there was any violence occurring, but I did see something else that warranted further investigation. Sitting at the dining room table was a man who was plainly engaging in the process of weighing and packaging marijuana.

I motioned for my backup officer to come see and we laughed for a moment before going to knock on the door. In response to our knock, the rather large man we had just seen bagging weed answered the door. He only opened it a little way and stuck his head through the resulting crack.

We told him that there was a report of a fight in his apartment. He said that everything was OK. I told him that I needed to come inside to discuss a secondary matter with him. He tried to slam the door. I stuck my flashlight in the doorjamb to prevent it from closing and the fight was on. My partner and I forced our way inside while the weed-bagger screamed something about how we needed a warrant. After a short scuffle he was subdued and we explained that when we see a felony in progress, no warrant is needed. The trial court concurred.

He had not only the massive amount of marijuana but also a fair amount of cocaine that we never would have found had we not looked before we leapt. Every officer owes it to him or her self to be well versed on search and seizure. There are many gray areas and nuances that can only be decided by a court but there are some concrete rules as well.

The plain view doctrine allows officers to act on anything that they can see in "plain view", provided that they have a legal right to be where they were when they saw it. If you choose to commit crimes in front of an open window where anyone walking by can see you, then don't be surprised when the police appear at your door.

Chapter 14

Spread Your Tiny Wings...

For civilian and police audiences alike, the quintessential car chase seems to fascinate and enthrall practically everyone. Therefore, I would be remiss by not dedicating a chapter to this glorious pastime. In practically every circle, the police chase will spark debates that I do not mean to ignite here. I will make a few short comments and cut to the proverbial chase.

The facts are that every day people around the world die. People around the world commit crimes. People who commit crimes, tend not to want to get caught. People who commit crimes and don't want to get caught tend to run away from those tasked with apprehending them. When they run away they sometimes hurt or kill other people. We must, then, decide if Evil will do more damage by getting away than he can do by running away. Often we don't know what particular act of Evil is causing a person to run away until we catch him.

The extremists on both ends of the "chase – don't chase" spectrum tend to have knee-jerk emotional responses to the problem and as always, the answer likely lies somewhere between the extremes. As in many aspects of life, moderation is the key, and, like the population of a hillbilly mining town, everything is relative. We reach moderation through education, training, and equipment, not through legislation or prohibition.

Before my department went from a "chase 'til the wheels fall off" policy to one that limits chase to **known** forcible felony perpetrators, I was involved in a great many car chases. I never wrecked and Evil regularly did. **None** of my literally hundreds of high speed car chases have ever ended in serious injury or death to anyone other than the fleeing Evil. Maybe I'm just lucky.

Since the adoption of a much more prohibitive chase policy, none of my chases have ended with serious injury or death to anyone other than the fleeing Evil. However, I have had several people explain to me after they have run from me and crashed that the only reason they ran was because they knew my department had a "no-chase" policy.

"How did they wreck if I wasn't allowed to chase them?" you ask. Well, just because I stop chasing someone does not mean that they stop running. As a result of the fight or flight response, many people who choose to run from the police in automobiles, get tunnel vision and stare intently at the road ahead of them to keep from crashing. (This phenomenon also occurs to a lesser degree in people who are just driving rapidly for no particular reason.) Therefore, it is quite common for a fleeing motorist to never look in the rear view mirror to see if the police are still there. Evil just assumes that we are and behaves accordingly.

As mentioned earlier, the fight or flight response causes the brain to do irrational things. It's bad enough if the Evil is irrational but if the pursuing police suffer as well, you have the recipe for disaster.

To reduce the effects of the immense stress suffered by all participants in a pursuit, I recommend the following: Whenever you feel that initial adrenaline dump, the first thing to do is take a deep breath and consciously try to calm yourself down. Let your rational mind stay in charge so that you can make good decisions.

One way to propagate the calm instead of the panic is to maintain a reasonable distance from the target vehicle. Human beings involved in any type of chase tend to revert to their base instincts. One of those instincts is that when we chase something, we want desperately to catch it. To catch it, we have to be close to it. That doesn't work with cars. Until it is time to perform some type of pursuit intervention technique, which is sometimes vulgarly referred to as wreckin' 'em, there is no reason for a patrol car to follow any more closely to Evil than he would at the same speed if there weren't a pursuit. In other words, back off!

Whenever I pursue a vehicle, I try to stay at least 300 feet back. At low speeds I may be closer depending on circumstances. Giving fleeing Evil a little room serves several purposes. First, the closer you are to Evil, the more Evil thinks he's about to be caught and the harder he tries to get away. This means that he drives faster and takes more chances. If you give Evil a little breathing room, he tends to slow down (a little) and take fewer chances. That means that he is less likely to crash.

Which brings us to point number two. If Evil crashes and you are right behind him, then you crash too. Some people call that a "no-brainer" but I would argue that one of the most common errors committed by officers in high speed chases is that they follow too closely.

Along the same lines, if you are too close to Evil and he turns abruptly, you don't have time to turn safely and either crash or let Evil get away. In any pursuit you need time to respond to Evil's actions, and distance is time.

Bear in mind that very few chases end with the suspect simply stopping and surrendering. When Evil crashes, runs out of gas, suffers catastrophic mechanical failure or just decides to get out of the car, he will likely run away on foot. Another interesting behavior for police is the "monkey see, monkey do" syndrome. For some reason (likely a result of the fight or flight response in the officer), officers in a car chase will park their cars and run after Evil if Evil gets out and runs. This is true even if Evil is running across a fifty acre parking lot. If you are far enough from Evil when he transitions from car to foot, then you can make the rational decision to follow him as far as possible in your car. If you can outlast Evil in the first few seconds of a foot pursuit you will likely win. What better way to win a foot chase than to start it in your car?

My last comment pertains to the perception of civilians and administrators that having lots of cars in a chase is worse than having a few. My department's current pursuit policy limits the number of actively participating officers to two. If the pursuit crosses jurisdictional lines, then we may add one car for that jurisdiction. That means that in theory there should be no more than three police cars in any authorized, active vehicle pursuit.

I see two problems here. First, if you have ever seen a car chase involving dozens of police cars it is truly spectacular. With all those blinkie-blinkies and woo-woos goin' together, citizens will scurry out of the way like frightened rabbits and the effect is magnified in the dark. When there are only two or three police cars involved, people sometimes don't even see them and very rarely try to move out of the way.

The second problem is that if there are three or more perpetrators in a fleeing car, which there often are, the police are automatically outnumbered when the chase hits the ground.

155

Hypothetically, if a carload of Evil sees two police cars in the pursuit, the smart thing to do would be to stop and let all but two perps file out of the car. Then, the two police officers will have to stay with those two if they follow procedure. That gives the other Evil the opportunity to either get away or worse, circle and ambush the two officers while there attention is directed at the Evil that did not flee. I always think that more is better, especially when it's more good guys and less bad guys.

Now, on to the chase stories. They say that no man forgets his first girl. I have trouble remembering what old what's-her-name looks like but I darn sure remember my first high speed pursuit.

I was still in the twelve week FTO (Field Training Officer) program, fresh out of the police academy and was a little perturbed that I was working the quietest part of the county with a training officer that had been asleep for the last two hours.

The radio burst to life as our dispatcher advised all units that the city of Atlanta PD was chasing one north on Highway 9 into the heart of our jurisdiction. I was pissed that I was working in the boonies and everyone else was falling into the chase. I was sure that the chase would never make it the fifteen or so miles to my patrol area.

I was wrong. One of our units joined the chase as it entered the county. I knew the roads pretty well and I could tell that with the frequency they were passing cross streets, they had to be flying. I kept thinking that Evil would turn off or divert to an Interstate, but he kept on going, full speed ahead.

Radio advised that there was roadblock being set on Highway 9 by a local department. Radio advised he blew through the roadblock. More and more units, now from three jurisdictions, were joining in as the pursuit passed by.

They approached another city and another roadblock. He blew that one too. With every new cross street announced over the radio, my adrenaline level rose. I was waiting at a main intersection on Highway 9 and he was coming at me full force.

One of our units shouted that he was approaching my intersection. I couldn't see Evil yet but took off in the direction he was traveling because I was determined to be in on this one and I needed time to get up to speed. As I was trying to get up speed in my crappy Dodge Diplomat, I had my gaze fixed on my rear view mirror. I saw nothing but empty road behind me and in front of me.

I kept looking and driving but didn't see anything. All of a sudden, around the curve in the newly widened, seven or eight lane Highway behind me, my eyes were blinded by the glorious highbeams of Evil. He was indeed flying. A second or so behind Evil was what I can only describe as a wall of blue lights, acting like a peristaltic wave, pushing our Evil excrement down the highway towards our mutual destinies.

About then I realized that despite my best efforts, I was going way too slow. I turned my gaze forward and had my accelerator foot glued to the floor. My FTO was finally awake and turned to look behind us. Our position was not unlike a person on a bicycle trying to outrun the tidal-wave deluge from a recently collapsed, nearby dam. I remember my FTO's voice becoming increasingly panicky as he said, "Here he comes! Here he comes! He's gonna ram us! Here it comes!!!"

I was expecting an impact and peeked at the side view mirror in time to see Evil jerk the wheel to his left. He narrowly missed us and his poorly executed evasive maneuver set him into a spin at an estimated 110 mph. As he screeched and spun by me toward the front yard of a newly constructed bank that was to be his car's final resting point, I think I said, "Whew."

His car crashed rather unspectacularly considering the circumstances, and as soon as the car came to rest, Evil was out the door running. He ran around the near side of the bank building so I drove around the far side.

While the roughly twenty-six police cars from four jurisdictions all tried to avoid running into each other like grocery bags in the trunk when you slam on the brakes, I tried to get out of my car but despite my best efforts could not. My door was open and I was trying with every ounce of energy to join the foot pursuit but something was holding me back. I kept trying but could not break free from the clutches of my patrol car so I took a moment to unlatch my seatbelt and I was off. About ten officers beat me to Evil, and beat Evil. He was subdued with a considerable amount of force but not nearly what he deserved.

Among the myriad traffic violations committed, Evil was wanted for the molestation and rape of several young children. We did not find that out until after the chase was over. If we hadn't chased him, how many children would have been his victims before he was caught again? These are the decisions we must live with.

Television has conditioned us to think that Evil is easy to catch. Just get the tag number or call a helicopter or radio ahead. What if there is no helicopter and the tag is stolen? Evil gets away. If you radio ahead he just runs from them too. Even if you get his tag number and it's on the right car, how do you prove who was driving? We have a fifth amendment right against self-incrimination and nothing can compel a car's owner to tell who was driving. I'm not saying that I have the answers, but these are all good questions. How would you feel if someone just raped your daughter or killed your spouse and the police couldn't catch him because of a "no chase" policy since all they knew at the time he ran the red light leaving your neighborhood was that he was a traffic violator?

#14.2 Muffin Man

One of my all time favorites and a story that I constantly use in training recruits, involves a pursuit where there were two rookies and two veterans involved with one stolen car that was chock full o' Evil. I happened to be assisting another unit in the apprehension of a separate stolen car perp when my brother, who was working the same shift that I was, called out over the radio that he was following a stolen car and was headed in my direction.

I turned things over to the primary officer handling the call I was on and ran to my car to join in. Evil was unaware that they had been spotted and there was no chase at the time. The standard plan was for us to follow the vehicle until enough police units could coalesce in the general vicinity. Then we would wait until they stopped in traffic or at a red light and we would "pounce". This strategy is not the safest in the world (for many reasons that I won't go into here), but it usually works and it avoids protracted vehicle pursuits. It is another dangerous side effect of a no-chase policy.

I fell in behind my brother's car and we followed them, quietly waiting for more units. Two other units were approaching from side streets at about the same time Evil stopped at a red light. Our plan was about to be executed in characteristically flawless, morning watch fashion when in came the unknown variable in the form of rookie officer number one. He came flying up behind us with all of his emergency equipment running. Evil figured that the police were coming after him and he took off through the red light.

He sped down a side street in his stolen, early eighties model Cadillac, (which incidentally is quite popular amongst the perpetrators due to its fast motor, large cargo capacity for fellow perps and stolen goods, and the ease with which they can be stolen). I took the role of secondary unit. That means that I would be responsible for all radio traffic pertaining to the chase until I voluntarily relinquished the role or fell out of the chase. The secondary unit is the only unit that operates without a siren so that radio traffic can be clearly understood. The secondary unit should be the only person talking on the radio. All other units should remain SILENT!

The primary unit is responsible for keeping up with Evil. He does not talk on the radio and always has lights and siren on. The rest of the pursuing vehicles work off of the primary and secondary units.

Our chase sped down a two-lane side road at a healthy speed. When we hit a long straight-a-way, rookie number one passed both me and the primary unit and got right on Evil's back bumper. I switched to our private line channel and called his car radio. He answered after a few rings and I told him to back off of the perpetrator and get back in line where he belonged. He acknowledged me and backed off but did not take the appropriate position in the pursuit line.

I switched my radio back to main channel to continue calling the pursuit. It wasn't long before rookie number one got right back on Evil's butt. Once again, I switched to the private channel and told him to back off before he caused a collision. He acknowledged and backed off a bit. I went back to main channel. We went back and forth several more times with me calling him on the private line telling him to back off and his doing so for a few seconds before going right back to his stress-induced, following too closely position.

By the time we reached a five lane main road heading into Atlanta, I gave up trying to get rookie number one to behave and concentrated on calling the pursuit. We were joined by the city police and had a fair number of cars in the pursuit when rookie number one decided that there were too many patrol cars behind Evil. At that point he did something that I could not believe. He passed Evil and got in front of him. Under certain circumstances, such an action would be warranted. If a rolling roadblock were being deployed to slow Evil down, that would be acceptable. Also, if he were speeding ahead to block off intersections to make the pursuit safer, that would be okay too. Rookie number one did neither.

I called rookie number one on the radio and told him that he was in a dangerous position and needed to get back behind Evil. Just then, Evil seized the opportunity and rammed rookie number one from behind, knocking him off of the roadway to the left. As I passed rookie number one, he was narrowly avoiding a collision with a strategically placed strip mall.

We continued our pursuit and I was somewhat relieved that rookie number one had been knocked out. That relief was short lived when out of the blue appeared, you guessed it, rookie number one. Once again he passed all the other cars in the pursuit so he could be up front and right on Evil's rear-end. I thought about calling him on the radio but figured, "What's the use?"

It wasn't long before Evil ran a red light and struck a taxi cab (no major injuries). Rookie number one plowed right into the back of Evil and totaled his patrol car. Staying true to established cop-rodeo principles, all of Evil's representatives got out and fled in separate directions on foot and were captured shortly thereafter.

As I was returning to my patrol car, which was abandoned near the escape site, I saw my shift commander looking at the wrecked patrol car and shaking his head.

About that time rookie number two chimed in on the radio. He said something like, "Radio, can you start a supervisor to……in reference to a 41 involving a county car." The shift commander looked puzzled since rookie number two had not been involved in the chase and was assigned to a beat that was 15 miles on the other side of the starting point of the pursuit.

As it turned out, rookie number two wanted to be in his first chase. He was flying down the roadway about three to five minutes behind us trying to catch up. He ran a red light without slowing down and clipped the back end of a bread delivery truck. He knocked the truck into a spin, which caused it to leave the roadway and strike a light pole, which in turn came crashing to the ground. As a result of the impact, little pastries, muffins and assorted breads were strewn all over the roadway.

The police car continued with its forward momentum and crashed through the lobby door of a popular Atlanta hotel where it came to rest.

After that, our chase policy became much more prohibitive. Thanks, rookies. By the way, no one else wrecked.

#14.3 Hot Pursuit

Another rather memorable pursuit occurred early on in my career. I was working the evening watch and was patrolling the main thoroughfare in my beat at about 4 o'clock in the afternoon. I saw a Porsche 944 turbo that was displaying a dealer tag. At the time, dealer tags were only allowed on vehicles that were owned by dealerships and the vehicles had to be on the way to or from a show for sale. (An example would be if a car was purchased at an auction and then driven back to the car lot, the dealer would put his dealer tag on the car.)

I had seen the car parked in front of a movie theater and figured that there wasn't a big car sale there that day. I activated my emergency equipment to pull the car over just as it was getting onto the ramp of the Interstate Highway. Instead of pulling over, the Porsche accelerated rapidly and took evasive action, leading me to believe that he might be attempting to flee.

My police package Chevy Caprice was normally a very fast and capable car but that day it seemed like it had a two thousand pound weight in the trunk. It just wouldn't go. Needless to say the Porsche left me in the dust. I did my best to keep up but my car was failing miserably.

As I crested a hill I could see the Porsche in the left lane nearly a mile ahead of me. It abruptly went from the left lane to the exit ramp without decreasing speed and as the car went out of sight around the turn of the ramp, I saw a huge cloud of smoke.

A great big grin consumed my face. I knew that he had out-driven himself and that if I hurried, I might be able to catch him after all. My car had managed to creep up to about 70 mph by that time and I kept pushing it. Something was definitely wrong with it, but I wasn't going to give up when I was that close. I pulled up behind the Porsche just as it was preparing to drive off. The driver saw me and did something completely unexpected. He stopped.

I cautiously approached his car and asked him to step out of the vehicle and put his hands behind his back. The businessman in the dark blue suit pensively inquired, "Can we talk about this?"

I said, "No" and handcuffed him and put him into the rear of my patrol car with nothing else said. I then returned to the vehicle to inquire of the nicely dressed female passenger if she had any idea why her companion had attempted to elude me. She said that they were on both their first and last date and that she didn't even know I was behind them.

As I sat talking to his passenger, I noticed the smell of something burning and heard the sound that police often associate with someone trying to break out of the back of a patrol car. I turned to look and saw that the front half of my patrol car was completely engulfed in flames coming from the engine compartment.

I am known for my tendency to under-react at times and this was no different. I could see the frantic look on my prisoner's face as he was yelling, "Heeeeellllllp" and bouncing up and down in my back seat. I keyed up my radio and said, "Radio, can you start the fire department to my location. My patrol car's on fire."

I then went past the menacing flames of the car-b-que to the passenger side front door and began extricating all my personal police equipment from the front seat of the doomed cruiser. While I was unloading my equipment, Evil was screaming, "What about me?"

I told him to quit whining and that since the fire was in front, my stuff would burn up long before he would and that if he would just be patient, I would get to him next.

About that time my shift commander rolled up with a fire extinguisher and recommended that I get my perpetrator out of the car. I complied. It turned out that Evil that day was the exception to the rule. He was just trying to show off for his female friend. His plan backfired and I made it into the newspaper police blotter headlines:

"Hot Pursuit Leaves Police Car in Flames"

#14.4 Pole Vault

Next we move to a night on the morning watch. I was sitting in the parking lot next to another patrol unit. That particular maneuver is called the "Adam 69". It is suggestively named after the old TV show and the fact that the cars are positioned with the rear of one car next to the head of the other so the driver's windows are next to each other.

There was a loud crash and, as we looked around to see where it came from, we saw a car in a parking lot across the street that looked like it had just struck a parked car. We watched for a second to see what the driver would do. We were neither surprised nor disappointed when the guilty driver inspected the damage he had just caused and then promptly drove away from the scene.

We immediately fell in behind him and activated our emergency equipment. He immediately ran two red lights and headed for the Interstate. He got on the Interstate, traveled about a quarter of a mile, and then stopped in the right emergency lane next to the guardrail. Since Evil often feigns a stop and waits for police to get out of the cars before continuing to flee, I stayed in my patrol car and positioned it near the driver's door. The reasons for this are two-fold. It adds an "in-your-face" intimidation factor and it lets me stay prepared for another pursuit while staying behind the cover of the patrol car.

Evil waited for the other unit to approach on foot before he sped off once again and the chase was on. Here we come across one of the other dangers of a "no-chase" policy. Officers hate for Evil to escape, so even if we can't chase, sometimes we follow to keep the car in sight until it enters a jurisdiction that has a less restrictive chase policy and can chase them. That is more or less what happened here.

We advised radio that the vehicle had taken off and our supervisor immediately told us not to pursue. We turned off our emergency equipment and conducted what we call a mobile vehicular investigation (or MVI for short).

The old American sedan was able to use the relatively vacant freeway to creep up to about 105 mph. We were behind him a considerable distance but had him in sight. As we left our jurisdiction and were preparing to call it quits, Evil made a beeline for an exit ramp. I noticed right away that I had not yet seen brake lights and thought to myself, "He's going to crash if he doesn't slow down."

As his car went up the straight exit ramp I still saw no brake lights until it reached the very top where there was an intersection and a red light. At this particular intersection, there is a concrete, triangular island that separates the left turn and straight lanes from the right turn lanes. Evil apparently suffered a moment of indecision. He slammed on the brakes just before reaching the island.

When you hit the brakes hard in an automobile, the front end characteristically dips. The harder you hit them and the faster you're going, the farther down the front end will dip. When the front end dips, the back end goes up. In this particular case, the back end went up, and up, and up.

Evil had struck the concrete island in such a way that the front bumper stuck on the leading edge of the curb, causing the car to do a pole vault and a subsequent aerial maneuver that would have made the Walindas proud. It was truly spectacular to watch as the car did something that very few people see in the course of a lifetime (except in Hollywood). The car flipped end over end. On its way up, the trunk struck the wires holding the traffic lights, ripping them down and causing two transformers to blow up in rapid succession.

As the car flew through the air, power at the intersection was extinguished and all the lights in the immediate area went out, except for the light from the exploding transformers. The car continued to flip until it met a utility pole about 100 feet away.

The point of impact on the pole was about 6 feet off the ground. By the time we got to the intersection, there were live wires popping on the ground and the car was upside down and in flames. The other patrol unit pulled up next to me and asked if Evil was still in the car. I said, "How should I know, it's too dangerous to go over there and check."

Since we weren't supposed to be following the guy in the first place, I told the other unit not to say anything. I called radio and said that it appeared as though the power just went out at the intersection in question and we would be on the way to see if there was a 41 (motor vehicle accident).

I waited a few seconds and told radio that there was indeed a 41 and to start the appropriate jurisdiction. They got there quickly and asked if Evil was still in the car. I said, "We don't know, it's too dangerous to go over there, etc." between all the live wires and the now fully-involved, car and brushfires.

As it turns out, drunk Evil had been ejected from the vehicle and had run away from the wreck that would have killed a normal human. That's what I call "perp-luck". We found him about a half-mile away hiding under a car in a hotel parking lot. The only injury he had was a fishhook in his big toe. The fishhook was on the floorboard of the car he wrecked and he wasn't wearing shoes. As he was floundering in to the port-a-perp (paddy wagon) for his ride to the Graybar Hotel, he did say that he was sorry.

#14.5 Challenged

Now that I am a training officer, I do my best to expose recruits to as much as possible in the ridiculously short time they have in the field training program. One night while training a recruit, I was stopped at a red light conversing with another officer when a motorcycle approached the same intersection, facing the same red light. He paused and then drove right through the red light. I looked at the other officer and said, "I think we have just been challenged."

He wished me well in my impending pursuit and went about his business (he was off duty) as my recruit and I went after Evil. The motorcycle was driving relatively fast but nowhere near its crotch-rocket potential. I did consider the possibility that he was drunk and/or oblivious and not actually running. I got to within a few hundred yards of him when he turned into the entrance of an apartment complex and stopped.

As I drew near to him, he looked over his shoulder, turned calmly back to the front and took off. That was all I needed to convince me he was indeed running. I got that familiar grin since I knew that there was only one way in and out of this apartment complex. I knew this chase would not take long.

The biggest obstacle facing my recruit and me at that juncture was a series of very large speed humps. The motorcycle could navigate them with minimal difficulty and maximum enjoyment but my much heavier Crown Victoria would bottom out if I went more than 15 mph. The cycle took advantage of my handicap and pulled way ahead. After successfully negotiating the speed hump minefield, I was surprised to see our friend, the fleeing cyclist, once again sitting there as if awaiting our arrival like a kid in an amusement park waiting for his parents to catch up.

As I pulled up behind him, he again turned his backward gaze forward and continued his flight. He went up a hill and into an even more constrictive parking area dedicated to three buildings. I lost sight of him and thought for a moment that he had ditched the bike and was already on foot. A careful scan of the area proved that assumption wrong.

We were in a small parking lot with one driveway for vehicles entering and leaving. The parking lot itself was sort of a circle with a big landscaped island in the middle. I was on one side of the island and Evil was waiting on the other side, barely visible.

The dilemma was that as soon as I went around the island one way, the cycle could go out the opposite side and get to the exit. The smart thing to do would have been to park the patrol car blocking the driveway and go after him (or send the recruit after him) on foot.

I chose full speed ahead in the patrol car and went around the circle to the left. Cocky little Evil waited a second too long before taking off this time. Just as he was trying to negotiate the curve to leave the parking area, I caught him. My front bumper impacted his rear wheel and gave him a little more of a push than either of us was expecting.

Man and machine flew through the air with the greatest of ease about forty feet before crashing back to earth again. The bike slid under a parked car and Evil hit the ground running. Thankfully, with no prodding from his FTO, my recruit was out the door like a scalded dog. Within minutes, Evil was subdued by my recruit and brought back to his wrecked bike.

It turned out that the bike was stolen. A few days later, that same Evil failed to appear in Federal Court to be sentenced on his bank robbery conviction. He wrecked another bike a few days after that without any outside assistance. His girlfriend came and picked him up while police were working the accident. It took several minutes for them to realize that their perp had left the scene and by then it was too late to catch him. I'm not sure where he is now.

#14.6 A Patriot On A Scud

After we dropped off the Evil from story #5 at the jail, we headed back to our patrol area. As we exited the Interstate and turned north to go do our paperwork, an old Lincoln Town Car came speeding south with no headlights on, weaving erratically from lane to lane.

I did an immediate, fishtailing U-turn and caught sight of the vehicle as it turned into an apartment complex. Like a Patriot missile on a SCUD, I was on top of him before he got too far into the complex. I had my lights and siren on and chased him to the center of the apartment complex, which has a circular parking area with, you guessed it, a landscaped island in the middle.

I was right behind Evil as it negotiated the first corner sliding into two parked cars. He continued around the circle twice more, hitting at least one car in each curve. He finally came to a stop in front of the site of his first collision. He got out of the car, threw his hands out, and said in broken English, "No problem, my friend. No Problem." With that declaration, heavily intoxicated Evil gave up and was taken into custody without further incident. My only regret was that the mountain of paperwork that followed prevented us from any more chases that night.

#14.7 Perp-Luck

Sometimes Evil hides right out in the open. That was the case early one morning when I was driving by one of my favorite locations, the donut shop. I admit that sometimes I am consumed with thoughts of the culinary delights that frolic behind the doors of our local baked goods retailer and those thoughts almost made me ignore the brand new Corvette convertible that was backed into a parking space in the lot next door with two suspicious characters inside. I caught sight of them as I was passing and watched my rear view mirror as I continued along my original path.

I was not a bit surprised when I got a block away and saw the Corvette pull out of the lot and proceed in the opposite direction. So as not to spook them with a u-turn that would let them know I was on to them, I made a left turn and went around the block. I quickly returned to the main roadway and was able to keep their taillights in sight. I noticed that they turned down a dead end street that I knew had no open businesses.

I knew they were up to something and called some other units, to give them the description and circumstances. Then I sat and waited for Evil to come back out. After waiting for several minutes I thought that perhaps they had gotten spooked, parked the car somewhere and run away.

I decided to investigate. As perp-luck would have it, just as I turned down the dead end street, Evil pulled out of a driveway heading toward me. I knew they knew I was after them and there was no more sense in pretending. As I went to u-turn behind them, they took off in the direction they had been traveling originally.

I notified the other units in the area that Evil was on its way. I started this pursuit less than two seconds behind Evil, but he was operating one of the fastest and best-engineered production cars in the world. Even though I knew the roads as well as anyone and had my accelerator hammered to the floor, all I could do was keep the rocket ship-on-wheels in sight.

For the first time in my life, I had a bit of perp-luck in that every traffic light was green for me. I was going well over a hundred miles per hour on a five-lane surface street but could not close the gap between me and Evil.

I could tell he was slowing down for unfamiliar curves, which allowed me to get a little closer, but then he would hit a straight-a-way and increase the gap once again.

One by one, units joined in on the vain endeavor to catch the low-flying Evil. We crossed five miles in less than three minutes, but Evil was out of his league. As he came down a long straight hill that leads into another jurisdiction, he did not set up correctly to take the turn at the bottom. He left the roadway at probably 100-105 miles per hour and flipped upside down while flying into the woods of a local nature park.

I came to a stop before striking the utility pole that he had knocked over. I immediately exited my vehicle and ran into the woods, careful to keep my distance from the flaming power transformer and potentially live wires. I made it to the demolished, upside down Corvette within thirty seconds of his improvisational cannonball impression and found no Evil. I immediately thought that

Evil was trapped under the car but that assumption was later proven incorrect.

While staring at the mass of space age composite and metal that moments earlier was such a beautiful and powerful machine, I listened for footsteps in the woods and heard none. We did not catch Evil that night but thankfully, he left his driver's license behind along with his wallet and jacket. Apparently he had run across the roadway away from the woods, which explains why I did not see or hear him. Evil stole another car before we could set up a perimeter to contain him. In this case, Evil was arrested without incident several days later in his apartment not 1 mile from the crash site.

I still cannot fathom how both perps lived through that crash, much less how they were able to run away so quickly.

#14.8 The Bigger They Are Etc.

I responded to a domestic dispute as backup for another unit. The woman who had called told us that her ex-boyfriend had broken into her house by pulling the screen off of an unlocked window. He had threatened her but had not done any physical harm. This woman was one of the biggest women I had ever seen. She was well over six feet tall and was as thick as an NFL lineman. Strangely enough, her ex-boyfriend actually was an NFL lineman.

While we were in her apartment taking the information for the report, her phone rang. As you might suspect, the person calling was her ex-boyfriend. He was calling and threatening her from a payphone in the area. I quickly left the scene to try to track him down. According to the description we had, he should have been easy to spot. He was driving a 1970's era Cadillac Fleetwood that was only a little larger than he was. I doubt that any lesser car could carry him, especially if he had his ex-girlfriend with him.

I drove around the block several times and was unable to locate the target of my search. My supervisor, who is quite a large man as well, had called me to meet with him in a nearby parking lot and we were discussing what we would do when we found the man. Just then, one of our units announced over the radio that he had the Cadillac in sight.

My supervisor and I launched toward the location and in the meantime, that unit and one other had initiated a traffic stop on the individual on the side of an entrance ramp to a limited access freeway. As I crested the hill that was the final obstacle separating me from the officers on the traffic stop, I saw the primary officer at the driver's window of the Cadillac.

The officer reached for his sidearm and stepped back from the vehicle as a whoosh of white smoke billowed from the ancient luxury car's tailpipes. The car lunged forward and nearly crushed the backup unit, who was at a position near the right front of the car, before taking off south on the freeway.

My patrol car was still moving so, naturally, I fell into place right behind Evil and casually activated the blinky-blinkies. Since we had a "no chase" policy and my supervisor was right behind me, I figured the order to disengage was forthcoming. To my surprise and delight, I was mistaken. I had forgotten that our suspect was wanted for aggravated stalking (which is a felony) and that my supervisor had seen him attempt to run over the other officer. That was all that was needed for a justifiable pursuit.

So off we went. The car that Evil was occupying had one of the largest engines produced since the Korean War. While traveling straight, it did quite well but, because of its excessive weight, it could not perform well while turning. Consequently, we had to squeeze every little bit of horsepower from our patrol units to keep up with him while he was on the freeway, but within about ten miles or so he had the brilliant idea to exit and try his luck on the side streets of downtown Atlanta where the odds were more in our favor.

His clumsy behemoth was no match for our relatively nimble police package Fords when it came to negotiating the winding side streets he had chosen as the avenue for his doomed-to-fail escape attempt. He took one particular left hand turn so abruptly that the tires popped right off of the wheels on the right side of his car.

Since his primary transportation was now hopelessly crippled, our 400+ lbs of Evil decided to give it a go on foot. Lucky for us, when he decided to bail out of his still floating land yacht, he picked a section of roadway in an industrial area that was bound by a large concrete wall topped by a chain link fence on the right side, and a tall chain link fence topped with concertina wire on the left side.

Nevertheless, the huge wrecking ball of a man gave it the old college try. The first police car stopped short of him and the officer dismounted for a personal introduction. I seized the opportunity along with another unit to pull past him and cut him off. He was surrounded and turned to advancing officers as if they were an approaching offensive line and he was the last defender protecting an imaginary quarterback. It was then that my supervisor slammed him with a body block that would have made him the envy of anyone in the WWE. He hit Evil so hard that Evil went up in the air at least two feet before crashing to earth with an impact that could be read on a Richter scale.

That was the only hit required to take the stunned Evil out of the game. When he regained his senses, Evil was actually a pretty nice guy. He apologized profusely for all the trouble he had caused and, before being carted away to answer for his sins, he told my supervisor that in all his years as an NFL lineman he had never been hit that hard.

If Evil hadn't been handcuffed, I think he would have "high-fived" my boss. I guess we were all impressed.

#14.9 Like An Episode Of "COPS"

I mentioned earlier how I love to give recruits the experience of a high-speed pursuit when I can be with them to give a running narrative and critique. That very thing happened one night when I had a female recruit riding with me. The City of Atlanta announced that they were chasing a stolen pickup truck into our jurisdiction. The truck was occupied by one representative of Evil and had a cargo bed full of stolen equipment.

Though our departmental policy would not allow us to be directly involved in the pursuit, I thought it would be a perfect time to just follow, watch and let my recruit learn. As soon as we fell in behind the lump of police cars, I immediately pointed out that the first few units were probably rookies since they were riding right on the bumper of Evil.

As the pursuit progressed, two of those units were disabled by heavy equipment falling from the truck bed. Another unit swerved to miss the first two and struck a fourth unit. As we passed them I looked at my recruit and said, "See what I mean?"

The pursuit continued and two more of the rookie units ended up running into each other. One was following the pickup too closely. Evil saw this and slammed on the brakes. The first rookie hit the truck and the second rookie hit the first rookie. Two more units were out and the pickup truck continued. As we passed them I looked at my recruit and said, "See what I mean?"

Evil turned into a parking lot and all the other rookie units drove right behind him. I and some other veterans continued on to the far side of the parking lot and sat waiting for him to emerge. We had all the exit driveways blocked so Evil made his own driveway right over a hedge of hollies. He was going so fast that he went airborne and crashed into the roadway losing the rest of his cargo and permanently destroying the truck's suspension.

It was then that my otherwise silent trainee let out a yell that I must admit startled me. When I looked at her to see what had happened she was clapping her hands and laughing and said, "Whoooo weee! This is just like an episode of COPS."

#14.10 Now I Get It

I was heading for the precinct one morning to turn in my reports. It was around the middle of the shift so it must have been about 0300 hours or so. While passing by an apartment complex, I noticed a car coming out the driveway that only had its parking lights illuminated and not its headlights. I thought about turning around to make an "investigative stop" but then decided that turning in my reports was more important.

I made it about a quarter of a mile further down the road when radio broadcast that there was an armed robbery/car-jacking that had just occurred in the very same apartment complex I had just passed. The victim told the 911 operator that the perpetrator was leaving the complex in the stolen car and that he was driving without his headlights.

I immediately slammed on the brakes and yanked my car around to head the opposite direction. I didn't bother even trying to get on the radio because not only were there too many other units already jabbering needlessly, but I needed to concentrate on catching up to Evil. Thankfully, Evil had stolen a crappy little Chevrolet that was no match for my police interceptor Ford. I caught back up to him quickly and joined the chase that another unit had started seconds before.

We screamed down the empty highway at ever-increasing speeds, blowing through red lights and using the entire roadway as if it were our own. With every other block we traveled, another patrol car joined the chase. The lead car happened to be one of our newer officers who had very little experience with high-speed pursuits. I had given him my standard pursuit speeches several times in the past but there's no teacher like experience.

The lead car was too close to Evil. That fact became painfully clear when Evil made an abrupt turn toward a highway on-ramp. Evil was going way too fast to perform such a maneuver and began sliding sideways. His tires screamed and squalled as he slid toward the outside curb of the ramp. When both of Evil's left side tires hit the curb, the car went airborne. It performed a spectacular barrel roll over a large shrub, crashed down the embankment on the other side and down onto the shoulder of the Interstate highway below.

I had strategically positioned myself near the rear of the pursuing pack and as a result, while everyone else was panic-stopping and trying not to crash, I drove around them all, onto the entrance ramp and parked my patrol car.

I jumped out of the car as fast as I could and ran down the hill to where the upright but demolished car came to rest. The faster I got to Evil, the less likely he was to get away. I was the second officer to get to Evil and he was still in the driver's seat. He was unconscious (or pretending to be unconscious) and was not moving.

The first officer to the car tried to open the car door that was between him and Evil but the car was so badly damaged that the door would not budge. He switched to plan B and struck the window with his wooden baton. The wooden baton did not break the glass so I stepped in and smacked the glass with my Glock. The window shattered instantly into a million tiny shards that rained down on the unconscious Evil.

I directed the unit next to me to cover him while I reached inside the car and felt his pockets for weapons. I found a pistol in his right front pants pocket and removed it before yanking the scumbag out the broken window. We slammed him to the ground as he regained consciousness and started to resist. He was handcuffed and dragged back to the closest patrol car.

A few minutes later, I was back on top of the hill where Evil's acrobatic performance had begun. I looked around and noticed that one patrol car had a badly damaged wheel. I later learned that the lead car had tried to turn when he saw Evil turn toward the ramp. Since he was traveling too fast, he also slid sideways out of control and struck the curb.

Before I said anything, the officer approached me and said something like, "I remember you preaching about keeping your distance in a pursuit but never really understood exactly what you were saying. Now I get it."

#14.11 Puppy Chow

I'll close out this chapter with a quick tale of a young man on a motorcycle who decided to run from one of our traffic units rather than stop to accept his speeding ticket. The traffic unit activated his blue lights for all of a few seconds before realizing that he would never be able to catch the high-speed motorcycle, even on the long straight road where he was running RADAR.

The young man on the motorcycle kept running even though the police weren't chasing him. He went around a corner too fast and lost control. The bike went airborne and our young thrill seeker went with it. The bike flew an incredible distance and I'm sure the rider would have too, if it hadn't been for the one-hundred year old oak tree that he hit just yards off the roadway.

The young man hit the tree so hard that his body broke into two pieces with one piece continuing its flight path on each side of the tree. When we arrived at the scene a few minutes later, after a unit had seen the skid marks and a cloud of smoke left by the out of control vehicle. We found the top half of the man first. A dog that belonged to the owners of the yard he had crashed into was gnawing at the man's intestines. Running from the police is never a good idea.

According to the National Highway Transportation Safety Administration (NHTSA) Fatality Analysis Reporting System, in a five-year period ending in the year 2000, 1,641 deaths were caused by law enforcement vehicular pursuits. Of those, 18 (1%) were police officers – which is unacceptable, 1,058 (65%) were occupants of the violator vehicle – which is justice, 565 (34%) were innocent third parties – and the fault of the violator.

My interpretation of these statistics is that over a five-year period, 583 people died who shouldn't have. When you add that there are an estimated 500,000 police pursuits in this country in any given year (depending upon whose statistics you want to believe), that means that approximately one out of every 4,288 police pursuits ends with the accidental death of an innocent party. Is that an acceptable number? Who knows for sure?

In my personal opinion, anyone who runs from the police is in effect perpetrating aggravated assault against society as a whole. Aggravated assault is a forcible felony and warrants the use of deadly force. There are a bunch of whiney liberals who say that police pursuits are so horribly and horrendously dangerous that they should be banned altogether. If they are so terrible, then why is running from the police still considered a misdemeanor in some states (like Georgia) and not the aggravated forcible felony that it is…and why aren't those same whiners lobbying for increased punishments of the true offenders?

How is propelling a 3000 pound missile recklessly down populated streets any less dangerous than standing in the middle of the roadway randomly firing a pistol? Do they make car-proof vests? Are you more likely to survive the impact of a car traveling at 88 feet per second (60 mph) or the impact of a bullet traveling at roughly fourteen times that speed? (Answer: I think I would rather try my luck with the bullet.)

Any time an innocent person dies, I think we all agree that it's bad. If we cancel all police pursuits, then how many criminals will escape to take someone's life later on? If we cancel police pursuits, how many people will run just because they can, or because they don't want a ticket that day? No one knows the answers to these and the many other pursuit debates.

We can never know. That is why, as I have said before, common sense and moderation are the best answer. I don't think that everyone who flees should be chased regardless of the circumstances. I also do not believe that police pursuits should be banned altogether. There is a happy medium somewhere, but no matter what we do, accidents will always happen. It's not the officer's fault if a perpetrator runs and wrecks. It is the officer's fault if he or she causes a collision through negligence. It's a tough decision but just another of the many that officers worldwide have to make every day. Let's not lose sight of the fact that the person who makes the conscious decision to run from the police carries the blame for the outcome.

Chapter 15

Name That Toon

Often times, as the cliché goes, "Life imitates art". Perhaps one of the world's most universal art forms is the cartoon. In rare but precious instances, people do things or get trapped in situations that tend to mimic some of my favorite cartoons. Some situations are so strange or ironic that they could almost be copyright infringements upon the works of William Hanna, Joseph Barbera, or the Warner Brothers. Other situations sometimes just have a cartoon-like flair.

This anecdote falls into the first category. There is a rare phenomenon that I like to call the "Wylie Coyote" maneuver. It is a privilege to witness this feat of legend and it is one most people would likely never forget. My introduction to that mythical maneuver happened one day when I responded to a domestic violence call at a ground floor apartment. The police had been called to the same residence numerous times in the past and, if I remember correctly, we knew that there was an outstanding warrant for the male of the household.

The apartment in question was at the edge of a large field, the outer boundary of which was a creek at the bottom of about an eight to ten foot deep ravine.

We knocked on the door of the apartment and the female of the house answered the door. She said that the man we were looking for was in the back bedroom. About that time, I heard what sounded like a window opening and immediately thought that he was running out the back.

I ran outside just in time to see that day's manifestation of Evil, sprinting through the grassy field. He was looking back at me while yelling some type of sophomoric taunt and extending skyward the middle finger of his right hand. I stopped in my tracks wearing a smile big enough to see across the some fifty-yard expanse between us, because I knew something he didn't know.

He was headed straight for the ravine. I was letting go with a full-scale guffaw by the time the ground disappeared beneath him. If I didn't know better, I would swear that he actually defied gravity for that split second of time it took to acquire a full appreciation of his current predicament.

Just after his surprised look disappeared into the ravine, I heard what sounded like a little girl screaming. I sauntered over to see what the matter could be, and lo and behold, it was Evil!

When he ran off the cliff, he happened to land right on top of a concrete storm drain, which promptly produced a compound fracture to his leg that was uncannily similar to the one in the movie "Deliverance".

I asked him if he was hurt and he continued to cuss at me, so I walked away. When he saw I was leaving, he became a bit more congenial and demanded that I call him an ambulance. He didn't know that I already had, so I figured, why not make the most of the situation?

"Say Please."

#15.2 "...Like I need a Hole in the Head"

The call initially came out as a signal 50 and 4 (person shot/ambulance enroute). Responding officers rushed to the apartment in question and were met at the door by a calm, seemingly normal man. They asked him what had happened. He proceeded to explain how things had not been going well with his wife and that they had been separated.

She was living at the apartment in question and apparently had a boyfriend whom she regularly brought up in conversation just to irritate her estranged husband.

That day, the husband just snapped. He came over to the apartment and kicked open the door. The wife came down the stairs to confront him and he shot her twice killing her rather quickly.

The boyfriend was in the apartment at the time and was understandably afraid for his own well-being. He sprinted toward the rear, sliding glass door of the apartment. Just before he reached the door, Evil fired two very well placed rounds that most marksmen would have been proud, of considering the circumstances. Both of the rounds struck their intended target in the back knocking him through the plate glass door. He was also D.R.T.

Then, despondent over the horrible sin he had just committed, Evil decided to take his own life. He put his six shot revolver in his mouth and pulled the trigger to fire the last of his bullets. However, Fate interfered with his plans.

Officers at the scene were perplexed and asked if the gun had misfired. Evil said, "No, it went off" and then he spit something out onto the floor.

Upon closer inspection, officers discovered that he indeed had fired his weapon in his mouth. The bullet had gone straight through the roof of his mouth and out the top of his head without killing him. What he was spitting out was something that used to be in the remaining hole.

As far as I know, the man lived to be prosecuted. When he gets out of jail, maybe he can travel with the circus.

#15.3 Elvis

I was just rounding the last corner in the roadway, making my way back to the precinct for the end of my shift, when I saw the car in front of me drive up over the curb. The driver over-corrected and ended up swerving into oncoming traffic. I activated my blue lights and the car kept on going. He jumped the curb a few more times before turning into the parking lot of a liquor store.

He parked the car and I pulled my patrol car in behind him to prevent escape. The driver got out of his car at the same time I got out of mine. He looked surprised to see me and after noticing me, he put up one finger as if requesting that I wait a moment.

I watched intently as the middle-aged man began gyrating his body. He looked like someone suffering from cerebral palsy doing an Elvis impression. At the end of the several second display, which I must admit had me intrigued, there was a very loud, very long, audible sound like that which we normally associate with the expulsion of noxious gasses from one's nether region. If I were grading the man, using the three "D" principal (Delivery, Depth, Duration), then his expulsion would have rated off the positive end of the scale.

Though I tried, I was unable to fight back my laughter completely as I asked for his license and insurance. The man was so intoxicated that he could barely stand up without using his car for support. He provided me with the requested documents and then politely refused all field sobriety evaluations. I placed the man under arrest and transported him to our precinct, which was only a block away.

I escorted the man into the holding area that housed our breath test machine. There were several other units waiting to use the machine so I asked my Evil to have a seat until it was his turn.

He waited quietly in his chair until his turn came to blow into the trusty machine. When I asked the man to stand up, he pushed up off the chair with both arms and immediately went into a repeat performance of his cerebral-palsy-Elvis impression. Needless to say, his contortionist jig attracted the attention of everyone in the relatively small and crowded room.

As the entertainment seemed to be winding down amidst the restrained snickers of both officers and perpetrators alike, that same unmistakable, ratcheting flatulence echoed through the halls of the poorly ventilated, rapidly shrinking holding area. The laughter turned to horror as the occupants of the room, officers and perpetrators, all clamored for the nearest exit.

I sat laughing uncontrollably and dreading the expected olfactory input. The responsible party was just standing there with a look that was a mixture of shame and irritation. It was then that he decided to explain to me emphatically, the only other person in the room at that point, "That was not a fart."

He had a prosthetic leg because his real one had been amputated at the hip. Whenever he stood up, he had to reseat the prosthesis and the process often caused trapped air to escape the joining region of hip and leg in a manner emulating a really big pooty.

I laughed a little more and apologized. I didn't bother to tell anyone else at the time because I had the holding area all to myself, and wanted to keep it that way.

#15.4 We are the Police. Really!

Serving warrants, like any other aspect of police life, can at times take a humorous turn. One of my beat partners had a warrant to serve on an individual for some type of financial fraud. The suspect was not from this country and had a pretty strong accent, though he spoke English rather well.

We had a total of three officers to serve the warrant. The primary officer, who had the warrant in hand, and a second officer positioned themselves at the front door to the ground floor apartment. I covered the only other means of escape from the residence, which were the patio area and an adjacent bedroom window.

The patio had a wooden railing around it to separate it from the common area of the apartment building. I stepped over the rail to get close enough to the sliding glass doors to see inside the apartment. Looking through the slats of the ubiquitous vertical blinds, I could see a lone suspect sitting on the large U-shaped couch in the main room watching television.

I signaled the other two units that I was in position and could see one occupant. With that, the primary officer knocked on the door, briefly but forcefully. The startled suspect turned his attention to the door and in a rather comical voice that hinted of Ricky Ricardo, almost sang the phrase, "Who is it?"

The primary officer attempted an amusing ruse. "Domino's," he said.

The suspect tersely responded with, "No order pizza. Fuck off!"

Since I could hear the entire exchange from my vantage point, I was chuckling to myself and wondering what the primary officer was going to do since Evil had called his bluff. The primary officer astutely switched to plan "B". He knocked on the door as before and awaited the response from the Evil within.

"Who is it?" he sang out again.

"Police," replied the primary officer.

"Yeah, right," was the retort from inside the apartment.

At this point my chuckle was a full-fledged laugh. While I was trying to regain my composure, there was a further verbal exchange between the involved parties and, the next thing I knew, I heard the unmistakable sound of somebody kicking something really hard.

Meanwhile, Evil had picked up his cordless phone and dialed 911 to report someone breaking into his house. Our dispatcher called to see if we were out at the apartment where the call came from. I was answering her in the affirmative when the door to the apartment crashed open.

What I saw from my vantage point was a scene straight out of The Three Stooges as Evil ran around his couch with the police hot on his tail. I am sure that my memory exaggerates when I say they ran around the couch four or five times with Evil intermittently hopping over the couch as if the shortcut would allow him to escape his pursuers.

All the while Evil had his cordless phone in hand and was yelling at the 911 operator to send the police. The operator kept telling him that the police were there. He kept saying that we weren't and that he was still being chased.

Finally, Evil zigged when he should have zagged and got tackled by one of the officers in the apartment. He fell over the couch and into the coffee table. No one was seriously hurt. After the tumult had subsided, the officers finally opened the sliding glass door to find me still laughing. I told them that I would have gladly joined in the foot pursuit but didn't want to miss the show.

#15.5 Hole-y Cow

Many people find the story that I am about to tell to be difficult if not impossible to believe. It is, however, one hundred percent true. It is the story of a man who committed suicide by shooting himself in the head six to eight times with a .45 caliber semi-auto handgun.

One of the officers on my shift responded to a call on a suspicious person sitting in a car in the parking lot of an apartment complex. After he arrived at the scene and notified the supervisor what he had found, we all had to go see. Inside the locked car, there was a man sitting in the driver's seat. His head was almost completely destroyed and there was gooey, semi-dried blood all over the interior of the vehicle. There was a .45 caliber semi-auto pistol in the man's hand and several spent shell casings strewn about the passenger compartment.

Detectives and the medical examiner determined the following: He had been despondent and had left a suicide note. He got into the driver's seat of his car and held the gun with both hands, resting on top of the steering column behind the steering wheel. He positioned the weapon so that the barrel was pointing at his head through the steering wheel. One hand held the gun from each side and he put both thumbs into the trigger guard to pull the trigger. The positioning of his thumbs in the trigger guard coupled with the recoil of the weapon and the subsequent jarring of his body from the impact of each successive bullet caused the gun to keep firing until the magazine was empty or near empty. In my experience, that is definitely one for the record books.

#15.6 Muddy, Bloody, Naked and Crazy

Fighting with naked people *at work* is never fun. At home is, perhaps, a whole 'nother story, but let's not go there. It always seems that when we encounter naked people in the line of duty, they are rarely, if ever, the kind of people that you would actually want to see naked. Take for instance a call I responded to with my beat partner that was dispatched as a 67 and 4 (person down/ambulance enroute) with no further information.

When we arrived at the scene, we had to look around the squalid apartment complex for a few minutes to find the target of our complaint. We found the little man lying (not laying - learn the difference) in the mud outside of one of the derelict two story apartment buildings. What made the scene unusual was not that the guy was completely naked, but that he was hopelessly entangled in a set of aluminum mini-blinds and covered in blood.

As he became aware of our presence, he began thrashing about. I assume he was either trying to run from us or wanted to fight, but since he couldn't free himself from his entanglements, he just sort of flopped around, grunting and squeaking and bearing a remarkable resemblance to a netted fish that had just been thrown onto the floor of the tuna boat.

My partner and I watched for a few moments trying to determine the best plan of action. We realized that with every movement, the aluminum slats in the blinds he was wrapped up in were cutting more severely into his flesh. Emergency medical personnel were already on the way so we decided that the best thing for us to do would be to try to keep him from injuring himself further by holding him down until they got there.

This type of situation is precisely why I recommend that officers wear gloves while on patrol. We constantly come across situations where, without warning, we have to go hands on with people or things that may be contaminated. Without gloves, you risk injury or illness and possibly even death.

I volunteered to hold the man's legs and the other officer went for his arms. It was difficult to keep him contained because not only did he have exaggerated strength due to his current mental condition, but all the blood, sweat and mud made it very hard to keep a grip on our slippery little flounder of Evil.

Medical personnel arrived after about a year and a half, and even though I was tiring significantly, naked bloody guy seemed to have all the energy in the world. We went to lift him from the ground to a waiting stretcher. I asked my partner if he had a good grip on the guy before we lifted him. He of course said that he did. Up we hoisted him, and he promptly broke free of the grip my partner had on him and slapped me square across the side of my big, bald head, leaving a perfect handprint in blood.

While no one can argue the humor in that particular situation, a more appropriate time to stop to laugh would have been after he was on the stretcher rather than while we were still holding him. That just made it take even longer to get him on the stretcher.

After the circus sideshow was over, we did a little investigating. It appeared (from the blood trail that led to a broken upstairs window) as though Evil had broken out of an apartment by taking a flying leap through the closed window that the aforementioned mini-blinds had been covering. He wallowed around on the upstairs walkway, likely trying to untangle himself from the blinds, until he fell over the rail and into the muddy yard below.

The apartment he came from was ransacked on the inside as if someone had just gone into a frenzied rage and begun turning over furniture and throwing things as you would expect someone to do in a frenzied rage. I was looking around the apartment for signs of drug use or possible victims when I came upon a closed door. Upon closer inspection I discovered that the door was not just closed, it was locked.

I fully expected to find either more Evil, or one of Evil's victims, behind that door. I quietly walked back outside the apartment and motioned for another officer to come upstairs with me. We approached the door together and with him as cover, I knocked sternly on the door. There was no answer. I beat on it one more time. Just as we were about to kick the door off its hinges, we heard a meek and mousy voice from inside. We identified ourselves and ordered the occupant to open the door.

A few seconds later, the door slowly opened to reveal a confused and tired looking female. She was startled either by us or by the realization that her apartment had been trashed. I asked her what had happened and she said that she didn't know. When she went to bed everything was fine and she didn't wake up until we knocked on the door.

We never did figure out exactly what had happened (the case was transferred to the detective division for expeditious placement in the inactive file) but we did discover that during the wrestling match with Evil we had been covered in blood. My partner took off his "not-fit-for-police-duty" neoprene gloves to discover that Evil blood had soaked completely through them and had covered his hands.

I took off my "made-for-police-duty" leather gloves and had no visible penetration. It was near shift change, so I called my wife and told her to implement our emergency decontamination procedures in anticipation of my arrival. That procedure is something I had worked out with her as a result of my having been covered in hazardous materials more than once in my career. Since our department has not seen fit to provide us with any means of decontamination, we have to do it ourselves.

My procedure is simple. My wife prepares the disinfecting solutions (either bleach, isopropyl alcohol and/or other chemicals designed for decontaminating things) in spray bottles and has lots of disposable wipes available. I drive into the garage, close the door and that's where I take off the contaminated uniform. Most of the time the uniform goes into the trash and I take a full disinfectant bath in my garage. Any salvageable equipment is also treated with the appropriate chemicals. Then I take a regular shower. I am not sure exactly how scientific the method is, but so far I have beaten the odds when it comes to blood-borne pathogens.

#15.7 Worse Than Going Blind

The individual in my next story made his exit into the hereafter in a rather humorous predicament. The call I received was to investigate a person down (signal 67/4). As is commonly the case, there was little additional information. When I arrived at the designated apartment, friends and family members of the deceased were gathered at the apartment across the hall and had not yet been made aware of his passing.

I spoke first to the lady who had called. She was the girlfriend and roommate of the deceased. She was visibly shaken and told me that her boyfriend, a man in his late 30's, had stayed at home from work that day because he was not feeling well. After repeated but unsuccessful attempts to contact him by phone to check on his condition, she decided to come home early from work to make sure that he was okay. When she opened the door to the apartment she saw him lying on the floor in the den. She got scared and immediately ran to the neighbor's house to call police.

About that time, emergency personnel were arriving and we went into the apartment together, leaving the girlfriend in the company of her neighbors. Immediately inside the door of the apartment was the den. There was a fireplace on the far left wall. Straight ahead was a couch and reclining chair with a small table between them. Beside the chair was an electronic keyboard with headphones attached. To the right was the kitchen and on the same wall as the entry door was an entertainment center with all the usual electronic components including a TV and VCR.

On the floor in the middle of the room, positioned between the couch and the entertainment center, with his feet toward the kitchen and his head toward the fireplace, was our victim. What made it interesting was that he was face down in the carpet and his pants were down around his ankles with his big ole butt stickin' straight up.

It didn't take the paramedics long to determine that he was stone cold DRT (dead right there). From the looks of things he had been dead for several hours. The blood in his body had already begun settling to the lowest point causing the skin closest to the carpet to take on a dark red color. The liquid that came out of his mouth as he lay face down on the carpet had already dried into a sticky mess that sounded almost like Velcro when we peeled his head up from the matted carpet. I'm not sure whether it was a result of a last minute grimace in the face of impending death or whether it was just gravity that gave his face the appearance of someone who had just tasted something very sour or who had seen something really gross.

The paramedics were quick to leave the "crime scene" and on the way out they made sure to tell the girlfriend that she was single again. At any rate, I was left in the apartment all alone with the dead guy with his pants down. My job was to notify the supervisor on duty, and to wait for the detective on call and the medical examiner to respond to the scene. After notifying the supervisor, all I could do was sit and wait. Since it was rush hour and I was in one of the most remote areas of the county, the wait promised to be a long one.

I sat down in the recliner with the dead guy sprawled out at my feet, and I waited. As you might guess, it wasn't long before I became a little restless and began looking for ways to occupy my time. As my eyes fell on the little table next to me, I saw the remote controller for the TV. I picked it up and turned on the TV. As I was watching, I couldn't help but think of the dead guy and the most likely reason that he would be on the floor in front of the TV with his pants down. So I made the next logical step. I rewound the tape in the VCR and pressed play.

Just as I had suspected, there was a rather explicit adult video that had to be completely rewound before I could watch it. The medical examiner would later confirm that he had a heart attack while pleasuring himself on his knees in front of the TV. He fell face first into the carpet and that was that.

My suspicions confirmed (and for fear of meeting a fate similar to the man on the floor in front of me), I turned off the VCR and turned on the news. I began to feel the pangs of hunger that always seem to coincide with rush hour and dead people, so I began looking around the apartment for something to eat. I looked for a minute but then thought it might be a bit more appropriate to call out for pizza. I called the delivery place that was a few blocks away and in no time at all, had my medium pepperoni enroute.

I must admit that for a few minutes I toyed with the idea of making that scene the most memorable pizza delivery the pizza man ever had. I thought of waiting in the closet when he knocked on the door and yelling out, "Come on in, I'm in the den!" I didn't have the heart and made sure I met him outside.

While I was waiting for the pizza to get there, I happened to look down once again at that little table. There, I saw an answering machine on which the message indicator light was blinking, indicating that there were several messages that needed to be checked, and beckoning me to check them. I didn't think there would be any harm in listening to the dead guy's messages, so I hit the "play" button.

The first message was from the girlfriend. "Hi honey, I was just calling to see how you were feeling. Call me when you get this message." BEEEEEEEP.

The second message was also from the girlfriend. "Hi honey, I hope you're feeling okay. Call me as soon as you can." BEEEEEEEP.

The third message was, you guessed it, from the girlfriend. "Hi honey, I bet your playing you're silly keyboard with the headphones on and can't hear the phone. Just call me as soon as you get this message." BEEEEEEEP.

The fourth message was, surprisingly enough, from the girlfriend. "Hi honey. I hope you're not lying there dead….."

#15.8 I Drink, I Get Drunk, I Fall Down; No Problem

I was dispatched to investigate a call on a person down (signal 67/4) in the parking lot of a fast food restaurant. It was in the early hours of the morning, probably around 0430 hours. Obviously, the restaurant was closed and so was everything else in the general vicinity.

I was the first person on the scene. What I found was interesting but unimpressive. In the middle of the parking lot, about halfway between the twelve-foot high, stone retaining wall and the building that was the fast food restaurant, was a guy lying face up. He was unconscious and breathing, but his breathing was irregular. There was no blood to speak of and the cause of his condition was not readily apparent.

He did smell strongly of alcohol. Thus, my first assumption was that he drank too much and fell down, a common occurrence among those who drink too much. The rescue personnel arrived shortly after I did so I abandoned my meager, half-hearted attempts to raise the man to consciousness. I backed off and let the emergency medical professionals do their job while I "secured the scene".

The man was quickly loaded into an ambulance and whisked away. As a formality, before pulling back in service "code 9 to EMS" (situation turned over to emergency medical personnel), I asked one of the paramedics, as he was climbing back onto the fire truck, if the guy was going to be okay. He gave a concerned look and said that the man was in serious condition and might not make it.

I was a little surprised and laughed as I asked if the paramedic was kidding. He said, "No" and off they went. I knocked out a quick report, checked the scene for any kind of evidence and, finding none, notified my supervisor and went back in service.

A few hours later, the guy died. The official investigative assumption of the cause of death was the following:

The man apparently spent several hours drinking heavily in a bar that was about 100 yards away from his final resting place, in a shopping center that was on a hill above the fast food restaurant. When the bar closed, he, like everyone else, left. He then walked straight across the parking lot from the bar toward the fast food restaurant. He then walked through a narrow band of trees and promptly fell off of the aforementioned twelve-foot high, stone retaining wall. He sustained his mortal injury when he plummeted head first into the asphalt parking lot below.

What a way to go!

#15.9 Pole – eese

A beat partner and I had assumed the standard Adam 69 position and were just passing time when all of a sudden it began to rain. This wasn't what you would call a gentle rain. On the contrary, it was what we in the South call a real "gully-washer". By the time we were able to roll up our patrol car windows, there was already so much water in the car that we would have needed a beach towel to dry it off.

We had a designated "dry" area that we always retreated to when it rained. The area was under a parking deck and offered excellent shelter from the elements. That's where I assumed we were headed when the torrents came. I began to pull forward through the parking lot and was watching my partner in my rear view mirror. All I could see of his car, through the preponderance of precipitation, was the dim glow of his taillights as he quickly drove away.

Imagine my surprise and confusion when those taillights suddenly flipped up on one side and came to a stop at a very unnatural angle. I carefully negotiated a 180-degree turn in the parking lot and went to investigate. When I saw what had happened it took me a minute or two to stop laughing.

When my partner had sped away from our previous location, he had forgotten that he was headed for an area of the parking lot where they had recently torn down a self-service gas station. The last step in the demolition, which hadn't been completed yet, was to remove those large concrete poles that such gas stations install around their pump islands to keep cars from hitting the pumps. The officer didn't see the concrete poles because of the intense rain and drove right into one of them.

He was going so fast that the car drove up on top of the pole and the pole jammed under the driver's seat of the patrol car. My beat partner had absolutely no clue as to what had happened until the rain finally stopped and he peered over the precipice of his driver's side door to have a look.

Surprisingly, the most damage was done to the car as the wrecker driver tried to yank it from its perch.

#15.10 Fuzzy Pink Slippers

I'll close out this chapter with an anecdote from recent history that some of you will swear I made up. Those of us working that night can hardly believe it ourselves. Nonetheless, it is 100% true.

One of our officers got a call on a signal 57 (loud noise/disturbance) at an apartment complex. No big deal. We answer thousands of those calls each year. It was what happened when he got there that will live in infamy.

The officer had no difficulty locating the offending apartment. The music coming from inside was indeed quite loud. He banged on the door a few times before the Eastern European resident came to the door. The resident opened the door part way and the officer asked him to turn down the music. The resident gruffly complied and the officer turned to leave.

Just as he got a few yards from the apartment, Evil, in a taunting gesture, turned the music up even louder than before. The officer, obviously a bit perturbed, backtracked to the apartment and banged on the door again. Evil actually opened the door and was verbally defiant to the officer, proclaiming that the apartment was his and he could play his music as loudly as he wanted. That assumption is not only patently incorrect, it also often causes one to fail the attitude test. The officer asked for the man's ID and walked him into the living room of the apartment.

Evil told the officer that he had no ID. The officer stood in front of Evil while Evil sat on his couch. Evil's roommate peeked out of a back bedroom and was told something by Evil in their mutual native language. The roommate went back into the bedroom and closed the door. Meanwhile, a verbal altercation between Evil and our officer ensued. At that point, the officer decided that he had had enough and was going to take Evil to jail.

The officer approached Evil from the front to handcuff him. We teach officers not to approach from the front to handcuff. What happened next is one of the reasons we teach that. Evil promptly kicked the officer backward over the coffee table. The fight was on. The officer had called for backup already and, while the fistfight (or possibly slapfight) raged, Evil's roommate decided to join the fray, thereby joining the ranks of Evil himself.

As the three men tussled, they worked their way toward the apartment door. At some point the officer had deployed his baton and was preparing to strike with it when somehow, one of the disciples of Evil took it from him. The officer began backpedaling for the door to escape the hornets' nest he had stirred up. As he backed over the plane of the doorway into the safety and freedom of the great outdoors, Evil slammed the door in his face.

The officer frantically called out over the radio that he had just been involved in a 29 (fight) with the 57 (loud music) perps. Then he added as a footnote, "…they 45'd (stole) my baton."

For whatever reason, Evil opened the door, threw the officer's baton at him, and then slammed the door again. The officer broadcast over the radio, "Be advised I got my baton back."

The officer, as a reaction, kicked the door, knocking it partially open. He hit the door again and it came open just in time for the officer to see Evil running to a back bedroom where it once again slammed the door.

The officer decided to wait for a backup officer to arrive. Consequently, enough time elapsed for a supervisor to arrive at the scene. The supervisor, exercising his supervisory abilities, told the officers not to go into the apartment and promptly called out the hostage negotiator and the SWAT team.

Once all the units were in place, the hostage negotiator carefully entered the apartment and approached the closed bedroom door that likely housed at least one perp. The hostage negotiator knocked on the door and got no answer. He said something through the door that was the functional equivalent of "you guys better come out or we're comin' in" and again got no response from the heinous loud-stereo-playing-baton-stealers.

With that, SWAT burst through the hollow-core bedroom door and laid the smackdown on Evil (which, by the way, offered less resistance than the hollow-core door). Both of the svelte, effeminate East-Europeans were taken out of the bed they were sharing and into custody with minimal difficulty.

As a lieutenant was looking around the apartment subsequent to the melee, he spied by the door a pair of fuzzy pink bedroom slippers that belonged to one of our brutal combatants. Without breaking a smile, he lit up the slippers with his flashlight, looked at the initiating officer and said, "So... just how tough were these guys?"

Chapter 16

It's Not My Fault...I Hydroplaned!

The title of this chapter is something that I hear all too often. The assumption that if a person hydroplanes, they are somehow magically absolved of any responsibility for the loss of control of their vehicle and any subsequent damage that occurs as a direct result of that loss of control, is self-contradictory. If a person hydroplanes while driving, then by definition that person was driving too fast. If that person was driving too fast, then any resulting accident is that person's responsibility. Therefore, if a person admits that they hydroplaned, they are in fact admitting responsibility for the accident. Bad weather rarely (if ever) causes traffic accidents. Bad driving causes traffic accidents. If you mix bad driving with bad weather, then you get more traffic accidents.

I would be failing in my duties if I did not offer some good driving tips. First and foremost, we must all remember that driving is an active and dynamic activity, not a passive one. Too many people get behind the wheel of their 3000-pound missiles and then never look past their hood ornaments. You always have to pay attention to your surroundings and try to minimize any outside stimuli that distract you from that goal. If you are not consciously looking as far down the road as you can see on a regular basis, then you are not a good driver. If you do not look in your rear view mirrors regularly to see what cars are around you, then you are not a good driver. If you do not look on the sides of the road for approaching vehicles, animals, pedestrians or obstructions, then you are not a good driver. If you have to look at your passengers (thereby taking your eyes off the road) to talk to them, you are not a good driver. If you use one hand to hold your cell phone while you are driving, you are not a good driver. If you do not regularly check your speedometer, you are not a good driver. If you are in America and people regularly pass you on the right, you are not a good driver. Just because you have had few (or no) accidents in your car does not mean that you are a good driver; it just means that you are lucky. When the weather turns bad, it increases the likelihood that anyone committing any of the aforementioned faux pas will cause an accident.

There is a physiological condition that also raises the probability that you will crash in inclement weather. Recent studies have shown that the area of the brain that is responsible for the perception of speed is also responsible for the perception of visual contrast. Consequently, when your perception of contrast is altered, so is your perception of speed. That is another reason why we see so many automobile crashes that involve large numbers of vehicles and severe amounts of damage during inclement weather, and in the fog in particular. As the driver's perception of contrast decreases with the increasing amount of fog (or rain or whatever), unless the driver pays conscious attention to the speedometer, the driver will unknowingly increase his or her speed in nearly direct proportion to the perceived loss of contrast. The result is that cars end up going much faster in bad weather than the drivers intend or even realize. The remedy is to make sure that as you drive, you pay attention to your speedometer, you leave enough room between you and the car ahead of you, and when the weather is bad, you drive **slowly**.

I am reminded of one incident in particular where one car was directly behind another in heavy traffic. The front car stopped for the red light and the rear car promptly proceeded to strike the front car from behind. When I asked what happened, the driver of the rear car told me that it wasn't really his fault because his car had slipped on the wet pavement (hydroplaned). After I gave him his ticket and counseled him on safe driving techniques, we all went about our merry way, which just happened to be south on the same road. In less than four blocks, the same guy ran into the back of yet another vehicle. This time, I didn't say a word. Neither did he. He just signed.

#16.2 Keep Your hands on the Wheel, Dear

Over the course of my career, my police car has been struck by other motorists approximately eight times. In every one of those times, my patrol car was stopped, with every available light on. Most of the collisions were on straight sections of roadway and several were in broad daylight. There is rarely an excuse for crashing into a stopped car, especially when it is lit up like a Fourth of July fireworks display.

My first patrol car collision happened while I was responding to a motor vehicle accident with injuries. I was driving with all of my emergency equipment activated. Behind me was a second police car that was also driving with all of his emergency equipment activated. Behind him was a rescue truck (which is a small fire truck) that was also running all of his emergency equipment. Behind the rescue truck were two full size fire trucks also running all of their emergency equipment.

We were on a seven-lane roadway that was perfectly straight and unobstructed. It was dark outside so all of our lights lit the surrounding environment with a multitude of silent visual explosions. There were no other cars on the roadway and ahead of us was an intersection with a green light facing our direction. There were three cars on the opposing roadway that were stopped for the red light that was opposite our green light. When I got to within 100 yards of the intersection, my light turned red. I slammed on the brakes and slowed to about 20 mph. I was watching intently to see if any of the cars that had just been given a green light were going to pull out in front of all those emergency vehicles. None of the cars moved for several seconds so I was sure that they had seen us.

I let my foot off the brake preparing to accelerate and at that same moment, I saw the car at the intersection on my right, pull out to make a left turn right in front of me. No problem. I hit the brakes and came to a full stop still inside my lane and still behind the balk line (the white line that tells you where to stop for the red light). I watched as the teenage female driver continued with her left turn. About half way through her turn, she decided to look in our direction. I could actually see the panic on her face as she took both hands off the steering wheel, covered her face with them, and drove straight into the front of my patrol car.

#16.3 Idiot Screaming Blindly…

Many of my patrol car collisions happened on the Interstate. Often, people driving in the passing lane (which is the left lane of any roadway that has two or more lanes traveling in the same direction) will, for some reason, stop in that lane if they experience mechanical difficulties. There are a fair number of auto accidents in the left lane as well. When I respond to either type of incident, I normally park my car about 150 feet behind the stalled or wrecked cars, using my patrol car as a buffer between the obstruction and all the oblivious idiots that I know are screaming blindly in my direction. Since my patrol car is likely to be the first thing hit, I usually get out of it and way from it quickly. Then, I do my best to clear the roadway as fast as possible so that I can get out of the danger zone.

One night I had done just that and was proud of myself for clearing the roadway with such superior alacrity. Just as I was returning to my patrol car, I saw death approaching in a late model Plymouth. Just prior to impacting my patrol car dead on, the vehicle swerved right and gave my right rear bumper a glancing blow before spinning out of control across the remainder of the five lane Interstate. After all the dust from the screeching, sliding, and spinning cars had settled, I asked the driver what had happened. She said that she thought my car were on the other side of the median wall. I started to point out that if my car were on the other side of the wall, she would need x-ray vision to see it, but I stopped myself thinking, "What's the use?"

Almost every other collision involving my patrol car has been a variation of that same story.

#16.4 Hold on, I'm Crashing

If you pay attention to the cars around you, you can often see accidents coming well in advance. One morning I was driving home after my shift in moderate traffic when I saw a car that I knew would soon be crashing. The person driving the little Honda was talking on the cell phone and doing two things that inevitably cause a car to go out of control: she was jerking the steering wheel when changing lanes, and she was slamming on the brakes for no apparent reason.

Before long my intuition came to fruition and the car spun sideways across all four lanes of travel before coming to rest facing in the opposite direction. Traffic came to a grinding halt, miraculously avoiding a collision. As she was pulling her car back into the correct position to continue her journey, I could see that she was still talking on the phone and driving with one hand.

It's all about priorities.

#16.5 Jerkin' and Slammin'

I mentioned in the previous story that there are two things that often lead to accidents: jerking the steering wheel and slamming on the brakes. Any good driver is aware that smooth and gentle steering is the way to maintain control of a vehicle. If you jerk the wheel, you cause an abrupt weight shift in the car, which can knock it into a slide. If you slam on the brakes, you often cause the wheels to lock up. Without what is called "rolling friction", you cannot steer a car. Many people tend to think that the brakes are a "cure-all" but improper use of the brakes causes a great number of accidents.

We often get people who, while driving in ice, snow or rain, begin to slide a little and panic. When they panic, they slam on the brakes. When they slam on the brakes, they lose all control of their car and crash. Then they say, "It's not my fault." The first thing to do when your car begins to slide or skid, is take your foot off the gas and the brake and just steer. That is the only way to maintain control. If you hit the brake when you strike a puddle or slick spot of any kind, your wheels will lock up with very little pressure, even if you have "antilock" brakes. When your wheels are locked up, your car floats out of control. The more slippery the roadway, the more severe the slide.

We had advance warning of a coming ice storm from the weather service. For once the meteorologists were correct in announcing the arrival time of the storm. Just before midnight the ice began forming on the roadway, making roads extremely treacherous at any speed. Roughly three hours after the storm began I was dispatched to handle a single car accident on the Interstate. When I arrived I found a man in his mid-thirties with his three-year-old son. Their car was about three hundred feet off the roadway in the woods. Thankfully they were not injured. I asked the man what had happened and he told me, "I knew that there was an ice storm coming so I decided to start on our trip [to Michigan] when I knew there would be few cars on the road. Since I knew there was ice everywhere, I was going pretty slow. I'd say I was doing about 60 mph."

That is exactly the kind of grotesque stupidity we have to deal with on a daily basis. In fact, if stupidity were people, I think that guy would be China.

#16.6 Bark Poisoning

It is bad enough not to pay attention while operating a passenger vehicle, but it's even worse when you're driving a motorcycle. Proof positive lies in the example set by a young man who was traveling at normal speed, in moderate traffic, down a main road on my beat. He didn't notice that traffic in front of him had stopped until it was too late. He jerked the handlebars to the right to avoid imminent impact with the car directly in front of him. He hit the curb and went slightly airborne. The shoulder of the roadway dropped off considerably and his mid air flight was extended as a result. His headlong improvisational acrobatic maneuver met an abrupt end when his helmeted head impacted with a very broad poplar tree, instantly snapping his neck.

Official cause of death – Bark poisoning.

Chapter 17

Gateway Drug?

Most often when people speak of a "gateway drug", their thoughts immediately turn to marijuana. Years of post WWII propaganda and mind numbing public service ads have convinced us all that if we dare even to try smoking the evil weed that we will all soon become heroin or cocaine addicts and die belly-up in a gutter somewhere before we turn 30. My experience has suggested quite the contrary. While I do not promote marijuana use any more than I promote alcoholism or cigarette addictions etc., I believe strongly in the principles of freedom that dictate not only that citizens should be allowed the freedom of choosing what they want to do with their bodies and their lives as long as it does not adversely effect the rest of us, but also that those same citizens are obligated to bear the responsibilities for their own actions or inactions. Using the previous statement as a qualifier, I would like to state for the record that, in my opinion, there is no logical reason for marijuana to be illegal, especially when alcohol isn't.

As the opening statement in defense of this thesis, I would like to declare emphatically that in all of the fights in which I have been involved in over fifteen years of working the street, none has been with a person who just got through smoking a joint. All the people I have ever encountered who are on strictly a marijuana high have been docile, content, and as darn near useless as a conscious human being can be. Virtually everyone I have known in my entire life who smoked marijuana as an adult (not those starting as children) has been an otherwise normal and productive member of society, and has not turned to harder drugs as a result. Most marijuana users I have been in contact with do not use harder drugs and most hard drug users I have been in contact with do not use marijuana regularly.

Nearly all of the individuals with whom I have had to fight, who were not fleeing the scene of a recently committed felony, have had one thing in common. The majority of them were drunk. Most of the hard drug users with whom I come into contact have one thing in common as well. When they are not high on their preferred drug, they are drunk. In my opinion, alcohol is far worse in the damage that it causes and the costs that it incurs for our society than marijuana ever will be. As far as the damage that either does to the individual, as I said before, that is the individual's responsibility. As we all know, opinions are a lot like armpits…most everyone has at least one and some of them smell bad. Crimes committed under the influence of any drug are still crimes, regardless of whether the drug in question is legal, illegal, or legitimized by a doctor's prescription.

After that long, three paragraph introduction, the following anecdotes deal with people and their chemically altered psyches. These stories are but a random few out of the thousands that are currently running amok in my memory banks.

I'll start with one of my personal all-time favorites. It is a situation that occurred early in my career while I was assigned to the evening watch. I happened to be driving through a local strip mall that housed one of those "neighborhood" bar and grill type restaurants. I saw what appeared to be a heavily intoxicated male staggering rather intently toward the parking lot with his car keys in hand. Behind him was another male who seemed, at first glance, to be much more toward the sober end of the spectrum. As I pulled my car near the two men, their attention shifted towards me as I asked the more sober individual, "He's not driving, is he?" The man assured me that his very drunk friend would not be driving. He ushered the man back into the restaurant, but not until after I issued my standard warning that I would be close by, and if I saw him driving, he would certainly be spending the night in the Gray Bar Hotel.

I would like to take a moment to explain that as part of my police philosophy, I have never been one to engage in entrapment. In some circles it seems to be perfectly normal and acceptable for police to watch drunks come out of bars, stagger to their cars, careen out of the parking lot and then pull them over to arrest them. I, however, have always been the type that if I see that kind of violation about to occur, I will warn the would-be violator and offer to call a cab. I believe that mentality is more in line with the spirit of police work. There are plenty of drunk drivers to choose from without taking the "fish in a barrel" approach. Watching an obviously intoxicated person getting into a vehicle and then arresting him after allowing him to drive may not legally be considered entrapment, but it certainly straddles the ethics line.

Anyway, it just so happens that about an hour later, after I had forgotten all about the encounter, I was driving past the same strip mall when a large white van came barreling out of the parking lot across the roadway in front of me. The van was sliding sideways as its tires wrote their signature on the five lane state highway. The van was traveling in the same direction I was originally going (north) and it made the first available right turn heading east to a major freeway.

I felt no need to witness any more bad driving so I immediately activated my emergency equipment (blinky-blinkies and woo-woos in concert) and pulled directly behind the van. To my utter shock and amazement, the van did not stop. Not only did it not stop, it sped up and was weaving from lane to lane, narrowly escaping a plethora of single vehicle accident opportunities.

The van continued east to the freeway junction where it got onto the limited access thoroughfare going north. I had notified radio that I had a vehicle refusing to stop. I only call out on pursuits when I am positive that a driver is attempting to elude me. Other than the mild increase in speed, there was nothing to confirm for me that the driver was trying to flee.

After traveling about two miles north on the freeway, the van abruptly pulled over and stopped in the right emergency lane. I saw two things that I always look for when initiating a traffic stop: the brake lights and a brief flash of the backup lights which suggests that the automatic transmission has just passed the "reverse" setting on its way to "park". Like a good policeman, I exited my patrol car quickly. If I remember correctly, some 25 % of officers killed in the line of duty are killed on traffic stops and over half of those are killed before they initially exit the patrol vehicle. A quick dismount is a tactical must.

As I approached the driver and asked for his license and proof of insurance, I noticed that it was the same drunk idiot to whom I had spoken in the parking lot earlier, only now he seemed even more drunk. At first, he was very friendly in addition to being very drunk. I asked him why he had gotten into the driver seat after I had warned him against doing so. He gave the usual apologies and pleaded with me to give me a break. He said he would be happy to take a cab home from there. Sadly for him, I am a man of my word. I explained to him that allowing him to take a cab would make me a liar, since I had already made it very clear what the consequences of driving drunk would be for him.

I asked if he would submit to some field sobriety evaluations and he ignored me. Drunks usually can only focus on one thing at a time so if they are contemplating their imminent loss of freedom, they often do not acknowledge anything else. Field sobriety evaluations are designed to exploit this condition by dividing the suspected intoxicated person's attention. With divided attention, the ability of the person to perform the evaluation decreases in direct proportion to the level of intoxication.

My driver, probably not evil when sober, was gradually becoming more of a problem. He first became sad and then angry, declaring that I was responsible for ruining his life. Very rarely do people, especially drunks, take responsibility for their own actions but that's a whole other book. The driver refused to perform any of the requested evaluations, so I placed him in the rear of my patrol car, under arrest for DUI.

Contrary to popular belief, I like it when people refuse sobriety evaluations. The reports are much shorter and there's less for an attorney to attack in court. It also seems that a lot of judges and juries assume that if someone refuses the field sobriety evaluations, then he must be hiding something. Nonetheless, the best attitude to have is one where you do your job to the best of your ability with the circumstances given, within the legal parameters, and try not to take anything personally.

On that note, as soon as he entered the confines of the back seat of my patrol car, he calmed down considerably. We talked while I wrote tickets and waited on a tow truck to arrive. Then came the next mood swing. The Evil in my back seat began to resurface. He asked me to do him a favor. More specifically he demanded that I, "...pull out [my] gun and just shoot [him] in the head." He was certain that his metaphorical "life" was over so he thought it appropriate that I end his literal life. Of course his request was denied and that seemed to irritate him considerably.

He responded to my denial by saying, "If you won't kill me then I guess I'll just have to do it myself." At first I didn't take him seriously and his subsequent actions are responsible for a fundamental change in my procedures from that point forward. Though I knew better at the time, I had acquired the attitude that I could always tell which prisoners needed to be handcuffed and which did not. I was confident at the outset that handcuffing this guy would not be required. Enter the unknown variable.

As he sat and contemplated his predicament, he became determined to make my life as difficult as he perceived that I had made his. The only implement left to him to effect that end was the cigarette lighter I had mistakenly left in his pocket. Once he realized that he had the lighter, he held it up to his head and began flicking it as though attempting to light it and then himself on fire. I saw this in my rear view mirror and thought to myself that things were about to get bad. I calmly picked up the radio transmitter and told radio, "I'm about to be involved in a 29 (fight) with my prisoner. Can you start another car?" While transmitting I smelled that all too familiar smell of burning hair. I looked into the back seat and can only remember a cloud of smoke and screaming Evil.

I exited the patrol car and went around to the passenger side to open the rear compartment. The rear compartment is divided from the front by a metal screen and roll bar. I went to the passenger side so as not to be on the traffic side of the car should the altercation spill out of the vehicle. As I climbed into the back seat with Evil, who was sitting on the far left side of the car, I began to realize just how little room there is in the back seat of a patrol car. I had training and experience fighting with people out in the open but never in such a confined space.

By the time I reached Evil, his hair fire was out but he was trying to rekindle it. I grabbed for the hand that held the lighter and the fight was on. We wrestled around in the confines of the Crown Victoria until suddenly the passenger side rear door flung open. It was my first backup unit. The officer reached in and grabbed Evil around the neck and worked him into a headlock. I worked my grip down to Evil's lower half and for a moment we thought we had him subdued.

The officer with the headlock on Evil suddenly shouted something that I will never forget (children please leave the room). "Shit! Mutha fucka's on fire!!!" With that he released his hold and I must admit that mine weakened as the result of channeling energy from my muscles to the repression of laughter.

At that point the second backup unit arrived. We yanked Evil out to the grass and hog-tied him. We were all none the worse for wear but Evil had a few contusions to go with the rather large blister on the now hairless, right side of his head.

I transported him directly to jail (without passing "GO") and the last thing that Evil said before being dragged into the bowels of the county jail by understandably less tolerant, waiting deputies was (while pointing to his burned, hairless and blistered head), "They did this to me."

#17.2 Out of the Car!…Ma'am?

I remember working the evening watch, patrolling aimlessly looking for some Evil while the thick night air threatened, or rather teased, with hints of the deluge to come.

It seemed as though everyone except me was doing something and quite simply, I was bored. My beat partner was working a traffic accident on the Interstate nearby. I was just about to drive to his location to view what carnage the waning hours of that cool, Fall day rush hour had delivered when he called out on the radio, "Are there any units near Roswell Rd and I-285 Westbound?"

As fate (or what I later referred to fondly as the DUI demon) would have it, I was at that very intersection. I replied to him over the radio and asked what he had. He stated that there was a vehicle traveling West that was driving without tires on the right side of the vehicle and that the vehicle almost struck him as it passed.

I didn't even bother asking for a 78 (description) because I figured that a car with no tires on the right side would be easy enough to spot. I told him I would stand by on the entrance ramp and stop the vehicle if it came by.

I parked and I waited for what seemed like too long, but since there was nothing else going on, I decided to sit a bit longer. Then I noticed little drops of rain appearing on my windshield and thought to myself that if it was going to rain, I wasn't going to play. I put the car into gear and began to drive slowly down the ramp toward some as yet undetermined shelter when I glanced in my side view mirror and saw a shower of sparks coming my way on the Interstate at a modest speed.

I stopped and waited for the car to come by. As it did, there was quite a dazzling display of fireworks emanating from both right side wheels, which were completely devoid of even a trace of tire. If you have never seen such a thing, it is truly a treat.

The car was only going about 30 mph, which accounted for the inordinately long ETA. I positioned my patrol car behind the soon to be paraplegic four-door sedan and activated the emergency equipment. As if on cue, the car began increasing its speed. As the car went faster, the rain fell harder. We kept speeding up until the last time I checked the speedometer we were going 75 miles per hour in the pouring rain and Evil only had two tires.

With the increase in speed, the car in front of me became proportionately more difficult to control. This was evident by the erratic weaving and exponential increase in spark deployment. Every time the driver applied the brake, the spark volume would surge and the vehicle would slide a bit before returning to a relatively straight line of travel.

I called in the pursuit to radio and gave a 78 of the vehicle. The funny thing about chases in our department at the time was that while we were allowed to chase fleeing motorists, we weren't really allowed to catch them. What I mean is that the term "chase" was a bit of a misnomer. The procedure would be more appropriately termed a "following" because that's all we could do. Follow Evil until he crashes, gives up, or runs out of gas.

I took a deep breath and settled in for one of those "followings". Enter the unknown variable. Out of nowhere appears an old Chevrolet coupe with tinted windows and unknown occupants. The coupe passed me, then Evil, then cut right in front of Evil and began to slow down. Evil hit the brakes and, amidst the showering sparks, lost control temporarily, swerved around the coupe, and continued on its merry way.

I cannot remember what all went through my mind at the time, but I know that I thought the person in the Chevrolet had to be either a police officer or someone whom Evil had hit on the roadway who was catching up for revenge.

We continued Westbound and the rain lessened in intensity. Before long I saw my old friend the Chevrolet approaching fast again from the rear. The Chevrolet passed me and again passed Evil and this time, cut Evil off and slammed on the brakes. Evil slammed on the brakes too and somehow avoided colliding with the Chevrolet.

Before I knew it we were stopped in the middle of the Interstate. I positioned my car as close to Evil as I could to keep him from escaping rearward. The Chevrolet was steadfast in front of Evil and I waited a few seconds to see what was next. No one did anything so I decided it was time to move.

I jumped out of the patrol car and ran cautiously up to the tireless car. It was dark and raining and I couldn't see inside. I was a bit apprehensive but had to act. Just then the car lurched forward as if it were going to ram the Chevrolet. I banged on the window with my fist and tried the door handle to no avail.

The car lurched forward again. I struck the window as hard as I could with my fist, and to my complete surprise, the window shattered. The car stopped moving so I reached inside and found the head of Evil, grabbed hold and pulled. With that, Evil came easily out of the window and onto the Interstate with me.

Adding to the myriad surprises of the evening was the fact that Evil just happened to have taken the form of a 50-year-old woman, drunk of course. I spun her around so that she was facing away from me and was pinned between me and her car. While I was placing her in handcuffs, she kept trying to face me asked rather casually, "Do I know you?" I quickly secured Evil in my patrol car and cleared the roadway to keep from becoming cop-pizza.

I then approached the driver of the mystery Chevrolet, had the sense to pull off the roadway with me. The driver explained with a heavy southern drawl that he was a truck driver who just wanted to help the police. I politely explained the hazards of such behavior but thanked him for his help (since it worked) and sent him on his way.

When I got back to the precinct, Evil was unconscious in a pool of her own urine in my back seat. I woke her up and walked her into the station. She sat down and, with a bewildered look much like a Miami Democrat on Election Day, she asked what had happened. She didn't remember anything.

When I gave her a brief synopsis of the evening's happenings she said, "That's impossible. I couldn't have been driving because my license is suspended," … for DUI no less.

#17.3 Why Don't We do it in the Road?

My next tale takes us to a night on the morning watch that became memorable just as I was traveling north on Hwy 9 approaching one of our infamous drinking establishments. Without warning a cruiser-type motorcycle came careening out of a business driveway on my right. The bike was making a left turn in front of me and swung so wide that after crossing the entire 5-lane roadway, he decided that he also needed the majority of the sidewalk to complete his precarious turn.

I immediately felt a smile sweep across my face because I knew that the DUI demon had struck again, and this one was bound to be a doozey.

By the time I completed my U-turn, the impaired ground pilot was flying southbound using every single lane at least once, though he seemed to be concentrating his efforts primarily on the center turn lane and the opposing traffic lanes. He narrowly escaped certain death no less than six times in less than a mile. I was able to catch up to the two-wheeler and activate my emergency equipment just as he was turning into the driveway of a local strip club.

This particular club is unique in that on the inside you will not be able to buy alcohol, but you will be able to see both women and men dancing all night long completely naked. …To each his own, I guess.

As that night's version of Evil made his turn into the parking lot, his inebriation finally got the better of him and he literally fell off of the still moving motorcycle. I had just enough room to position my patrol car in the driveway next to him and out of the roadway. I quickly exited my patrol car to find Evil preparing to upright his bike. I calmly asked for his license and insurance and told him in no uncertain terms that he needed to put the bike down.

He looked at me and said something like, "Oh no, I can't go to jail. I just can't." He then proceeded to try and pick up the bike.

As he got the bike upright and began to straddle it, I again said in a calm but much firmer voice, "If you don't get off the bike, I will be forced to knock you off." He ignored me as drunks usually do and prepared to start the bike.

I gave one final, still unheeded warning before making good on my promise. With one swift shove, Evil lay prostrate before me on the cold, cold ground. The reason that I know for a fact that he was Evil was that any normal person would have realized at that point that they were in both a physically and philosophically indefensible position and would have relented, but not my perfectly possessed new friend. He was determined to fight to the finish.

It's good that I ates me spinach before work because the next thing I knew, we were in a full blown wrestling match that found its way from the driveway, to the parking lot, to the sidewalk, to the curb, to the outside lane of a busy highway, at night, in a curve. I remember thinking as we went from curb to asphalt that this could very well be the grizzly end of us both. It was certainly the end of the shine on my brand new $125 boots. There's something about getting new boots that always attracts people who want to scuffle.

The thought of dying for a DUI arrest gave me the adrenaline that I needed to subdue that clown once and for all. I quickly dragged Evil out of the roadway to the sounds of clapping and cheering doormen and patrons who were crowded at the front of the nearby strip club. I thanked them for all their help and off to jail we went.

The main reason I included this story in this collection was that about two weeks prior to this writing, one valuable young officer and one worthless hunk of Evil, became involved in almost the exact same set of circumstances, but with a starkly different outcome. Both the police officer and the perpetrator were run over and killed by multiple vehicles.

As I have said before and will say again, I could not care less that Evil perished, but our nation (and more specifically, the city of East Point, GA) lost one more of its heroes in that senseless encounter. No perpetrator and no arrest in the world is worth the life of a law abiding citizen, and definitely not worth the life of a Sheepdog.

#17.4 Old Pumpkin Teeth

Let's go now to another non-descript night of evening watch police work when I'm patrolling the interstate and happen across a vehicle traveling 35 mph in a 55 mph hour zone and using every bit of three lanes out of five to do it. I immediately suspected another drunk and activated the blinky-blinkies etc.

The vehicle, staying true to form, continued westbound, apparently oblivious not only to my presence, but also to my visual and audible request that it pull to the side of the road.

I followed the vehicle to the exit ramp, through the red light and about a block north to where it finally came to rest, occupying the only two vacant parking spaces in front of a busy liquor store. I quickly dismounted the police cruiser and positioned myself just to the rear and beside the driver's window. I could see clearly that there was a single elderly woman occupying the vehicle. I waited for her to acknowledge me.

I waited and watched while she fumbled with her keys and began looking for something in her purse. Fearing I might root to the spot if I stood there much longer, I knocked on the window. The old lady jerked in startled amazement at seeing someone so close to her. She then looked as if she had some sort of epiphany and a calm and jolly grin took over her wrinkled face exposing her nicotine stained teeth and bad gingivitis. I must have jumped too when startled by "old pumpkin teeth" with her smeared topcoat of rouge and her runny mascara.

She opened the door and greeted me like an old friend. Among other old-people-type sayings, she said that I was so cute and that I reminded her of her grandson. When she reached up to pinch my cheeks I had to step back. She asked what she could do for such a nice boy.

I asked her for her license and insurance. I could see her glee turning to fear as she whimpered, "What for?"

I told her that I suspected that she was driving drunk and needed to check. She said, "Oh no you don't, you just run along. I had a couple of pink ladies earlier (I'm still not sure what that means) but I'm fine now."

We went back and forth with forced congeniality until I finally told her that if she did not comply with my request, I would have to place her into my patrol car. We each continued with our rhetoric and all the while I was thinking of the old Andy Kaufmann debate about fighting with women. There's really no way to win.

If you beat them up, you are a bully and if you let them beat you up, then you are a wimp. I tried to escort grandma Evil casually to the back seat of my patrol car, but the closer we got to it, the more she began kicking, hitting, biting and screaming. I was afraid that I would break her but I had to get her contained. I managed to open the door and stuff her inside, much like trying to compress a spring snake into an "assorted nuts" can. She kept trying to come out.

When I finally got the door closed, she was smearing the rest of her roller-applied makeup across the rear window of my car. Having gone completely berserk by that point, she was screaming and clawing at the window like a child who had just been snatched from its mother's arms to be carted away by a stranger.

As I regained my composure and surveyed the astonished crowd, all I could think was, "Could be worse - Could be raining."

#17.5 Entirely Too Much to be Driving

I am including this story because for me it illustrates a point. I have long maintained that police should be more interested in upholding the spirit of the law rather than the letter. I also cannot stand it when people lie to me. I am much more likely to "go easy" on someone who is honest and remorseful rather than someone who lies to my face.

As far as traffic law goes, I thoroughly support all traffic laws and think that they are invaluable for finding true Evil and for keeping the roadways safe, but tickets are not always necessary to effectually do your job, especially for the small stuff. Warnings are usually enough.

In reference to DUI's, I learned early on that every drunk lies about drinking. When you pull over a car that's weaving, or driving on the wrong side of the road or any other of the indicators of intoxication and you ask the driver, "How much have you had to drink?", the standard response is, "Two drinks".

I got so tired of hearing that response and then, after arresting the person, finding that their blood alcohol level was three to five time the legal limit, that I made a promise to myself. I had to keep to that promise about five years after I made it but have not had to do so since. I was driving down the Interstate when I noticed a car ahead of me exhibiting all the signs of a heavily intoxicated driver. He was driving so poorly that he was a serious threat. I activated my emergency equipment right away. The car lethargically and deliberately pulled to the right shoulder. I approached the driver and asked him, "How much have you had to drink tonight, sir?"

He sat for a moment, likely contemplating his current predicament, started to speak and then stopped. He looked at me, looked forward, and looked at me again. Then he said, "Ocifer, I'll be honest with you."

I thought, "Oh boy, here it comes."

He continued, "I have had entirely too much to be driving."

You could have knocked me over with a feather. In all my years, I had never heard that admission and I haven't heard it since. I remained true to that promise I made myself and I called the man's wife to come pick him up. Sometimes, it pays to be honest.

#17.6 Snakes Inside Me

I could probably write a book just on "drunk encounters", but since that is not currently the objective, I will move on. My next story marks a movement from the humorous into the macabre. It started when my entire shift was leaving roll call to pull in service when radio dispatched my beat partner and me to a signal 51 and 4 (person stabbed/ambulance enroute). There were no other calls to handle at the time so our backup consisted of the entire shift.

The apartment complex was close to the precinct, so we were all there in a matter of minutes. I remember approaching the apartment door. I got one of those eerie feelings as we found the door slightly ajar. We listened for a moment and could make out the quiet, muffled sound of a female crying. With officers positioned on either side of the doorway, we slowly and quietly pushed the door open to reveal the main living room of the apartment.

There was a wall on the "hinge side" of the door, which was to our right. The rest of the room opened out to our left. In the corner to our left and along the front wall of the apartment was the source of the crying that we heard. It was a young woman who was wearing what looked like her pajamas. She was sitting on a mattress which I assume was the only bed in the apartment and she had her head in her hands, crying quietly.

She did not respond to us. Within a few seconds of opening the door we heard a noise coming from the hall which led off the main room to our right, about twelve feet from the door. The aforementioned wall, which stretched from the door area to the hallway, had a large smear of blood across it.

The following sequence of events varies slightly depending on who is remembering the story, but the key elements remain intact.

From down the hallway, a completely naked man ran into the main room. He stopped, turned towards the platoon of police officers gathered in his doorway and froze for a split second. No one knows what was going on inside his chemically altered and seriously deranged mind when he said, "Oh shit! I gotta get my gun!" He then ran straight for the kitchen. The kitchen ran off the left side of the main room toward the rear.

Not wanting Evil to get out of our sight, we all followed him and regrouped at the kitchen door. I remember watching as Evil rummaged in a drawer intently looking for something. We all had our new Beretta 9mm pistols pointed at him which must have induced in him a hint of lucidity because, when he finally turned his attention from the drawer to us, he once again froze. This time, however, he had a steak knife in his hand.

He was shaking and screaming uncontrollably. He then screamed, "Help me…I've got snakes inside me!" With that he plunged the steak knife into the upper part of his right leg. He paused for a second, then ripped the knife upward enlarging the already gaping wound. How he avoided any vital arteries I will never know. He slung the knife to the floor and, amidst his own deafening howl, he used both hands to pry open the wound he had just made. He then began pulling out amorphous chunks of flesh from inside his leg. I can only assume that he did so in an attempt to remove the phantom serpents. Before he did too much more damage to himself, we all pounced and the fight was on.

Fate relegated to me the task of securing his feet and, though it was quite a struggle, I managed to maneuver his legs into a position where I could get a pair of handcuffs around his ankles. Once his feet were secured, I just applied my weight to his legs while the other officers tried to control the rest of him. It was not until he lost consciousness from excessive blood loss that we really had him completely controlled.

When he finally fell unconscious, I stepped away from his bloody mass to catch my breath and hopefully swab off the sanguine residue. I stood next to my supervisor who had been standing above us all acting as a "cover" officer. I looked at my sergeant as I was about to comment on the preceding fracas, but he beat me to the punch.

He said, "Rich. I think I'd like to party with that guy. Know what I mean?" Then he walked away.

#17.7 Look Ma, No Hand

During the same week as "snake man", we had another incident that was apparently the result of the same batch of bad drugs. One of the morning watch FTO's was driving down the road when he saw something that you don't see on the side of the road every day - a naked man.

The naked man was walking as if there were nothing wrong. The officer stopped to investigate. As he approached the naked man, the officer realized that the man was exhibiting signs of mental instability (other than walking down the road naked) and proceeded with caution. As he got nearer to the man he noticed that the man was missing his right hand. As he got even closer, he realized that the wound was fresh.

The officer started emergency medical personnel and began talking with the man to keep him occupied. During the course of the conversation, the naked man revealed that the missing hand was possessed by the Devil so it had to be removed before the Devil could infiltrate his entire body.

Before the man was carted away to the psych ward, we determined he lived in an apartment not far from where he had been discovered. A couple of officers decided to go to his apartment to see if there might be something there that would be of interest.

Upon arrival at the apartment, officers discovered that the front door was open. Just inside the open door was a coffee table in the main room. On the coffee table was the allegedly possessed, severed appendage. Apparently the man's exorcism had worked because the hand showed absolutely no signs of being occupied by Satan. Even if he had wanted it to be reattached, it was too late.

#17.8 Some Things You Can't Run Away From

Illegal drugs do all kinds of things to a body and a mind; none of them are good. Their effects range from a false sense of euphoria, to psychosis, to death, not to mention the adverse physical effects. For those witnessing drug-induced behavior, it can at times be entertaining, surprising, frightening or downright deadly.

One night while sitting in a parking lot waiting for Evil to go by, I saw something that struck me as curious. There was a man on the other side of the street, on the sidewalk, who was running. Usually, when I see people running I assume that there is a situation requiring a police presence, so my attention focused on the man.

I watched as he ran about fifty feet at full sprint speed and then stopped. He kneeled on the ground visibly gasping for breath. Then sprang up to run about fifty feet in the opposite direction where he repeated the drill. After the third or fourth trip, I went to investigate.

I parked my car away from him and approached him on foot during one of his "resting" cycles. I posed my favorite and most commonly used cop question, "What er you doin'?"

He replied simply, "Running." And with that he took off for another relay. He did not seem to be a threat at the time but you never know. I stayed put and stayed ready.

His pattern soon repeated and landed him back in front of me for another resting phase. I seized the opportunity to take my investigation a bit deeper, "What are you running from?" I asked.

"Just running," he said as he took off again.

I waited where I was. He was back after a few moments so that I could continue my "one question at a time" interrogation. "Why are you running?"

Pointing to the root of his current dilemma he said, "I've been smokin' crack for three days straight and I can't stop or my heart will explode."

"Fair enough," I thought as I started an ambulance to the location. By then there were more officers there to help contain the man and we directed him away from the roadway to a small building that he could run around unmolested.

We put an officer on each corner of the building to keep the man contained and allowed him to keep up his heart explosion prevention course until medical help arrived.

Apparently, our concerted efforts reached the intended goal and since it's not against the law to be on drugs, it's only illegal to have drugs on you, he was transported to the local hospital and never seen or heard from again.

#17.9 Harmless Sleep Aid

My first interaction with the drug GHB was also the first arrest for GHB in my division's history. GHB is the acronym for gamma-hydroxy-butyric acid or gamma-hydroxy-butyrate. It was originally sold in health food stores as a bodybuilding aid that was known to induce a very deep sleep.

The state of Georgia was one of the first to classify GHB as an illegal drug. To my knowledge, many states have still not yet followed suit. The liquid drug is still available widely on the Internet, marketed as a sleep aid, an anabolic supplement, a plant food, a floor cleaner, and maybe some other things as well.

GHB can and often does cause heart failure and coma, even in strong, young adults. The effects are greatly magnified when you mix it with alcohol. It is not uncommon for individuals to sneak some of the colorless liquid into an unsuspecting person's alcoholic beverage. The alcohol covers up the taste and the unsuspecting drinker normally has no idea they have ingested a life threatening substance. GHB is sometimes used as a "date rape" drug or as a simple prank but it is very dangerous any time it is used.

There was at one time, a restaurant/bar in our jurisdiction where the GHB dealers seemed to congregate. It was at that bar that I had my introduction to GHB. The call I was responding to was on a 67 and 4 (person down/ambulance en route). The call is not an uncommon one at bars, as young people often tend to drink too much and pass out.

That was my impression of the situation when I first arrived to find a young woman unconscious in the parking lot. She was breathing and appeared uninjured so I stood by awaiting the ambulance. Without warning, the young lady burst to life and began yelling and screaming and thrashing about. Attempts to control her were only moderately successful. Then, as abruptly as she had started her rampage, she fell back unconscious.

One of her friends got the courage to tell me that she saw the young lady put some sort of liquid into her own drink. My curiosity was piqued and about that time, Evil sprang back to life. She was cussing and threatening and gyrating in a manner much more indicative of a drug induced psychosis than a basic alcohol intoxication. She ran and jumped on to the roof of a car and began dancing and screaming something unintelligible. Then she went unconscious once again.

The roof of a car is never a good place to lose consciousness and this case was proof positive. Her completely limp, spaghetti-noodle-like body, crashed to the pavement and sustained minor but visible injuries. The medical personnel arrived and provided me with my first education on GHB. A cursory inspection of her purse produced the suspected controlled substance. I looked it up in the criminal code and applied the appropriate charge to the woman as she was carted off to the emergency room where by all accounts, she narrowly escaped death.

Chapter 18

By the Light, of the Silvery Moon

Most police officers, at some point in their careers, rely on extra jobs for extra income. They perform police related duties for private individuals or corporations and are paid for their efforts by those entities. Some departments forbid their officers to do this type of work entirely while others seem to allow it with no restrictions. As you might guess, it is my opinion that the best policy lies somewhere between the two extremes.

We all know that police work does not provide an excess of monetary compensation and many officers' lives are greatly improved by their ability to work extra jobs. Many of the establishments (like bars and nightclubs) that require police for security purposes are loaded with individuals of questionable character. If the officer working an extra job in one of the less respectable establishments can keep his ethical and moral compass pointed in the proper direction, then there is not likely to be a problem. However, some people feel that if you wallow in the slime long enough you can't help but get some on you.

Let's also bear in mind that as police officers, we deal with people at their worst, all the time. When things are going well, no one needs us. Certain places are magnets for criminal and anti-social behavior and a police presence helps maintain order. When that police presence is paid for from private coffers, then we all benefit from an increase in police protection without having to pay for it with tax money.

I worked extra jobs at nightclubs during the first few years of my career. At first, I enjoyed the atmosphere but it did not take long for me to get fed up with the drunk idiots. At this phase in my life I try to avoid working in any place that serves alcohol. From the owners, to the operators, to the employees, to the patrons, the bar business attracts the criminal element like poop attracts flies. Not everyone in a bar is Evil but every bar has Evil in it - guaranteed.

One of the first bar jobs I ever had was also one that I worked for the longest. It was at one of Atlanta's most infamous live rock 'n' roll clubs and it provided me with some colorful experiences. I met many of the music stars and superstars that I had grown up listening to and many that were still on the charts. I made some good friends and also made a few enemies, but that is true of my entire life.

There was a pair of professional wrestlers that I came to know while working that job. They were brothers and they were both huge. The younger brother was also the smaller brother and he was six foot five and weighed in at 250 pounds. Most of that weight was muscle. He and his brother were monsters but they were also two of the nicest, most non-violent individuals you could ever meet.

One of the brothers happened to be dating a waitress at the bar, so for a while they were at the place a lot, even on the slow nights. One such night, early in the evening (about midnight) there were only a few patrons in the bar. Two of them were the wrestlers. They were each sitting at the bar with their respective girlfriends and they comprised about fifty percent of the patronage at that time. I was standing at the front door with one of the bouncers when a large black limousine pulled up out front.

Out of the limousine stepped another very large man. He was also about six foot five and 250 pounds but he was old and mostly fat. He also happened to be about as likeable as a Palestinian at a bar mitzvah. Under normal conditions, he would have been denied entry based solely upon his attitude, but since it was such a slow night, the doorman decided to let him in.

He promptly proceeded to plant his obnoxious butt right beside the younger of the two wrestlers. He sat and stared at the wrestler for a few minutes and then without warning, invitation, or provocation, reached up and put his hand on the left shoulder of the wrestler and planted a kiss on the wrestler's left cheek.

I know many men who at that point would have opened up a can of whupass on that guy, but the wrestler kept his cool. He calmly laid his hand on the man's chest and pushed him away gently. The wrestler even went so far as to move one stool over to get away from the man. Little did he know, the encounter was just beginning.

Evil, as he would come to be known, sat quietly at the bar for the next few minutes. He would stare forward and then back at the wrestler and then forward again. Then, once again, he made up his mind to act. He reached over the bar and grabbed a thick glass beer mug. Holding the beer mug in one hand, he used the other to tap on the wrestler's shoulder. As the wrestler turned to face him, Evil brought the beer mug to bear, slamming it into the wrestler's face. The glass mug shattered and shards cut deep into the wrestler's face causing a huge gash that poured blood from the exposed muscle and the artery that was severed in the process.

With more than ample provocation, the wrestler sprang into action in true sheepdog fashion. Unconcerned about his injury, the wrestler fought back fiercely. His massive, sledgehammer-like hands pummeled Evil and I would bet that the first blow rendered Evil unconscious. The speed with which the devastating follow-up blows were delivered allowed several more to impact Evil as he was falling into a heap on the floor.

The wrestler's big brother was close by when the altercation began and, with lightning speed, he also joined the fray. The waitress ran up to me and was screaming for me to do something. I was already in the process of formulating a plan that would allow me (a guy who tips the scales at 200 lbs max with all my stuff on) to somehow stop the collective 750+ pounds of tumultuous flesh.

In the heat of the moment I developed, and subsequently executed, a brilliant plan. I approached the older and larger wrestler from behind as he was kicking the unconscious Evil with his cowboy boots. I gently tapped on his shoulder and called him by name. He stopped abruptly as if being startled back to reality and turned to face me. I said, "Can you please stop, I think he's dead."

The wrestlers looked at the purple grease spot that used to be Evil and said that they guessed I was right. Then they apologized and helped pick the man up. While the older wrestler and a bouncer dragged Evil, whose face resembled more an eggplant than a human head, out of the bar, I sat with the younger wrestler taking the appropriate information for a report. While I was talking with the younger wrestler, I felt something touching my face. At first, I didn't pay much attention to it but it persisted and was becoming more noticeable. I reached my hand up to brush away whatever it was and discovered blood.

There was a good bit of blood and it surprised me because I couldn't remember being near anything that could have injured me. Further investigation revealed that the blood was not mine. It was spewing forth from a severed artery in the wrestlers face and with each beat of his heart, another spurt of warm blood would strike me in the face. I got him a towel and continued my interview.

When I got through obtaining his information, I walked him outside to await the arrival of emergency medical personnel. Evil was still unconscious and propped up on a bench against the front wall of the club. I walked the two wrestlers down to the end of the sidewalk to keep them separated from Evil.

While we were waiting for the ambulance, the older wrestler took the towel from his little brother's face to examine the damage in the brighter light of the sidewalk. When he saw just how serious the injury was, he got that fire in his eye again, let out a generic curse, and stomped off in the direction of Evil. I tried to stop him but was grossly unsuccessful. He stopped in front of Evil, took a standard strong side fighting stance, reared back and let loose with a closed fist punch that knocked Evil into next week. The sound of the impact hurt me.

I don't think Evil felt a thing as his near lifeless body collapsed from the bench to the unforgiving concrete. The ambulance still had not arrived, so the wrestler drove himself to the hospital. Evil finally got his medical attention. He recovered eventually and remembered nothing. Evil was charged with aggravated battery and the wrestler declined to prosecute, saying that Evil had already been punished and that there was no need for more. I happened to agree. The wrestler returned to the bar later that night to finish his beer. He had nearly three hundred tiny stitches in his face that despite the plastic surgeon's mediocre effort, would become one bitchin' scar.

#18.2 Is that a Pistol in Your Pocket?

Although it may be astonishing news to some people, I firmly believe that in any bar, in addition to alcohol and drunk people, you will find illegal drugs. I am neither dismayed nor surprised at the phenomenon and often took advantage of it to increase my monthly arrest statistics. The management supported me in my endeavors, at least on the outside, and I did my job. Drugs seem to be so common in some nightclubs that the people who use them and sell them behave as if they are not doing anything wrong. That makes it easy for the officer to make a case if he so desires.

I was working at the door of a particular nightclub when an employee approached me and said that some man was dealing drugs in the men's bathroom. The employee described the perp in exhausting detail and after gathering the necessary information, I went to the end of the hall leading to the bathrooms to patiently await the emergence of Evil.

Within moments, a scumbag precisely matching Evil's description came out of the bathroom and was walking toward me. He looked at me briefly before training his eyes on the floor. He tried to walk by me and I stepped into his path. He did not make eye contact and tried to go around but I positioned myself in his way again. He stopped and looked up and said, "How's it goin'?" I guess that he didn't quite realize that there was a plastic baggy containing a white powdery substance that was hanging out of his right front pocket.

I smiled as I said, "I'm doin' good."

Then, simultaneously looking him dead in the eye and reaching for the plastic bag, I said, "What's this?" and yanked the bag out of his pocket.

"Awe man…" he said as I grabbed him by the back of the neck and forced him into a side room. "Can't we talk about this?" he pleaded as I cuffed him and began my search incident to arrest.

In his first jacket pocket was a small pistol (loaded). In his second pocket was a large switchblade knife. In an inside jacket pocket were a half dozen plastic bags containing about a half ounce of marijuana each. In his front pants pocket was some more of the white powdery stuff that later proved to be methamphetamine. He also had an assortment of pills and a little cocaine that he said was for personal use.

He kept promising that if I would just let him go, he would never come back to Georgia. I am about as lenient as they come but no way was that guy going anywhere but jail.

#18.3 A Smackdown and $20

I was working another bar off duty when my brother, who was on duty at the time, stopped by for a visit. He was in a marked patrol car and parked right outside the front door. We were standing by the front door when the manager stepped outside to tell us that he thought someone inside was about to walk out on a $120 tab. The manager was still talking to us when out came Evil. The man the manager had warned us about was indeed walking out without paying for his drinks. He walked right by the club manager, two uniformed police officers, and a marked patrol car, and casually strolled down the street as if nothing was wrong.

The manager said, "That's the guy," so we went off on foot to subdue him. We called for him to stop but he just kept walking. We ran up behind the tall, wiry thug and just before we tackled him, he turned around to try to fight. He was grossly outmatched and went down quickly but continued to resist. He struggled all the way back to the police car. When we finally got him to the car, he refused to get in. His obstinance was quickly quelled by a right hook that knocked him off balance. He went face first into a puddle, but it did little to improve his attitude. I picked him up and shoved him head first into the patrol car.

After that brief display of force, the small crowd that had gathered outside the bar began applauding. One man walked up to me and said, "I just wanna shake your hand. I'm from Kentucky and that's how we like to see things done." Then he handed me a $20 bill as a "tip". I thanked him but told him that there was no way in the world I could take his money and I recommended that he give to the waitress who had been stiffed by Evil. The man agreed and took his southern charm back into the bar where he convinced everyone inside to donate enough money to cover the unpaid bill so that the waitress would not have to.

#18.4 Drop the Gun, or I'll Drop You - Spanky

Most bars in the Atlanta area close at about 0400 hours (4:00 AM). In one of the bars where I worked, at 0400 hours, we shoved everybody out the door and were completely closed by 0415 hours. Then I would meet the manager in the office and get my money for the night. As soon as I was paid I was normally out the door and headed home. On one night in particular I was following that plan to the letter and was closing out the final phase in the manager's office when a waitress ran into the office screaming, "Come quick. There's a fight in the parking lot."

I would be lying if I said I wasn't a little irritated by that development but since I had to traverse the parking lot where the fight was to get to my car to go home, I reluctantly started toward the area of the reported altercation.

As I exited the bar into the parking lot, I noticed immediately that there was a conspicuous lack of persons and vehicles. Normally, after closing, certain people would hang out in the parking lot and some would leave their cars there until the next day. Not this night.

The only thing that I saw in the parking lot besides my car was a very large, fat, hairy, overalls-wearing man. He also happened to be holding what turned out to be a Dan Wesson .357 magnum revolver with an eight inch barrel. Just as I gained a complete grasp of the situation, the hand cannon let loose with a thunderous explosion and its operator recoiled as a result. Once he had recovered from the recoil and regained a stable shooting platform, he fired again.

He still was unaware of my presence but I changed all that when I bellowed, "Police, drop the gun or I'll drop you. Do it now." He turned his head to the left and glanced at me without moving the rest of his body. He looked like a kid that had been caught with his hand in the cookie jar. He slowly and carefully laid the weapon on the ground and said something like, "Awe man."

I quickly secured both Evil and weapon and asked just what it was he though that he was doing.

He said, "Well, they shot at me first."

"Who?" I asked since there had been no one in sight at the time that the shots were fired.

"That car getting' on the highway."

The highway was over a half mile away and if there really had been someone there, then they were long gone. Evil was very apologetic and promised not ever to do it again. He was not intoxicated and had no criminal history. It was time for me to go home and go to bed so I gave the man a ticket for reckless conduct, confiscated his pistol (he could get it back after the court hearing), and let him go home.

#18.5 Which One's the Idiot?

A person's innate stupidity is generally magnified exponentially when he consumes alcohol. I cannot remember the number of times I have watched a drunk stagger out of a bar with his car keys in hand and stopped him to implore him not to drive, only to have the idiot jump behind the wheel and take off when he thought I wasn't looking.

I want it to be perfectly clear that when I see one of these idiots getting anywhere near a vehicle, I make every effort to get them to find a ride home. I will offer to call them a taxi. I will tell them at least three times in no uncertain terms that I will be watching them and that I will arrest them if they drive. Like the sun rising in the East, they never fail to try to drive anyway. With the same enduring reliability, I never fail to lock them up when they do. (Well, almost never.)

I was working an extra job at a bar early one morning when I saw such a man with keys in hand, walk into (not in through, but into) the exit door of the bar. He bounced off the doorframe and fell over. He picked himself up and aimed for the opening and made it out the door with all the grace and accuracy of an albatross landing on an aircraft carrier.

His forward momentum was soon interrupted by an unseen curb, which caused him to submit to the effects of gravity once again as he fell onto the asphalt of the parking lot. I approached him and told him not to drive and pointed to a waiting taxi. He said that he had no intention of driving and that he was just going to get some fresh air.

I watched as he made his way to a car in the parking lot. As he desperately yet unsuccessfully tried to get the door key into the lock, I approached him from behind and tapped him on the soldier. He looked as if we were meeting for the first time and said, "Don't worry ossifer, I am not driving."

I repeated my warnings and stood by to watch. He wandered off from his vehicle and I went back to my post at the front door of the bar. It was not long before Evil was back at his car. I approached him yet again for "same song, different verse". He actually agreed to get into a cab that was waiting in the parking lot. The cab drove out of the parking lot and I assumed my troubles were over.

Within three minutes, the cab driver returned to inform me that the man had gotten out of the cab just as they left the parking lot. I looked, and there he was, back at his car again. I walked up to the car and by that time he had gotten the ignition started and was backing out of the parking space. I yelled for him to stop and he did. He again said that he wasn't going to drive.

I said, "Too late. Get out of the car."

Drunk idiot Evil complied, but left his car running. For some reason that I still can't remember, I began to administer field sobriety evaluations and did not turn off his car. About half way through the evaluations, he jumped back into the car and we began fighting over control of the vehicle. I was on the outside of the car, struggling through the open window. He got the best of me, got the car into gear and began to drive away.

My decision to hang on and fight the good fight was probably not too smart either. Off we went through the parking lot. As he headed for the main road I was struck by a lightning bolt of sensibility and disengaged from the car. As I rolled across the pavement, I caught a glimpse of the patrol car that I had called to transport Evil to jail for me. The patrol car was coming into the parking lot from a driveway opposite the one that Evil was exiting. I bounced to my feet and pointed to the fleeing Evil. The on-duty officer took off after him.

The ensuing high-speed pursuit went on for about twenty minutes and through three or four more jurisdictions before Evil finally just stopped and said, "I give up. You got me." The officer, who just so happened to be my brother, locked the guy up and did all the paperwork.

…and laughed at me for hanging on the side of the car.

#18.6 Burnin' Love

There was a female security guard hired to patrol the parking lot of the bar where I was working an extra job. She guarded the outside while I guarded the inside. She came running in to get me, laughing hysterically.

She said, "Offica, Offica, you got ta come quick. Theys two people in a car out here and they are makin' luv."

I smiled and walked with her into the parking lot where she pointed out the offending vehicle. It was stealthily and inconspicuously parked in the crowded lot, thirty feet from the front door, right under a streetlight, with the windows down. I cautiously approached the vehicle and could hear some muffled moans shortly before I was in a position to view the immodest occupants in "flagrante delectus" (burning love).

I stood outside the driver's window thinking that they would see me and stop. They kept going. The man was sitting in the front passenger seat and the woman was sitting on top of him and was actually facing me with her left arm on the top of the seat and her right hand gaining support from the dashboard. From the waist up, her movements were not unlike those associated with someone riding a pogo stick.

I bent down to look directly into the window of the car at the closed-eyed woman. I cleared my throat with no response from the occupants of the vehicle. I then stuck my head in, breaking the plane (not pane) of the window to where I almost felt like a part of the action and cleared my throat again.

This time, the woman snapped to reality and shrieked, "Oh God, please don't do this." I am still not sure exactly what she meant.

I felt like I had finally gotten my point across and told them not to do that out in the open where everyone could see. While the woman was still muttering, "oh god, oh god," the man said, "Yessir, sorry sir."

I went back into the bar thinking that the encounter was over. Within minutes, the man was walking back into the bar and the rumor of what had occurred had spread by then. There were a few people who applauded him as he returned to his barstool.

Then in came the woman. She received much the same accolades as the man when she walked through the door, but she responded in a very different way. I was trying to retain some semblance of professionalism but allowed a smile to creep onto my face as she was dealing with the embarrassment heaped upon her by her adoring fans.

She gave me an angry look and said, "You think this is funny?"

I have a character flaw that requires me to be honest with people even when it is not in my best interests and I said, "As a matter of fact, ma'am, I do find it amusing."

She responded with an increase in hostility and a hint of a whimper, "You think it's funny that I got raped?"

"Whooooooaaa. Wait a minute," I said. "You mean to tell me that the guy you were riding not thirty feet from here, under a streetlight, with the windows down, moaning with your eyes closed, was somehow raping you?"

She gave a humble but assertive, "Yes...and I want to prosecute."

I explained to her that I would be more than happy to take a report but that if an investigation proved she was lying, she would be going to jail and not him. At first she was persistent in her claim, but a little counseling from friends and officer Friendly, helped convince her to tell the truth.

As it turned out, she was in the process of going through a divorce. She thought that her husband would find out that she was screwing a strange guy in a parking lot and that it would hurt her divorce case. (How he would have found out, I do not know.) She said that she "hadn't had it in a while" and that it was just a one-time fling. She didn't even know the guy's first name. She apologized and repented and we all went about our business.

As far as I know, none of us told her husband....who or wherever he might have been.

Chapter 19

People Are Idiots

One seemingly universal axiom is that everywhere you go people are idiots. They might not always be idiots, but at least once in every person's life, he does something so incredibly stupid, that his continued existence suggests divine intervention. Some, however, are not so lucky.

I'll start with a young man who by all accounts was an intelligent and productive member of society. He had chosen a particular Friday night to go out to an infamous live rock and roll club where I worked security in uniform after my shift. This young man was approaching the front door to the club when a pickup truck pulled up next to him in the parking lot. The driver of the pickup truck asked to borrow a dollar so that he could go and buy some cigarettes.

The young man in the parking lot reached into his pocket and grabbed a wad of bills. He peeled off what he thought was a dollar bill and handed it to the driver of the pickup truck. As he handed the bill to the man, he realized that it wasn't a one-dollar bill he was giving him, it was a twenty.

As the realization hit him that he was giving away the equivalent of several drinks with tip, he tried to snatch the bill back but the driver of the pickup truck had other plans. The driver of the pickup truck sped away.

I would imagine that the young man might have behaved differently if he had stopped to think. Instead he impulsively jumped into the bed of the pickup truck as it sped out of the parking lot. The pickup truck driver was as determined to keep the twenty dollars as the hapless donor was to retrieve it. So off they went.

The pickup truck driver headed straight for the Interstate Highway on-ramp with his unwelcome passenger. Once on the Interstate, the pickup truck driver became more intolerant of his passenger's persistence and began jerking the steering wheel from side to side.

I am sure that the young man in the bed of the truck began having second thoughts about his chosen course of action, but by that time the truck was going too fast for him to get off. As the pickup truck's speed increased, the jerking of the steering wheel became more violent. About three miles down the Interstate, the young man in the bed of the pickup truck lost his fight with inertia and spilled out of the truck bed onto the highway.

It is quite possible that the young man would have survived his high-speed ejection if it hadn't been for the eighteen-wheeler that was right behind him as he flew off his perch.

For the grand total sum of twenty American dollars, the young man prematurely ended his night and his life literally wrapped around the rear axle of a tractor-trailer rig. When at last we were able to separate him from the implement of his destruction, his body was still relatively intact but had been stretched to several feet longer than its original design.

The things a body can do are indeed curious.

#19.2 Why do They Call it a Gore?

One night at about four o'clock in the morning (which happens to be the time that most of the bars in our jurisdiction close) a man and his wife got into an argument over something genuinely stupid but all too common. If I remember correctly, the man had the nerve to stare a second or two too long at one of the scantily clad waitresses at the bar and his wife became irrationally incensed as some wives have a proclivity for doing.

The verbal altercation that ensued was one that plays itself out countless times across the face of the earth every day. The ending, however, was a bit out of the ordinary.

You can imagine the dialogue that led up to the phrase, "Well you can just walk home, mister." Being a man and behaving like one, his response was, " Fine with me." He started walking. It was dark and he was drunk. He headed straight for the Interstate to begin his twenty-or-so mile hike.

He walked down the left side of the nearby entrance ramp perhaps fully expecting his wife to come along and apologetically offer to give him a ride. He kept walking. She never came.

His path led him to what is ironically referred to as the "gore" area separating the entrance ramp lane from the other lanes of travel. Since the entrance lane becomes an exit lane not too far down the road, vehicles often travel over the gore so that they can be first to get into the exit lane.

That's exactly what a taxi driver did. Had the taxi driver been paying a bit more attention to the roadway, he might have seen our intoxicated friend before the man's head struck the car frame on the right edge of the taxi's windshield.

As fate would have it, there was a patrol car traveling a few seconds behind the taxi. I was a block away from the accident scene when that patrol officer calmly announced on the radio, "128 to radio…hold me out on a signal 48 (person dead) on 285 eastbound at Roswell Rd."

The officer was so nonchalant about it that it took us all a minute to process what he had said. I went directly to the scene thinking that he must have had a dead animal in the road. I fully intended to chastise him for using the wrong radio signal. When I got to the scene, however, I found that he had indeed used correct radio procedure, for in front of me lay one poor slob who was DRT.

A peculiar thing about the human body when it suffers a high-speed impact is that it has a tendency to explode. Bones often fragment or pulverize and liquid tissue violently evacuates. This case had an all too common result. The skull dissolved as the brain matter erupted outward, leaving lots of little chunks strewn down the highway. The skin of the head and face remained intact. If you have never seen the phenomenon, the remaining fleshy mask looks more like a latex Halloween decoration than something that was a walking, talking human moments earlier.

The only remnants of life were the clouds of steam rising from the unrecognizable goo that had until recently been someone's husband. When officers went to his home to notify his wife of his premature departure, she thought he had finally made it home. After the officers left, I believe she realized all too late that some things just aren't worth fighting over.

#19.3 It's Rainin' Man

There is a phenomenon that defies all explanation not only in the magnitude of its inherent stupidity but also in the frequency with which it occurs. That is the phenomenon where people drive the wrong way on the highway. I call it the "Wrong Way on the Highway Phenomenon" (strangely enough).

I don't care how drunk you are, how stupid you are, what country you come from or what chemical substance has altered your brain, there is no excuse for accidentally getting on a limited access highway going the wrong direction, especially in traffic! Nonetheless, it happens all too frequently and usually ends in a really good wreck (or bad, depending upon your point of view).

One such incident started well outside my jurisdiction. By all reports, the offending driver traveled a minimum of eight to ten miles on a five lane, limited access Interstate highway. Throughout the duration of his trip, this particular driver was driving in the left lane (which to him would have seemed like the right lane) next to a five-foot median wall. Aside from the tell tale signs of having the median wall to your right rather than your left and aside from the fact that he saw only headlights when he should have seen taillights, he should have also noticed that the little reflective lane dividers were bright red instead of white. (The Department Of Transportation does that on purpose so that hopefully someone going the wrong way will realize that red means stop.)

Our confused little driver undoubtedly had quite a surprise when his highway trek and his life met an abrupt and violent end in the form of a fully loaded, tanker truck. Milliseconds before impact, the tractor trailer tanker truck driver veered to the right. If he had made it about ten more inches to the right, he might have missed the guy. Instead, his massive rig sheared the little pickup truck longitudinally and cut the driver of the pickup truck in half in much the same manner.

When we arrived on the scene, the tanker had pulled to the right side of the roadway and what was left of the wrong way driver's vehicle was in the left lane next to the median wall. The wrong way driver was strewn about two lanes wide and two hundred and fifty feet long. As is characteristic of a high-speed impact with a body, the tremendous hydraulic pressure tore his clothing off and caused his torso and cranium to explode. Little bits of his innards and their accompanying liquids then rained down upon the roadway. Most of the remaining chunks were no bigger than beef tips.

After the initial investigation was completed and the medical examiner arrived, we all had to help him pick up the pieces. I tried to requisition a wet-vac for the job but my request was denied. We laid a big sheet out on the roadway and started dumping pieces of the stupid guy onto it. The biggest piece I was able to find was the man's shoeless left foot. It had been severed about half way between the knee and the ankle and was about two hundred and fifty feet down the roadway from the impact site.

When we were pretty sure we had most of the big pieces (anything larger than a thumb), we had the fire department wash the rest into the storm drain. The first patrol car to leave the scene went down to the next exit to turn around. As he passed by our location going the opposite direction, he raised us on the radio and said, "Advise those units that there's some, uh, debris, on this side of the wall too."

He splattered a lot farther than we thought.

#19.4 If Stupidity Were People, These Guys Would Be China

Not only are some people incredibly stupid when they drive, they seem to be incredibly stupid when they break down. If your car breaks down on the highway, the first priority should be to get it out of the roadway. If the mechanical failure is so sudden and/or catastrophic that you cannot drive it off the roadway, then you must decide whether to stay in the car or get out. If you stay inside, keep your seat belt on and prepare for impact. If you can get out safely, get as far from the vehicle as you can and prepare for impact.

One thing I would recommend that you not do is something that proved nearly fatal for one particular brain surgeon whose vehicle broke down in a curve in the fast lane of an Interstate highway. While he sat next to his car waiting for help to arrive, a rocket scientist showed up and parked his car in the fast lane in front of the broken down car. Then the rocket scientist and the brain surgeon combined their immense intellect and determined that the best course of action would be to push the car across five lanes of traffic to the right side of the roadway.

The blithering idiots got across roughly two lanes before being struck at full speed by another driver who probably wasn't paying much attention to the roadway in front of him. The rocket scientist was pushing the car from the back bumper and got his right leg amputated just above the knee by the impact. The brain surgeon sustained minor injuries since he was in the driver's seat steering the car.

When all the emergency personnel arrived at the accident scene, we couldn't figure what had happened to the rocket scientist's missing leg. Just as the ambulance was preparing to take genius to the hospital, one officer decided to take one more look for the missing limb. He looked under the front of the car that had hit him and saw a shoe hanging down behind the radiator. He pulled on the shoe and the whole leg fell out. Surprisingly, the leg was in pretty good shape. He carried the leg back to the ambulance and set it on the gurney next to the still conscious rocket scientist. The man had been relatively calm and possibly was not aware of the magnitude of his injury up to that point, but when he saw his severed limb, he began screaming uncontrollably.

As the ambulance hurried away, I could swear his screams drowned out the siren.

#19.5 Woad Wage

Though it rarely seems to happen, it's always nice when you get a call on a crime in progress and you are less than a block away. In one particular incidence, I was dispatched to a 29 (fight) on the side of the Interstate. I was so close that I barely had time to broadcast my code 26 (officer on scene) before I was in sight of the fight.

For once, whoever had called 911 was dead right on the location. To add to that miracle, the communications center relayed the information correctly as well. As I approached the area of the highway I had been dispatched to, I could see two cars in the right-hand emergency lane. As I got closer, I could see that there were two people between the two cars and very near the guardrail. As I got even closer, I could see that the two people appeared to be embracing one another. Even closer, I could see that one of them had some kind of shiny, liquid looking substance all over his head and face. Closer, the liquid began to take on a dark red hue, very much like blood. By the time I was close enough to see that that liquid substance was indeed blood, I could also see that the guy who wasn't bleeding had a huge revolver in his right hand!

I slammed on the brakes and quickly exited my patrol car with my pistol drawn. I was trying to maintain visual contact with both individuals and trying to stay near the cover of the cars while at the same time, I cautiously approached the men. Neither subject seemed to be actively engaged in any violence. It almost looked like the guy with the gun was assisting the bloody guy.

As the focus of the two individuals seemed to shift from them to me, the guy with the gun somewhat nonchalantly tossed it over the guardrail into the dense kudzu patch that sloped down the hill on the other side. As soon as I was close enough that I was confident both parties could hear me over the roar of the Interstate, I yelled for them put their hands up. Reluctantly, they both complied.

I quickly checked the four-door late eighties model Cadillac that was directly in front of my patrol car for suspects, victims, bodies, guns, bombs, vicious dogs and whatever else we look for out of instinct. Nothing caught my attention. I instantly returned my focus to the two individuals by the guardrail. I later learned that the Cadillac belonged to the bloody guy.

I then worked my way past the two men to check the late model, full-size Dodge pickup that was in front of the Cadillac. I later learned that the pickup belonged to the guy with the gun. About that time, all of my backup showed up and we began to investigate the rather curious scene.

The man occupying the Cadillac was an Asian man with a heavy accent that was a little difficult to understand. The other man was a Georgia native. The odd thing was that after I was able to talk to both of them independently, their accounts of what had occurred were almost identical. It is hard enough to get people who are on the same side of an argument to agree to the specifics of what transpired. There I had two men on opposing sides of a confrontation who actually agreed to almost every detail of the sequence of events. Both of them thought that their respective courses of conduct were justifiable and both of them, in my opinion, were wrong.

The whole incident had started about seven miles previously on the same Interstate. The man in the Cadillac was driving down the highway and the pickup truck was merging in from an entrance ramp. The pickup truck cut off the Cadillac and caused the driver of the Cadillac to make an evasive maneuver. The guy in the pickup truck said that he didn't see the Cadillac and the guy in the Cadillac said that he thought the pickup truck driver did it on purpose.

The guy in the Cadillac took it upon himself to administer what he deemed an appropriate punishment to the driver of the pickup truck. The Cadillac driver pulled past the truck, then abruptly cut into the lane in front of the truck and slammed on the brakes. This action, of course, precipitated an evasive maneuver on the part of the pickup truck driver.

As you might suspect, the pickup driver had no idea that he had offended anyone and thought that the Cadillac driver had just cut him off as an unprovoked act of aggression. No self-respecting pickup truck driver could let such an action go unrequited, so the pickup truck driver sped around the Cadillac to return the favor.

This imbecilic, point-counterpoint behavior continued down the Interstate to the point where the idiot in the pickup truck decided that he had had enough. He pulled over to the side of the road and stopped. The moron in the Cadillac made the brilliant decision to pull over behind the guy in the pickup truck.

When the idiot saw the car pull in behind him, he allegedly became fearful for his personal safety so he drew his pistol and exited his truck. He pointed the pistol toward the driver's seat of the Cadillac where he assumed the moron was waiting. When the moron saw the idiot pointing the pistol at him, he got mad and jumped out of his car to confront him.

At that point, both Idiot and Moron were between the Cadillac and the pickup. Idiot really didn't want to shoot anyone, especially an unarmed man who was half his size and for some reason, Moron wasn't afraid of the big idiot with the gun. As Moron approached Idiot, Idiot had the startling realization that perhaps his weapon was about to make things worse rather than better. Idiot also wasn't familiar with basic gun safety rules because he had his finger on the trigger (something only done by competent gun handlers when they are in the process of firing the gun, and something that is done by incompetent gun handlers almost all the time). Anyway, when Moron got within arm's reach of Idiot, Idiot decided to smack Moron on the head with the butt of the gun. What happened next is one reason why competent gun handlers keep their fingers off the trigger. Under the stress of the impending fight and the action of tensing his muscles while striking Moron, Idiot unintentionally pulled the trigger as he was smacking Moron on the head.

Thankfully, the gun was pointed in an inconsequential direction and the only injuries sustained from the unintentional discharge were a few strained eardrums.

The impact of the butt of the gun with Moron's cranium caused a laceration that did no major damage but produced a good bit of blood (as head wounds are known to do on occasion). The deafening report of the discharging pistol was apparently enough to bring both individuals to their senses and make them realize that things had gotten just a little bit out of hand. They were in the process of reconciling with one another when I arrived at the scene.

My chosen course of action was to charge both individuals for their part in the childish fray that very nearly turned to tragedy. Either party could have made the conscious choice to disengage at any time but neither party did. In my opinion that makes them both responsible. The man with the gun obviously received a higher charge.

What happened here happens all the time, I am sad to say. Not so much as the specifics of the incident are concerned but more as the underlying theme. An accident led to a misunderstanding, which led to a fight over something that was not worth fighting for in the first place.

Think back a few chapters to when I discussed perceptions. Just because you perceive something one way does not mean that is the way that it really is. Before you decide to resort to violence, you owe it to yourself and to everyone else to make sure that the situation *requires* violence. If you think that being insulted justifies violence (especially deadly force violence) then there's a good that you need some professional psychological help.

Furthermore, if you decide that a situation is serious enough that violence is the only answer, make sure that you are not only justified in committing that violence, but that you are also prepared to commit that violence. Many times, police and civilians alike operate under the gross misconception that you can threaten violence to solve a problem without ever intending to follow through with the threat.

What happens when the person whom you are threatening calls your bluff? There had better be a backup plan.

#19.6 Virtual 63

I have mentioned previously that things often are not as they seem. Before you leap to an assumption, at least make an attempt to gather as much information as possible. Misperceptions, like all mistakes, are inevitable, but many would be preventable if people would just take a little time and use some of that dormant gray matter in their heads.

Take, for instance, the officer who responded to a signal 29 (fight call) in an apartment complex. Our dispatcher advised us that the complainant (caller) was reporting that their next-door neighbors were involved in a fight that could be heard clearly through the paper-thin walls that separated the two apartments.

The primary officer responding to the scene was not one of our most stellar performers. He never came close to attaining even junior sheepdog status before he resigned with only a few years experience. Nonetheless, he was the first car at the scene. When he got only a few yards away from the front door to the aging apartment, he could hear the sounds that prompted the resident to complain of the fight inside.

He stood outside of the apartment listening to the curious sounds emanating from within. He heard blood curdling screams, sounds of furniture being broken and sounds of fists impacting flesh. There were the antagonizing taunts exchanged by the combatants as they each tried to subdue the other. The officer was horrified at what he imagined was going on inside the apartment. Instead of investigating further, he promptly broadcast a signal 63 (officer down/needs assistance) over the police radio.

Several of us were already close by since we had been dispatched to the alleged melee already. A little extra pressure on the gas pedal got us there that much more quickly. As we ran to the building and to the apartment in question, we found the officer just standing outside, apparently unscathed. We asked why he had put in the 63 and he responded with, "Listen. It sounds like somebody's gettin' killed in there." That was still no justification for abuse of the

237

sacred 63, but there were other more pressing matters requiring our attention.

We stood outside the door for all of a second or two before several of us started to laugh. The primary officer looked a little offended and confused at that reaction. Before he could put the question in his mind into words, I went ahead and knocked on the door. A couple of us had immediately recognized the montage of sounds on the other side of the apartment door. The door opened to reveal the two teenagers just inside the living room that were facing the wide screen projection TV.

They had no idea that their video game could cause so much trouble. How's that for humiliation?

#19.7 Dying To Get In

I think that most every guy in America, at one point in his life, finds himself locked out of his house for any number of a multitude of reasons. Some guys wait for a relative to bring a key, some guys accomplish a covert entry with no damage to the dwelling, and others simply break out a window or use some other, equally destructive means of entry.

One particular individual had spent the night out drinking with friends and had become considerably intoxicated. When he arrived at his townhome, he realized that sometime over the course of the evening, he had inadvertently misplaced the keys to his house. He was drunk and tired and just wanted to go inside and climb into bed.

He did what many guys in the same situation would do. He balled up his fist and put it through a pane in the back door. As is often the case, when he punched out the glass, a shard of glass cut into his forearm. He was drunk so the pain was undoubtedly dulled.

He immediately went to the bathroom to dress his wound and found that despite his best efforts, he could not stop the bleeding. He was a little worried about his predicament but didn't want to overreact. Instead of calling 911, he dialed "0" and got the operator. He told the operator that he needed an ambulance for the cut on his arm and was just about give her his address, when he passed out, unconscious from the loss of blood combined with the over consumption of alcoholic beverages.

By the time authorities were able to trace where the call had come from and dispatch the appropriate personnel, the young man had bled to death in his own bathroom.

In my opinion, the cause of death was sheer stupidity.

#19.8 Glass Or Plastic?

A beat partner and I were sitting back in the local donut shop, enjoying some fresh pastries and a cup of coffee, when radio dispatched my beat partner to a signal 2 (silent alarm) at a liquor store that was two blocks away. I feel it appropriate to comment quickly on alarm calls. Usually, from the time the alarm goes off, to the time the signal reaches the central monitoring station, to the time the operator at the central monitoring station calls the police, to the time the police are dispatched, to the time the police actually arrive, it's rarely less than 4 minutes. Consequently, police usually arrive to find a freshly broken-into building, with Evil that has long since left the premises. Nonetheless, when you work an area long enough, you learn which alarms are likely to be "good" alarms (i.e. the result of a break-in) and which ones do not warrant a rapid response (i.e. are likely false alarms).

The alarm at this particular liquor store had never gone off before so on the off chance that it was a good alarm, we dropped our donuts and ran to our cars. We were so close that we didn't even bother turning on our headlights. As we simultaneously rode into the parking lot of the liquor store we both saw the conspicuously broken front glass door.

Since I was the backup unit, my actions were in response to the primary unit. He went to the front door so I went around to the back. Just as I had determined that the back was secure, I heard the primary unit say that he had someone inside the business. I quickly went back to the front in time to see a very drunk and very homeless idiot crawling out of the hole he had broken in the front door. He was covered in blood from multiple, deep lacerations to his wrists and forearms and was struggling to get to his feet after crawling out of the business. We yelled at him to stay on the ground. The ensuing conversation between primary unit and I went something like this:

"I'll cover him. You go cuff him."

"I'm not goin' to cuff that bloody bastard. I'll cover while you cuff."

"I'm not cuffin' him. You cuff him."

"You found him first and it's your call. You cuff him."

"Let's both cover him."

"Good plan."

So we called for paramedics and both assumed a cover position. The drunk, stupid, homeless, idiot kept yelling at us that we were public servants and we had to help him. From a distance we kept telling him that help was on the way and that he need to stay on the ground until it got there. He would have none of that and kept trying to get to his feet while inching closer and closer to us.

After a few more unheeded warnings to "get down or else", I finally ran over to him and gave him a gentle kick to the head, which knocked him over to the desired position. Of course, he did not stay down for long so we went back and forth a few more times until the ambulance arrived.

After we got the pillar of the community on his way to the hospital, we began investigating the scene and determined that he had broken out the front glass door with a large rock that we found just inside the store. Then, instead of reaching in and unlocking the door and pulling it open, he decided to crawl through the hole he had created. So far, so good.

He ran right for the expensive whiskey. He picked up four, one-gallon glass bottles and headed for the door. He crawled back out the way he had come in and was almost home free. So far, so good.

As he ran around the side of the building, he slipped on an oily spot in the pavement and fell on top of the four, one-gallon bottles of whiskey. When the bottles hit the pavement they broke into a million pieces. When the drunk, homeless, stupid, idiot hit the glass that used to be the whiskey bottles, he got cut deep and wide. (I guess the whiskey puddle sterilized the wounds though.)

Naturally a bit perturbed that his sophisticated liquor heisting plans had been foiled so quickly and so completely, he decided that the proper course of action would be to return to the store, again through the hole in the door, and retrieve four more gallons of whiskey. On his second trip he was smart. He got plastic bottles. He also stopped for a couple of packs of Marlboro Reds. By the time he crawled out the door the second time, the police were waitin' for him. The rest is history.

Chapter 20

Cuckoo, Cuckoo

Those whom we all used to call crazy people are now more sensitively referred to as emotionally disturbed people (EDPs). A rose by any other name… Years of intense study led me to develop what I call "Nable's planetary scale of mental instability". This highly complex and evolved, totally scientific and perfectly accurate method, uses our solar system as a way to categorize a person's sanity. Earth represents the norm. Those few people who show more mental stability than the average human, rate toward the Mercury and Venus end of the scale. Those individuals who are less stable than average person score to the opposite end of the scale in varying degrees. The maximum attainable instability rating is "Planet 10".

Perhaps the most difficult thing for officers who score near Earth to understand is that people who score toward the outer reaches of our solar system are by nature unpredictable. Their perceptions of reality are not the same as ours. We cannot fall into the trap of trying to "reason" with those people because their brains don't work like ours do. Their "reason" makes no sense to us and our "reason" makes no sense to them. If you somehow have a way to decipher their "reason" (which is what psychologists and psychiatrists do for a living) then you may be successful in talking with them.

Officers of the law are not therapists who engage in solving long-term problems. We are more concerned with solving the short-term problems and steering the participants in the proper direction for resolution of their particular, individual malfunctions. One thing is for sure; EDP's can be anything from deadly to down right hilarious.

The following accounts are presented in no particular order and are strictly for entertainment purposes only. The characters involved are trained professionals. Please do not attempt these stunts at home. Performing these actions in an unsupervised environment could lead to injury, death or loss of freedom.

There was an older lady who by all appearances was a normal and productive member of society. She apparently had enough money to sustain herself moderately well. She even worked occasionally as a nanny. The first time I ran across the woman was several years before I became a police officer. She walked into the retail store where I worked and began looking intently around the tools and miscellaneous auto parts that were displayed for sale.

After a few minutes, my boss decided to approach the out of place lady and see if he could be of assistance. He asked if there was something in particular that she was looking for and as if that was all the validation she needed to speak, she turned to him with a sudden almost frantic look and said, "Yes. Do you have any reflectors, reflecting tape, or anything that burns?"

My boss was a bit taken aback. He explained that if he knew what application she would be using the items for, he could be more helpful in his sales advice.

She said, "I need something that they will be able to see from the air."

My boss gave her a strange look and before he could answer she said, "Never mind," and walked out the door.

The next time I saw her was in much the same context. She walked into the store where I worked and approached one of the employees. She got right up in his face, looked him dead in the eye and said, "I-99-I." (eye ninety-nine eye).

The employee said, "What?"

She said again, "I-99-I."

The employee obviously had a bewildered look on his face as he asked if that was some kind of part or stock number.

As if not hearing his question, she immediately barked, "Why do you cut your hair like that?"

The employee just shrugged.

The lady then proceeded to go on a nonsensical rant about some CIA operation code named I-99-I that pertained to some type of conspiracy involving the President and people who "cut their hair like that".

I would love to have been privy to the things that were running around inside of her head at that moment, but alas I am bound to a different reality.

Fast-forward a few years to when I had graduated college and the police academy and was on patrol in the heart of my old neighborhood. I was driving down the road wondering why traffic was so heavy when it was normally light. Just then I happened upon the answer to my unspoken question. There was a car parked in the middle of the road. The car looked as if it had been intentionally parked in the middle of the five-lane roadway and left. I impounded the car and didn't think much about it.

Within a few weeks, I happened upon the exact same car parked in the middle of another intersection. The car was registered to the same woman and was impounded as before.

A few more weeks went by. I was in the parking lot of the police station when I noticed a familiar looking car driving through the parking lot. It was the same car. It drove around the parking lot several times and on one of the rounds it drove right by me. The woman driving looked familiar and she looked a bit confused. She was driving with her right arm over the top of the front seat, seemingly reaching toward the floorboard of the back seat.

She drove by in this rather peculiar and unnatural position twice before she stopped at the curb in front of where I was standing with my shift supervisor. She rolled down the window and we asked if we could help her with something.

She looked right at us but I could tell she was venturing out to at least Neptune when she said quite frankly, "They won't let go of my arm."With that she drove away.

Countless times in the years to come she would call or write the police department in reference to gremlins stealing English muffins from her freezer or some sort of government spies invading her privacy. As a joke, most officers began referring her to one of our detectives in particular for the resolution of her problems. Whatever her problem was, that particular detective became the specialist. Gremlins, aliens, government conspiracies etc…he was the detective that handled it all.

The last time I saw her, she was driving a different, car at night, without headlights, down the middle of the road. I made a traffic stop on her and realized who she was as I approached the window. She started talking about some aliens that were disguised as barstools and how they preferred mosaic black and white tiles. After a minute or two of enduring her invasion dissertation, I feigned a frantic look on my face and said, "I-99-I…I can't talk right now, they're watching," and I ran back to my patrol car and drove away.

I never saw her again.

#20.2 Wanna Race, Baby?

I was on my way from the precinct to my beat when I was forced by a red light to pause my journey. As the light turned green I casually accelerated. I noticed via my rear view, that there was a suspicious looking car pulling out of a gas station into traffic behind me.

Then, like a fiery horse with the speed of light, a cloud of dust and a hardy, "Hi Ho Silver", the car galloped past me. I thought at first that it might be an off-duty or undercover officer messing around with me but followed it anyway. The car kept going faster and faster and got to nearly 90 mph. I thought that anyone playing a prank would have given up by then so decided to make the traffic stop.

I activated my emergency equipment and the vehicle pulled off into a parking lot and stopped. I pulled in behind him and parked. I cautiously approached the driver, half expecting to see a familiar face behind the wheel. I got to the driver's window and realized that the driver looked 100% unfamiliar. My first question was, "What er you doin'?"

The driver looked completely natural and said, "Oh, I thought you wanted to race."

I looked around briefly for Alan Funt and his camera crew but did not see anyone so I asked the next natural question, "Why would you think that?"

He said, "No reason."

I got his driver's license and told him to stay put while I went back to my patrol car and tried to think of a reason not to put him in jail. I sat for a few minutes and returned to the driver. I said, "Well, I couldn't think of one," and I pulled him out of the car and arrested him.

During the course of our interaction he said that he thought I was an officer that he had a crush on and wanted to date, but then realized his mistake. (I'm not sure what he meant by that.) Then he went into a spiel about how Bill Gates was trying to steal his computer programs and was going to get him if he went to jail.

When he came to court, the judge honored my recommendation for therapy.

#20.3 Seven-Foot Jesus

I think that virtually everyone, even non-Christians, has an image that comes to mind when you mention Jesus. I know I do. Before the late nineteen-eighties I always pictured him as a kind looking, robe-wearing, long-haired, Middle-Easterner with a beard. Boy, was I wrong. I actually met him in vivo on a call one day. It turns out that he's a seven foot tall, 290 pound white guy with curly red hair...and boy is he strong.

I don't want to question the Almighty openly, but I really don't think that hiding in the woods next to a roadway intersection, then jumping on the hoods of stopped cars yelling "Repent or die!" is an effective way of getting your point across.

I tried to explain that to him but was not successful. I may have sealed my eternal fate when about eight other Lilliputian officers and I expended darn near all of our physical and mental energies convincing him to go to a happy place that would be more receptive to his philosophies.

He sure did damage a lot of officers and equipment for such a peaceful guy.

#20.4 Smart, Crazy People Scare Me

I responded to a call from a man who was a psychiatrist. His wife was also a psychiatrist and, ironically enough, their son was at least a Uranus on the Nable scale. They called me because they had filed the appropriate paperwork to have their son involuntarily committed to a psychiatric institution and were afraid that he would not respond well to the news. Providing that the paperwork was in order, I would be required by law to transport the man to the designated facility. To my dismay, the paperwork was in order.

They explained to me that their son was in the basement of the house and was alone, with no known weapons. Then the family waited outside the house for me to go and get him. I was already a little apprehensive because of the family's behavior and the fact that no backup was available. I decided to give it a go anyway.

I made my way down the only staircase that led to the recently finished basement of the 1950's era house. As is the case in many similar places, the ceilings were very low and the rooms were crowded with furniture and personal belongings.

At the foot of the stairs was the largest room in the basement, which, incidentally, was where the object of my search was located. He was sitting on the other side of a full drum set. Behind him, draped across the wall, was a large red flag bearing a black swastika on a white background. I will only say at this point that the man in question was not white. I, on the other hand, am white and whether or not that is why he greeted me with a "Heil Hitler" and the accompanying salute, I will never know for sure.

He began espousing the virtues of fascism. I could tell immediately that he was an intelligent and well-educated, though very misguided, person. Smart crazy people scare me and this guy had the hair on the back of my neck standing at full attention. I was convinced that there was going to be a knock-down, drag-out fight before our meeting was over. I engaged him in a debate concerning his political views while he began getting ready for his journey to the hospital.

As he was looking for his shoes to complete his clothing ensemble he stopped abruptly, looked me dead in the eye, and asked, "Do you believe in God?"

Outside I said, "Yes" without hesitation but inside I was thinking, "Here it comes."

I honestly expected his next phrase to be something like, "...well get ready to meet him," but instead he took off running through the cramped basement. In my mind I was convinced that he was running for a weapon of some sort and I tried to keep up with him as he ran through a small hallway, into a bathroom and then out the door on the other side into a bedroom.

I had my pistol out and was psychologically prepared for a life or death confrontation when he calmly sat down and donned the tennis shoe that he had just picked up from the floor.

I tried to hide the physical manifestations of my recent adrenaline dump as I handcuffed him for both his and my safety. I transported him to the hospital without any difficulty whatsoever and had a big drink after work.

#20.5 Strong, Crazy People Scare Me More

A nice middle class family only a few blocks from where I spent the majority of my childhood had an only son. He was a very large man who was about nineteen years old. He had a history of mental illness which resulted in a history of crime, mostly theft and drug use.

When he began acting erratically, his family wanted him taken somewhere for treatment. They had become afraid for their own safety. Junior did not want to leave the comfort of home sweet home. We had the makings of a standoff.

When he heard the police were coming, the teenager sat down in a chair in a corner of the kitchen wielding a large steak knife and warning everyone not to come near him.

Another officer tried to "talk him down" as I stood by as backup.

We also had paramedics from the local fire station with us along with a full compliment of firemen that accompanied the fire truck. The officer and the teenager had a cordial conversation and the officer thought he was about to talk some sense into the boy. Trying to show concern and friendship and get a reason to approach him, the officer made note of a small cut on the boy's hand and asked if he wanted the waiting paramedics to take a look at his injury.

The boy asked, "Why?"

The officer answered, "Because you are bleeding."

The boy said, "Bleeding...Bleeding? You call that bleeding?"

Obviously preparing for a trip out of the galaxy, junior raised the steak knife as high as he could while remaining seated. He got that distant look in his eye as he began to shake, silently mustering whatever psychological forces were needed for the task at hand. His hands thrust downward, driving the steak knife deep into his left thigh.

His look changed to one of rabid determination as he paused for a second before yanking the kitchen utensil out of his limb.

"That's bleeding," he said as he pointed to the freshly cut meat.

I must say that we all agreed with him on that particular observation. We made a tactical withdrawal from the negotiating table.

Before he bled to death he was subdued with a full strength water blast from a fire hose (that knocked the knife out of his hand) and a subsequent, carefully orchestrated, dog-pile maneuver.

#20.6 Bubblegum for a Book?

I received a rather cryptic call to meet with a man who said that he wanted to give an officer some information. My dispatcher said that the caller wanted me to bring him some bubble gum. There was no further information on the call.

Without stopping to acquire any chewable confections, I responded to the call. I knocked on the door and heard some rustling inside. Then, the door opened as wide as the inept burglar chain would allow and a very curious man stuck his head through the resulting crack.

"Did you bring the gum?" he asked.

"No. I did not." I replied

"Then you can't have the book," he said as he slammed the door.

I heard him yell as I drove out of sight, "Bring me the gum and you can have the book. Good night."

Who knows what literary treasure I was deprived of for not having a pack of gum? Who cares?

#20.7 Just Plain Weird

Who can really say what mental machinations lead people to do the things that they do? An eight hour shift is rarely enough time to get even a momentary glimpse into the minds of normal people, much less those of the less stable. The behavioral manifestations of their particular malfunctions can be funny, surreal or down right spooky.

One in particular that comes to mind is a young man who called police in reference to a domestic dispute. I was the primary officer on the call and had one backup unit. The apartment complex in question was unusual in that every apartment in it was a small, one-bedroom apartment.

As mentioned previously, it is my policy when responding to any type of disturbance call to approach quietly and to look and listen as much as possible before attempting to make contact with the involved parties. I did that on this call and did not see or hear anything out of the ordinary.

I knocked on the door. My knock was quickly answered by a calm, relatively lucid individual who seemed quite normal. He started by saying that he was not sure that I was going to believe him (which is a good indicator that something unbelievable is about to be presented) but that he was afraid for his personal safety. When I asked the logical question, "Why?" he said that he thought his family was trying to do something to him.

There were no signs in the apartment that it was "over-occupied", and I assumed at that point that he lived there alone. I then asked what would turn out to be a key and pivotal question in our encounter. I asked where his family was.

He nonchalantly replied, "Oh,… there in the bedroom. You'll probably have to go in there to see what I'm talking about."

I asked in a facetious sort of tone attempting clarification, "Your whole family's in the bedroom?"

"Yes," he said, "I made them."

"Really!" I said, immediately thinking that I was about to walk in on a scene that would bear some semblance to an Ed Gein – Norman Bates slaughter and taxidermy party. I could tell that my backup officer was also intrigued. As he kept an eye on Mr. Freaky, I cautiously stepped into the bedroom.

I was a little relieved, in an odd sort of way, when I walked into the tiny bedroom and saw no corpses. The bedroom was filled nearly to capacity by a large bed and a bedside table. There was just enough room for an average size person to walk around three sides of the bed and that was it.

The items on the bed were what made the scene eerie. Across the width of the bed were four pillows that were propped up against the headboard. Upon each pillow was taped a photograph of a different alleged family member. Flowing down from each photo was an effigy of the respective family member, precisely constructed from seemingly random household objects. Those objects included but were not limited to, packages of tea candles, two steam irons, lots of wire and plastic coat hangers.

I told the man that in my professional opinion, his "family" was of no real immediate threat to him and that he might consider going to the free clinic for an evaluation. I think he rated at least as far out as one of Jupiter's moons.

#20.8 Electronic Body Cooker and Stink Machine

There are a number of what we call "standard" psychoses that have some common elements to them. Some such psychoses include the nebulous government conspiracy that results in 24 hour surveillance, wire taps, bugging etc., the attempts by mysterious beings to steal a person's thoughts, the beaming of radio or other signals into a person's home or head, and other stereotypical, irrational paranoias too numerous to enumerate.

The same night I met the man from the previous story, I had a call from a woman who had an interesting twist on some of the classical aberrations. She was an elderly woman who was blind or very near blind. She lived in a public housing project with her jobless son who suffered from some of the standard chemical dependencies and some serious dental problems that left him nearly toothless.

She had a very serious problem that according to her was being caused by the upstairs neighbor. The neighbor had some type of electronic device that he used to beam energy through the floor that would cause the lady's body to heat up to the point of nearly bursting into flames. The neighbor could somehow track her every move through the floor and followed her around the apartment blasting her with his directed energy beam weapon.

When the police came to the building, the neighbor dismantled the machine and put part of it in the pantry and part of it in the cupboard. (She knew because she could hear him.) Also, at some point during the torture, the neighbor had to either refill the machine with water, or clean it off in the sink. (She knew because she heard the water running.)

This same neighbor also had a device that he could use to create a horrendous smell in her apartment. The stinky machine would only work when all the doors and windows of the victim's apartment were closed. Whenever outside air came into the apartment, it nullified the effects of the stinky machine. The stinky machine also seemed to function off of her son's pillow, which was where the stink would originate.

I recommended that she just leave the windows open, but of course that wouldn't work because then the neighbor would use the open window to come into her apartment and do whatever Evil does. That was apparently the nefarious intent of both devices…to get her out of her apartment.

As for the heat gun dilemma, I modified the standard tin foil hat recommendation and suggested a tin foil blanket, shiny side out, of course.

Chapter 21

Wolves in Sheepdog Clothing

Wherever there are people, there are good people and bad people. Regardless of race, color, sex, occupation etc. etc. there is both Good and Evil everywhere. Consequently, from time to time, Evil worms its way into the ranks of those who are sworn to fight it. I would argue that one of Evil's most insidious forms is when it disguises itself as a police officer.

Police officers around the world do Good every day. They save lives and property and selflessly give of themselves every second of every day. They guard the tenuous line between order and chaos. They fight to prevent Evil from overpowering Good and they do so with little promise of material reward or societal recognition.

However, let a police officer be accused of something bad and he is plastered all over the news. Articles and books are written about how awful the police are in general. People march. People file lawsuits. People cry and moan and before long, they begin to think that because a few police officers do bad things, all police officers must be bad. If they are all bad then they must be hated. That reaction seems to be particular to our profession.

If a plumber gets arrested, people do not generally begin espousing the evils of the plumbing profession, they just go find a different plumber. That's not true if the Evil is a police officer. Though not necessarily fair we must accept it as a truth. People do not like authority and they love to strike back at it when given the opportunity. Also, police have a power that everyone wants at least once in their lifetime. Think back to the last time someone cut you off in traffic and how much you wished you could write him a ticket or put him in jail. The power to take away a person's freedom is an awesome thing that I personally think far too many people take for granted.

Freedom is the most precious thing a person has and in America it has a very special meaning. Freedom is sacred and should only be taken from someone as a last resort. A person's freedom is not something to be taken lightly. Police should put people in jail only if they have no other choice, not simply because they can. Many department heads and police officers get into the habit of putting people in jail because they can and the more people you put in jail, the better police officer you are. I disagree.

Jail should be for criminals. People who, by the nature of their crime, are a danger to the general law-abiding public or who, for whatever reason, are not likely to appear in court, should go to jail. Anyone else should be given some latitude. Warnings or a summons to appear in court to answer charges are, more often than not, sufficient to solve whatever problem necessitated police presence in the first place.

A man who shoplifts $50 worth of merchandise is no real threat to the general population. If he has a verifiable local residence and does not have an extensive criminal history, why bother taking him to jail? Give him the benefit of the doubt and issue him a summons to appear in court. If he fails to appear, then get a warrant and put him in jail for that.

On the other hand, if he has no verifiable address, then he may be considered unlikely to appear. An extensive criminal history may indicate that though his current crime is minor, he may have a proclivity towards failing to appear or toward committing more violent crimes. All these things should be taken into account when deciding to deprive someone of their most precious asset: Freedom. If an officer has to make a mistake, it should be in favor of the citizen (or perpetrator), not the other way around. That is the way the system is designed to work. Though the system may not be perfect, it is the best system in the world.

With all that being said, I also feel that police officers who commit crimes that victimize any person should receive much harsher penalties than the same crime committed by an ordinary criminal. When a police officer commits a crime, he makes all police look bad and makes all police suffer.

His crime against a person becomes a crime against Society at large and against the very fabric of our profession. It is a betrayal of the worst kind.

The first time I had an opportunity to witness this type of Evil in action first hand was when I was a rookie working the evening watch. I was coming to work one night and was outside the police station when two morning watch officers burst out the back door carrying a handcuffed perpetrator. This particular perpetrator had committed the heinous crime of talking too much in the holding cell and the two officers decided to take upon themselves the role of "attitude adjusters".

The primary officer involved had less time in the department than I did and the other officer was about one year my senior. Their chosen form of punitive action against the restrained man was to throw him in the back of the paddy wagon and begin beating him. Perhaps the physical harm done to the man was not so severe, but the harm done to our profession was profound. If you have to beat someone, at least make it a fair fight. Exercising grossly unfair advantages is the way of the sissy, the bully, and the coward. Some would argue that this particular behavior is not so serious and not that far out of the norm. However, in this particular case (and I imagine in many others), the behavior of at least one of the involved officers was merely a symptom of a far greater Evil.

I tried to discuss the incident with the officers' supervisor. He basically told me that if the alleged victim did not file a complaint, nothing would be done. I never heard anything else about the incident.

It was not long after that, maybe a year or two, before I overheard those same officers laughing with each other and discussing a situation that was unfolding among their ranks. The primary officer mentioned previously was boasting about how he and a select few officers had found a prostitute who was working out of an apartment on his beat. He had worked out a deal with her where he promised her that she would not be hindered in the continued practice of her profession, provided she serviced him on occasion.

I am not generally what you would call a "tattletale" but Evil is Evil, regardless of whether it wears a badge or not. I was so offended by that officer's behavior that I went to a supervisor hoping that something would be done. I had no proof other than the conversation that I had overheard. I was assured that I had probably misunderstood and that none of our officers would do something like that.

I feel it necessary to comment that I do not believe that investigations should be launched based solely on the unsupported testimony of one or two individuals, especially when those individuals are not the victims of the alleged crime and when that testimony has no real concrete factual evidence. That is the stuff of witch-hunts. It is not my intent to imply that the aforementioned supervisors were complicit in the wrongdoing in any way. I merely think that they were naive. As I have said before, most police are good people. We do not want to believe that one in our family is Evil without compelling evidence.

Within a few months, our detectives made a raid on the apartment that was the center of operations for the aforementioned lady of the evening. As she was being arrested, she told detectives that they were making a mistake because she was supposed to be "protected". She allegedly told the detectives about the deal she had with the morning watch officer and once again nothing was done. At that point I believe that someone should have investigated. To my knowledge, no one did. Even if they had, it would have been a difficult allegation to prove.

It wasn't long before the officer in question was transferred to detectives. While he was assigned there, I heard no more about him. I did occasionally run into officers from neighboring jurisdictions who had known him before and no one spoke well of him.

Within a few more years, detective sycophant was promoted to lieutenant and it wasn't long before he was transferred to my watch as a supervisor. I had heard rumors from reliable sources that some of our detectives had linked him to some nefarious behavior that revolved around a local strip club. The allegations were that he had been offering police related favors to the management in return for money and sex from the dancers. It was under the cloud of those allegations that he was transferred to my shift.

I distinctly remember one night when he was the supervisor on my shift. We got a call to a local bar on a fight involving a man with a gun in the parking lot. When units pulled into the parking lot, a man matching the description we had been given immediately took flight into the adjacent woods. The allegedly armed suspect crawled into a briar patch and was lying down in an entanglement of dense vegetation when we finally located him. One of the other training officers on the shift had a trainee with him so the trainee was elected to go into the briars to make contact while the rest of us covered.

The trainee performed as directed and contacted Evil. The suspect refused to give up his hands. Since Evil was likely armed with a handgun, the trainee felt an appropriate sense of urgency. He struck the suspect twice in the back with a closed fist and repeated the command for the perpetrator to put his hands behind his back. The suspect did not comply and was struck two more times. The lieutenant was there and yelled at the trainee, telling him not to hit the man. I remember thinking back to the time when the lieutenant was striking a handcuffed prisoner for no good reason and thought how ironic this situation was.

The trainee was completely justified in striking the suspect in the manner in which he did and had the full support of all those present. I was fully prepared and positioned to shoot the man should the circumstances require, but thankfully, the blows delivered by the trainee produced the desired effect and the suspect complied. He was taken into custody without further incident. The lieutenant then had the nerve to reprimand the trainee verbally for his behavior right there in front of all the officers and witnesses.

Afterward, we all assured him that his actions were perfectly justified.

Within a few months of that incident, the lieutenant was promoted to captain. We all heard that he was going to be placed in charge of the detective unit, which includes the investigating of vice related crimes and all undercover work. Those of us who had heard the rumors of his history of misbehavior were all amazed.

Within days of the announcement of his promotion to captain, I was at home on a Friday evening watching the news before dinner. The breaking news was that the FBI had just arrested our illustrious captain for a number of crimes revolving around the aforementioned strip club. Though he was accused of many crimes, including trading sensitive information for sex and money, he ultimately pled guilty to one count of extortion.

Rumor has it that his wife's father had financed his defense and just prior to trial, the father asked the government prosecutors for the "smoking gun" evidence they claimed they had against the captain. The prosecutors allegedly showed the captain's father-in-law a video/audio tape of the captain extorting money from owners of the strip club. The philanthropic father in law after seeing the tape, instructed his son in law to take the plea or lose his financial support. His sentence was fourteen months to serve. Not enough but better than nothing I suppose.

I (along with many others) was elated with the news and to this day still wonder how he made it so far, so fast; especially when there are good officers who are forced to serve ten or even fifteen years or more without being granted so much as a single transfer request.

#21.2 Looks Like Evil, Smells Like Evil: Must be Evil

As a training officer, I get to meet and subsequently get to know most of the new hires during the training process. One in particular stood out because not only did people think that he looked like me but we also shared the same first name. That is apparently where the similarities ended.

The first suspicious circumstance involving this individual occurred when his roommate, who is also a police officer, expressed some concern about the officer's behavior. He told me that the officer had a habit of drinking heavily and could become irrational and violent. He also told me that the officer would go out of the house at all hours of the day and night wearing his uniform. Though he could not say specifically that the officer was involved in wrongdoing, he was suspicious of him.

I advised the concerned officer to distance himself from the suspect officer and report any law breaking, but until he was sure there was criminal behavior afoot, not to mention it to anyone. I make it a policy never to complain on an officer unless I have overwhelming evidence that he or she is involved in criminal behavior. My personal feelings about an officer are irrelevant when it comes to Evil police.

Time went by and that original complaint faded into obscurity until one day I saw an old acquaintance at a local restaurant. We dispensed with the usual greetings and began reminiscing. My old friend then brought up the officer of whom I have been speaking. She told me that she couldn't believe that we would hire someone like him as a police officer so naturally I asked her why.

She said that she had been to several get-togethers where he had also been present and that she knew for a fact that he used illegal drugs. She also told me that he sold drugs. She then began to relay a story about how the officer had been ingesting some controlled substance at a party in a local apartment complex. He allegedly "went crazy", ran out of the apartment, down the hall to another apartment, kicked open the door and committed a burglary in front of everyone.

She said that they were afraid to report him because they thought he might kill them. Needless to say I was a bit astonished and thought that she must be embellishing the facts a bit. I told her that she should file a complaint. She said she was too afraid. Again, without proof or a witness no action could be taken.

Not long after that, I answered a fight call involving an intoxicated female. During the course of her arrest she blurted out something about crooked police and mentioned the same officer's name. I asked her what she meant. She proceeded to relay a story that was scarily similar to the one my old acquaintance had told me.

Within a week or two, I happened to be at the precinct and answered a phone call from a concerned citizen who lived in New Jersey. She said that her daughter was fighting with her boyfriend and that the daughter was afraid to call the police because her boyfriend knew this police officer who was very crazy and very violent. Then, the anonymous lady from New Jersey proceeded to relay a story that her daughter had told her that was exactly like the other two.

Even for me, hearing the same story three separate times from three seemingly unrelated people was too much to be coincidence. It was then that I reported the incident to a lieutenant whom I knew I could trust to do the right thing. We decided that he would have some detectives investigate the complaints without filing any formal paperwork. We wanted to expose him if he was dirty but not tarnish his reputation if he was not.

So the investigation went forward. An informant was contracted to attempt a drug buy from the officer. The day the deal was supposed to go down, the informant disappeared. The investigation was essentially terminated.

Several months went by with no action taken. Then one day, as if acting on a tip, the officer was summoned for a "random" drug test. He failed miserably and was given the opportunity to resign quietly. He wisely accepted the offer. The informant resurfaced some time later unscathed. Rumor has it that she was too afraid that the police were setting her up and not the officer, so she went away.

That one officer has deeply and negatively affected the lives of so many people whose perceptions of police will be forever tainted.

The allegations of criminal behavior extended far beyond the few things mentioned here. I'm just glad that we got rid of him even though, as is customary, he was never prosecuted.

Though it would be possible for me to tell a few more stories about Evil that has disguised itself as Good, I will refrain. It does more harm than good to reopen old wounds and serves no real purpose. The most important thing to keep in mind is that we all share equally a responsibility to ferret out Evil wherever it may seek to hide. Evil in a police uniform is not something that should be hidden or protected. It is Evil, plain and simple, and should be treated as such.

Chapter 22

63!

Young men tend to develop a sense of invincibility. That is one reason why they make such good soldiers and police. When you have the attitude that nothing can or will hurt you, then you can accomplish some astounding feats. When you accomplish those astounding feats and regularly lay the smackdown on Evil, that sense of invincibility is fueled. The intense emotions and adrenaline rushes associated with certain aspects of the lives of police officers and soldiers lead them to form strong bonds with each other.

We speak of a brotherhood when we speak of soldiers and policemen and there is perhaps no more appropriate term. The bonds that can form between individuals fighting to achieve a common goal can grow in a matter of a few months to rival the bonds that true brothers create over the course of a lifetime. It is nearly impossible to explain this phenomenon to someone who has never experienced it, and for those who have, the concept needs no explanation. We become, for all practical purposes, members of each other's families and as a result, form one very large family.

These bonds are what make it so traumatic when a police officer loses his or her life. When a member of our family is killed in the fight against Evil, it not only causes the extreme emotional response usually associated with the loss of a close family member, but it also shatters that sense of invincibility. The result can be a catastrophic blow to the mind. It can also be a learning and a growing experience if you allow it to be.

In the late 1980's this country experienced what I call the "crack explosion". The new cocaine derivative (crack) was taking the nation by storm and communities everywhere suffered from a rise in violent crime as a result. My area was no different. Crack dealers congregated on street corners like roaches on a garbage heap. With them they brought crime and violence in a wave that crashed on all levels of our society. Our police department was shorthanded, as were many, and officers often had to handle dangerous calls by themselves or with only one other unit. While not a particularly desirable environment to work in, it forced us to be self sufficient and independent.

On my shift, there were five police officers who worked very closely with one another. We ate, drank, worked and played together and were as close a family as any. I remember one afternoon when the five of us took advantage of an uncommon lull in the action to go for a quick bite to eat at a local Mexican restaurant. As was often the case, our conversation turned to the violence on the street and the fact that several police officers in previous months had been killed in the line of duty. Most of the officers killed had worked in jurisdictions that bordered ours. That day a close friend and brother offered an ominous bit of foreshadowing. In the context of the abnormally large amount of officers killed nearby in recent months, he said, "...you know, we are about due."

What he meant was that somehow all the departments around us had had officers killed in the line of duty, but our department had been lucky and had not lost an officer in over ten years. While briefly contemplating our own mortality, we all vowed to each other that should any of us meet a similar fate, the remaining four would do whatever was necessary to even the score.

Within a matter of a few months, that officer, Christopher B. May, would embody the fulfillment of his own prophecy. On Monday, August 19, 1991 at 2001 hours, the 911 center received the call that set into motion a chain of events that would forever alter the lives of so many. The caller had a foreign accent, which made it a little difficult to understand her, but anyone who paid attention could clearly hear nearly everything that the woman said. Since she dialed 911, the address that she was calling from would have been displayed on the call-taker's computer screen. The following is a transcript of that call. The words in brackets are garbled on the tape but the other words are perfectly clear.

911 Operator: Fulton County
Caller: Hallo
911 Operator: Fulton emergency 911
Caller: Hallo
911 Operator: Hello
Caller: Somebody from up at the house [from our house] ...
911 Operator interrupts caller: Calm down.

262

Caller (continuing): ...has shot a friend of mine.

911 Operator: Ma'am, calm down so I can understand what you're saying. What's the problem?

Caller: Somebody shot at her with a gun or something. They shot a friend of mine.

911 Operator: Someone shot someone there?

Caller: She is shot too much in the leg.

911 Operator: She's shot in the leg?

Caller: In the leg [with a gun]. Five Five Five River Valley Road in Sandy Springs.

911 Operator: Okay. We on the way. Buh bye.

I would like to comment at this point that for nearly my entire career, police officers in my department have been complaining that our 911 operators do not keep callers on the line and fail to get even the most basic information needed for the responding officers. In many radio rooms, operators are trained to ask pertinent questions and, in the case of "serious" calls or crimes in progress, the operator keeps the caller on the phone. This is done for several reasons. The officers can get real time information on the incident from the source and can be kept apprised of any developments that may change the officer's approach tactics.

Sadly, our radio operators to this day have not changed. You will see from the transcription that there is a miscommunication that starts with that 911 operator and her miserable failure to perform her duties. While it is not my intention here to assign blame to anyone for the death of my very close friend, I cannot help but think that perhaps things might have turned out differently had the call been handled properly from its inception.

For the reader to understand, the three digit numbers are the officers involved. Unit 312 is the shift commander. Units 324 and 326 are the beat officers who responded to the call. Unit 166 is a traffic unit that was close by who went to assist the beat cars. The KDT is the in-car computer that officers use to receive calls and perform other work related functions. The call was immediately dispatched and a transcription of the dispatch is as follows:

Dispatcher: Three twenty four.

324: Twenty four

Dispatcher: Three twenty four, five zero five River Valley Road signal fifty and four rescue en route. Complainant's advising the perpetrator was a passing motorist. No seventy eight.

324: Twenty four clear.

166: One sixty six, I'll go with him.

Dispatcher: One sixty six Okay.

312: Unit 312's clear on the fifty and four.

Dispatcher: Receive

324: Repeat the call and the numbers, the KDT's not working right.

Dispatcher: Three twenty four it's five zero five River Valley Road. I just checked back with the complainant – she's advising they were outside in the garage. They did not see the vehicle. They also could not provide a direction of travel.

To this day, no one knows where the idea came from that this shooter was a "drive-by". The caller never said anything to that effect. Also, the caller never said anything about 505 River Valley Road.

324: I'm on River Valley.

Dispatcher: Okay.

312: Three twelve, all the walkie-talkies are showing "out of range". Can you have the system checked…see if there's a repeater or something down that can be corrected?

312: Three twelve confirm the number's 505?

Dispatcher: Three twelve affirmative.

312: The printout from the uh KDT shows…911 shows five fifty five.

Dispatcher: Three twelve, complainant called in from five fifty five advising the fifty occurred at five zero five.

312: We couldn't get anyone to the door at five zero five can you call 'em back?

Dispatcher: Receive.

During the next eleven minutes, the officers were able to locate the victim at #555. The shift commander had units 326 and 324 go to the house next door, which was #575, to look for possible witnesses. Sometime during the confusion, the officers realized that the shot must have come from #575 but were still operating under the assumption that it was a "drive by". One of the dangers of a high stress situation is that information you are given from a source that you subconsciously trust (like radio) works its way into your thought processes. Even though we know not to assume anything, the initial suggestion of the shooting being a drive-by no doubt affected the way that officers responded to this call.

312: Got shots fired next door where the original shot came from…Start us some more units.

320: Three twenty I'm clear.

312: Shots fired next door!

Dispatcher: Radio's clear.

312: Give three twenty six and twenty four an eighty nine.

Dispatcher: Calling three twenty four and three twenty six.

Dispatcher: Calling unit three twenty four and three twenty six.

Within approximately 47 seconds from the time the shots were fired, the following was transmitted.

326: Twenty six officer down. Subject's got a high-powered rifle. Sixty three.

Dispatcher: Radio's clear on signal sixty three.

326: Twenty six, start rescue and a four up here immediately. Officer shot in the face – Down.

It is important for me to remark here that unit 326 gave an outstanding performance. He was calm and clear, despite the fact that he had just seen a close friend get shot in the head with a rifle. He was less than twenty feet from him when the fatal shot was fired and he managed to return fire at the suspect and take cover.

The rest of the radio traffic was full of police telling radio that they were responding. To me, that is a very dangerous thing to do. Normally, if an officer puts in a help call, everyone goes. Sometimes they even start from neighboring jurisdictions. If an officer puts in a help call, the radio should go silent. That officer is the most important thing in the world and he may only have a split second to transmit vital information. However, it never fails that officers have to justify their existence by talking on the damn radio. We don't care if you tell radio you are going. Just go!! It is what is expected.

The following account is taken solely from my memory of the incident and from a question and answer session with officers involved. Minor details may be fuzzy but the story should be accurate.

The house in question had brick facing and sat on a hill. It had a very steep driveway that traversed the front of the house before wrapping around to the left side (as you look from the front) where the garage was situated. The garage door opened to the left side of the house. There were windows on the front side of the garage and a pedestrian doorway on the back side of the garage that opened to the back yard.

When facing into the garage from the driveway, on the back wall on the right side (which would coincide with the front of the house) there was a storage room. There were two cars parked facing into the garage. There was just enough room on any side of the vehicles for a person to walk. Evil had stationed himself in the front of the vehicle on the right and was using the hood of that vehicle to support and aim his rifle. He fired down the passenger side of the vehicle. The officer was hit just as he stepped into Evil's view from the driveway. He was only inches away from the brick faced corner of the house when he was hit.

After watching his close friend collapse from a fatal wound to the face, unit 326, Officer Jeffrey D. Wright, was able to return fire into the garage. There were no lights on in the garage so in the waning hours of daylight it was difficult to see inside. He managed to hit Evil but the wound was not severe. Evil then shut the garage door.

Shortly thereafter, the entire area was teeming with police and SWAT team members. No one was sure where Evil was in the house but SWAT decided to start with the garage area. The pedestrian door on the rear of the garage was open. One of the SWAT team members told me later that he thought Evil left that door open to entice them to use it, perhaps drawing them into another ambush. He decided to take a less conventional approach.

The lone SWAT officer made a hole in the garage door that allowed him to crawl into the garage directly behind the vehicle on the right side of the garage. He went in by himself because there would not have been room for more than one person. The SWAT officer told me that when he crawled into the garage, he immediately noticed that there was a doorway in the ceiling that led to the crawl space above the garage and that he thought Evil might be waiting up there. He soon discovered that assumption was false.

As the SWAT officer looked around the right side of the car he was behind, he could see the doorway to the aforementioned storage room. The light was on inside the storage room and the door was part way open. Apparently, his initial assumption about the pedestrian doorway being an invitation to ambush was correct. Evil was sitting with his rifle trained on that doorway. The SWAT officer announced his presence and Evil opened the door to the storage room to greet him. Evil let out a few curses while attempting to bring his weapon to bear on the SWAT officer.

The SWAT officer stayed behind the cover of the car and let loose a barrage of gunfire from his fully automatic .30 caliber carbine. In roughly three seconds, all thirty rounds in the magazine had been dispatched in Evil's direction. The majority of them struck Evil. Evil fell to his knees but was still a potential threat. The SWAT officer discarded his machine gun and pulled his pistol. sixteen rounds of 9mm ammo screamed in Evil's direction. Again the majority of them struck Evil, but Evil was still not down. The SWAT officer discarded the empty pistol and drew his .357 magnum revolver. As he advanced on Evil's position, all six rounds slammed into Evil's head and body and Evil finally went down. Out of approximately fifty-three rounds fired, Evil was hit forty something times. One round or fifty, dead is dead. We keep shooting until we perceive the threat to be eliminated.

Fourteen months later, I was working a night time extra job at a local bar when I got a call from a fellow officer who told me that there had been a shooting involving one of our officers and that he was being transported to the hospital. No more information was available. It just so happens that the officer was one of the five who was part of that original group that Evil had already reduced to four.

I told the manager of the club where I was working that I had to go and jumped into my recently restored 1963 Ford Thunderbird with a 390 cubic inch power plant. In moments I was doing mach 10 up the Interstate towards the hospital where the ambulance had taken my close friend. I really don't remember anything about the drive to the hospital other than an overwhelming feeling of dread.

When I arrived at the hospital, I was ushered to a small, dark waiting room where my other two close friends were waiting. We sat for what seemed like an eternity until a supervisor opened the door. He paused for a moment before he said solemnly, "He didn't make it." The supervisor backed out and closed the door. The atmosphere was thick and silent for a few moments while the tears welled up in our eyes. For the second time in less than two years we had lost one of our closest friends and brothers. He had apparently been drinking and began playing with his pistol. Some say that the resulting fatal wound was intentional while some say that it was accidental. I say that all that matters is that he was my friend and he too is gone.

And then there were three.

Chapter 23

Eeeewww

This chapter contains a few stories that I couldn't fit into any of the other chapters. I'll start with a call I received on a traffic accident with injuries. I had a trainee with me so I figured it would be a good learning experience for him. When we arrived at the crash site, there was an ambulance standing by and the remains of a Honda Accord that were stretched about thirty feet.

I honestly thought that our rescue units had been there already and had cut the car open to try to extract the driver. As it turned out, he was going so fast, when he left the roadway and hit the utility pole, that the car just disintegrated. The driver was still pinned in the wreckage, jammed butt first in the front passenger floorboard between the seat and what was left of the dash. All the doors were gone as was the roof.

The medical examiner arrived and requested some assistance extricating the body. I, naturally, volunteered… my trainee. The M.E. needed someone to stand on the hood of the car over the body and tug on the arms while, from a different vantage point, she tried to free the carcass from the area it was wedged into like a cork in a wine bottle.

I sat and "supervised" while my trainee tugged and the M.E. pried and prodded. The dead guy finally broke free of the death grasp the car had on him. The body shot upward toward my trainee. The dead guys pants were ripped and they came off leaving a big puddle of poo and other fluids to splash all over the three of them.

My trainee was not happy but I got a kick out of it and that's all that counts I guess.

#23.2 Head And Shoulders

I had just started toward the precinct near the end of my ten-hour shift. My chosen route took me down one of the main, limited access thoroughfares in our county. That main thoroughfare would also take me through a small city on my way. Just before I got the boundary line that divided the incorporated city from the unincorporated county, radio broadcast that the city police department was requesting assistance with a 41/4 (traffic accident with injuries) on the highway south of my location. At the time, the city department had a total of only about eight officers on that shift.

As I approached the scene of the accident moments later, I realized why they were going to need help. On this particular highway, there were four concrete lanes going in each direction and a large grassy median separating the northbound lanes form the southbound lanes. Traffic in both directions was completely shut down. Several city officers were needed to divert traffic onto the nearest exits before the accident scene in both directions.

I was a rookie of about two years at the time, and the scene before me was quite impressive. There was a slew of mangled cars on both sides of the freeway. Unrecognizable debris was scattered as far as the eye could see in both directions on the highway. A number of undamaged cars had stopped to try to assist, provide their eyewitness accounts to authorities, or just to gawk at the carnage.

I will attempt a cursory recap of what apparently happened. The whole thing started when a young man, who was under the influence of whatever controlled substance he had chosen to alter his perceptions of reality that day, was traveling northbound at over 120 mph in his Mercedes sports car.

As he crested a slight hill underneath an overpass, he apparently either didn't see the car in front of him or didn't realize how fast he was going (or both). He rear-ended that car, which by all accounts was traveling the posted 55mph speed limit, without even touching the brakes. That car was knocked hundreds of feet forward and off the roadway to the right, into a clump of trees. In the process, it hit one or two other cars that remained disabled in the roadway. If memory serves me correctly, the occupants of that vehicle, though injured and obviously shaken, all lived to tell of their ordeal.

After impacting with the first car, our young, impaired Evil went out of control and across the grassy median into the opposing lanes of southbound traffic. His forward momentum was immediately stymied by the compact car that was traveling in the left southbound lane. The Mercedes struck the little car head-on and instantly killed the entire family of four that was inside. The impact was so great that the Mercedes broke in half just behind the driver's seat, something that the manufacturer later sent engineers to investigate, since it apparently had never happened before.

What was left of the Mercedes ricocheted off the compact car and spun sideways. It soon impacted with another southbound car that was one lane over from the first. The little maggot driving the Mercedes was ejected from his car into (not onto) the hood of the second southbound car. The impact with the hood of that car sliced Evil into two pieces just below the shoulders.

Left behind in the twisted wreckage was Maggot's body from the shoulder's down. His "head and shoulders" were at the time unaccounted for, but he did see fit to leave a good number of his teeth behind, embedded in the sheet metal of the hood of the car that had sliced him in two.

Since the rest of the county units and I were merely support personnel, after the scene was secured, we had the liberty to move around. Naturally, we began the hunt for the head and shoulders. I concentrated my effort to the first 100 feet or so around the final impact. Another officer went a bit farther. We all looked unsuccessfully for an indeterminate amount of time until one of our officers called out from a point just inside the woodline some five hundred feet away.

We turned to see where he was as he simultaneously reported that he had found the object of our search. In his hand were the man's head and shoulders, still attached to each other. Part of the dress shirt and most of his tie were still on the "bust". With his typical, comical, morbid irreverence, the officer hoisted up the head, looked it in the face and gave a noticeable inhale through his nostrils.

"…Smells like he's been drinkin'!"

#23.3 It's Not The Fall That Gets You…

Of all the ways in the world to kill yourself, why anyone would choose to jump off of something very high up onto something very hard is especially curious. To me, that form of self destruction would be right up there with slowly burning to death. Even more curious, is when someone decides to leap to his or her death off of something that isn't quite high enough to ensure that the desired result is achieved.

271

Take for example, a young woman who for whatever reason, decided that she would depart to the hereafter via a short flight off of a highway overpass onto the pavement below. I guess that she figured if the fall didn't kill her, then a car would surely run over her and finish the job. She was wrong.

When the call was dispatched of a woman who had possibly leapt off the bridge in question, I was close and was, therefore, the first car to arrive. It was dark and traffic was light. Lying in the middle of the Interstate, right below the bridge, was a little blob of stuff that used to be a woman.

I positioned my car to prevent anyone from running over the blob or me and got out to investigate. There were a few bystanders that had gathered for whatever reasons bystanders gather. I approached the blob.

I'll admit that I was a bit taken aback when I noticed that the petite young woman was still breathing. She was also moaning a little and was not exactly what you would call conscious, but she was definitely alive. Paramedics arrived quickly and began working on her, though I could see the sense of hopelessness in their eyes.

As a result of the impact on the freeway, the woman's leg bones had pulverized and essentially disintegrated. The hydrostatic pressure from the enormous impact had caused her body to explode outward through the bottoms of her feet, which were apparently what she had landed on. There were chunks of whatever had come out of the splits in her feet. Small fragments of bone were mixed in with the chunks. I have no insight as to what had happened to her internal organs but assumed that since she essentially no longer existed from the waist down, that would likely be enough to kill her. The rest of her body was surprisingly undisturbed.

Perhaps if one of the two cars that had stopped to "help" had not swerved to avoid running over her, she would not have suffered for the four to six hours that I was told it took for her to finally pass. She was real-life proof of the axiom that says, "It's not the fall that gets you, it's the sudden stop". It's what we in the biz call Sudden Deceleration Trauma (SDT).

As an interesting side note, that same bridge was the site of another suicide that had an interesting twist. The man was sitting on the bridge rail, threatening to jump. The police and fire department had to close both the roadway on the bridge and the Interstate beneath. Negotiations were going nowhere and the man had traffic tied up for a very long time. One of the officers at the scene got fed up with the standoff and went in for some face-to-face negotiations. I can only imagine the dialog that lead up to the officer saying, "Well go ahead and jump then. I don't think you've got the balls."

The officer turned to walk away and the man jumped off the bridge. The road was open soon after.

#23.4 The Dentist

I had trouble deciding where to put this particular story so I just decided to put it here. There was once a low-level drug dealer who had some friends over to smoke some weed. He made the mistake of allowing his friends to see how much weed he had. It was a lot. After the party was over, everyone went home. That night, the "friends" decided to come back for a visit to get what was left of the weed.

They got their guns, put on their ski masks and kicked open the front door to the apartment. In this particular apartment, to get to the bedroom where the resident was, you had to go in the front door, turn left and walk a few steps. Then you had to turn right and go to the end of a long hall to where the bedroom was.

This particular drug dealer kept a high-powered rifle by his bed. When he heard his front door crash open, he immediately picked up that rifle and prepared to defend himself. The would-be robbers ran single file down the long narrow hallway, into the waiting ambush.

The lead bad guy (Evil) fired one round from his Smith and Wesson semi-auto pistol at the drug dealer and the pistol promptly jammed, a failure common to those particular pistols. Evil turned to run back out of the apartment and was able to make it almost to the end of the hallway, when the drug dealer fired down the hall with his high-powered rifle. His aim was true and the bullet struck Evil square in the back of the head, right at the base of the brain. Evil was likely dead before he hit the floor…and was probably dead before the rifle bullet exited through his mouth, blowing most of his teeth forward into the closet door at the end of the hall.

When we arrived at the apartment, the drug dealer had secured his rifle. He was congenial and moderately cooperative. Evil was lying in a puddle that was a mixture of his brains, blood and other gooey stuff. His teeth were still sticking out of the closet door.

Chapter 24

_____

...But Seriously Folks

We have all heard how stressful a police officer's job can be. We as police must endure the inherent shortcomings of a political system burdened with bureaucracies and budget constraints. We must deal with citizens who have their own hidden agendas or who just plain don't like police. We see people at their worst almost on a daily basis because, after all, people don't call the police when things are going well. We are expected to remain calm while we are yelled at or called names that would provoke the common man to fight. We are expected to take risks cheerfully that would cause most people to curl up into a fetal position and cry for their mamas. We are expected to settle disputes that would challenge the most seasoned diplomats and solve problems more fittingly relegated to a think tank. We are expected to be doctors and lawyers, therapists and mediators, writers and investigators, and the list goes on and on.

I knew all that when I signed on, though I must admit that I had no idea of the magnitude of the things to come. Any officer who spends more than a year or two on the streets will see things that alter the lives of most people. We see death and destruction on a grand scale. The insidious nature of that which we see is that it comes in seemingly small doses. But, those doses are regular and their effects can last a lifetime.

Becoming emotionally involved in every tragedy or circumstance an officer faces would send even the strongest to the mental ward in a very short time. As a result, we tend to develop defense mechanisms that distance us from the troubles we see. The public often mistakes these defense mechanisms as shallow callousness or insensitivity, not realizing that our behavior is necessary for our very survival. We joke about car crashes and dead people. Not because we truly think those things are funny. We do it because subconsciously we must distance ourselves from and attempt to dehumanize the tragedies we encounter, from the smallest to the largest. In essence, we must create a bullet proof vest for our minds.

One of my earliest law enforcement memories has to do with a story told to me in the Police Academy by one of our instructors. It is one of only a few stories in this book that I repeat without having been involved in the actual incident. At the time, I didn't really think it was that funny and most people would likely be horrified. So here goes:

A local detective arrived on the scene where a young woman had been beaten, raped, tortured, murdered and sodomized with a broom handle (not necessarily in that order). His eyes met the crime scene with curious detachment. Lying in front of him was the dead woman and she still had the broom handle protruding from her privates. Unaware that her family members were in the next room and without missing a beat, the detective asked, "So - What happened - Witch have a crash landing?"

This is a classic example of the aforementioned defense mechanism. I seriously doubt that anyone but an accomplished sociopath would not be affected by such a sight. To cope with such horrors, people often joke or pretend not to care. We have to do it to survive so don't take it personally. If we truly didn't care we would have different jobs.

I have seen people's entire lives go up in flames. I have had to tell them that their loved ones will never come home again. I have had to pick up pieces of bodies that were dismembered in extraordinary acts of violence or by freak accident. I have looked Evil dead in the eye and without hesitation, have given it the smackdown. Simply put, I have freely and voluntarily put myself into situations that most normal humans would run from. I am not special; officers across the globe do the same thing each and every day. People call us heroes but they really have no idea.

I do not regret my chosen profession. I am proud of it and I know there is no nobler cause. It is not what I do it is what I am. I have enjoyed almost every aspect of it but I must admit that there are a few things that have affected me negatively. Most of those things involve the deaths of innocent people. They are my Achilles' heel.

Most people who know me realize that I am far from being the most sensitive little flower in this great garden. I don't really give a damn about the guilty. They rarely get what they deserve anyway. The drunk who careens off the roadway at 0200 hours and dies in the twisted metal doesn't bother me a bit. He made his choices and suffered a fitting end. Better him than someone else. An intoxicated driver who wrecks does not have an accident, he merely wrecks. There's nothing accidental about driving drunk.

The perp who runs from the police in his car, flips over and dies in the fiery crash also has met a fitting end. The burglar, rapist, armed robber, or other miscellaneous felon killed by his would-be victim gives me a special delight like no other. I have no sympathy for these people. Let them die as they may. It is their own fault. (Also, just because someone happens to be dead doesn't mean that I am going to speak any more or less highly of them than I did when they were alive.)

However, take for example, the first person I was ever forced to watch as she died. It was a female in her late twenties. She was driving on a wet roadway just after a rain. No one knows for sure exactly what happened but something caused her to veer off the roadway. Going no more than the posted speed limit and perhaps less, her car drove up the guy wire of a utility pole. The car didn't violently flip over, it just sort of tipped over. For some reason she wasn't wearing her seatbelt that night. As the car tipped, her torso fell part way out of the open driver side window. The edge of the roof fell across her until then flawless face. It crushed her skull. The car itself barely sustained a scratch and could have been driven from the scene.

As I sat with her it began to rain lightly. Emergency personnel were doing their best but their efforts were in vain. All I could do was sit with her and hold her hand as she passed. She was conscious and whimpering. She was trying to speak but her damaged face could not form the words that were in her mind. I'll never know if she was pleading for help, asking what had happened, or wanting me to give a loved one her final farewell. For a rookie with only six weeks on the force, it was a rude awakening and one I will never forget. I had never felt such sadness or such utter helplessness. Little was I to know that those feelings would not be a stranger to me in the future. That which does not kill us, makes us stronger.

One of my favorite authors used a poem to describe a similar instance. It is as follows:

> *One cell.*
> *One single cell.*
> *Made mortal only by its wounds.*
> *Daddy can you fix it?*
> *Out of reach of human kind,*
> *To be a free spirit soon.*

#24.2 Just Plain Evil

I was traveling westbound on I-285 in the early morning hours. A call came out over the radio of a signal 50/4 (person shot/ambulance enroute) at a restaurant that was less than two minutes away. I was not the unit dispatched but, like a good officer, I went as fast as I could.

Radio advised that the caller kept getting disconnected but that the victims were in the rear of the building. I was the first officer on scene. I did a quick sweep of the entire parking lot and found no people and only one truck parked in the rear. As usual, radio was little help.

By then a backup officer arrived and we began a more thorough check of the building. We couldn't see anyone and all of the doors were locked. We were beginning to think that the call was a hoax when radio advised us that the victims were locked in the back office of the restaurant.

My backup officer and I had recently graduated SWAT school together and worked near each other for quite some time. He pulled on the locked front door and when it didn't budge, he began seeking other avenues of entry. I, on the other hand, was thinking that if there was someone inside who was shot, we needed to get in fast. I grabbed the handle of the front door and, with every ounce of strength I could muster, I yanked. The door popped open with a loud crack, and my backup joined me at the newly opened door.

I took a second to rib him for not being able to open the door (and nicknamed him "tool man", which is a term used to describe a SWAT team member who is responsible for carrying and using the tools needed to make forcible entries into whatever needs to be forcibly entered). We proceeded to clear the interior of the business. We systematically worked our way to the rear and when we were confident that Evil was not present, I called out, "Police, where are you?"

I heard a muffled sound from behind the only locked door in the building. The voice inside screamed for help. My backup officer kicked the door twice and it did not open. He stepped aside. I kicked it once and it came open (I joked that the tool man had loosened it for me). Something behind the door was keeping it from opening. I pushed gently on the door until it opened and found two people on the floor inside. One male and one female were both lying on the floor of the tiny office. They both had their hands and feet tied and both had been shot. The male had good color and could respond to my questions, though he was a bit incoherent from the shock of his ordeal. I could tell he was scared (as anyone would be) and I cut the ropes off his feet. I was conscious to leave the knot intact in case it could be used as evidence. I told him to lie still and asked if he had any information about who had assaulted him. He was delirious and in shock and could not tell me anything.

I then turned my attention to the female. She did not look so good. Her eyes were red and glazed. She looked like she had been crying but there were no tears. She was turning purple and though she tried to speak, her mouth moved but no sound came out. Wrenching from her unimaginable, excruciating pain, she made motions as if she were trying to scream but again no sound. The inside of her mouth was pale and dry. The veins on her neck and head were unusually pronounced. Words cannot adequately describe the haunting look that was on her face. It was a look of sheer agony that arose not just from the fatal gunshot wound she had in her lower back and the thoughts of her own mortality, but from the natural fear that any expectant mother has for the life that grows inside her.

I reached for her hand and tried to tell her that everything would be OK, even though I knew better. I can't help but think that my feeble words were of little consequence. People who are about to die have a very special look about them. It's hard to describe, but once you have seen it you will never forget it. I went to cut the ropes off her feet and I think that's when I realized that she was pregnant.

The next few minutes were chaos. Emergency medical personnel arrived quickly. There was very little room in the cramped office and since the police at that particular place and time were non-essential personnel, we evacuated the immediate area to allow paramedics to do their jobs. They did everything that they could but before long, the young mother of two who was five months pregnant with her first baby girl and working her last night shift as the restaurant owner/manager, was gone forever. Evil, in its purest and most despicable form, had struck again.

That week I relied heavily on my support group as I had done countless times before (and since). My support group consists of my magnificent wife and my two beautiful children. We share everything, whether it's good or bad, and it helps to keep us together.

#24.3 I Still Don't Get It

Suicides offer a strange panoply of emotions. On the one hand I am angered by a person's total disregard for not only his own life but for the lives that are affected by his actions. So many of God's creatures fight to survive on a day to day basis yet some choose to simply throw their lives away.

On the other hand, I am bewildered as to why Man seems to be the only creature who is capable of or concerned with taking his own life. How can anything be so bad that a person would give up everything that they have and everything that they ever will have? What drives a person to override the single strongest and most basic instinct of any living creature; the instinct of survival?

Though I have witnessed suicides and their after effects more times than I care to remember, several of them come to mind. One week in the late 90's I had the misfortune to witness two separate suicides in less than a week. First, I was leaving roll call one night when my supervisor told me that he had received a call from a local psychiatrist. The doctor told my supervisor that a long time patient had contacted him, stating that he wanted to meet the doctor at his office and that he was thinking of killing himself. The doctor wanted the police to check out the situation first to make sure that the patient would not be in a position to harm himself or anyone else.

I gladly accepted the assignment and took one other unit with me. I'm sorry to say that I was not expecting what was to transpire. I pulled into the office complex that housed the doctor's office. It is a complex that has nearly twenty identical square brick buildings that are three stories each and randomly placed in a maze of asphalt, bushes and young trees. I made my way around to the building in question and could see a car parked on the curb in the parking lot near my destination. As I made the final turn that put me in close proximity to that vehicle, I lit it up with my spot light.

In the driver's seat was a young man. In the young man's hand I could clearly see a revolver. He was holding the revolver with the barrel pointed into his mouth. I quickly accelerated past the car to the other side of the parking lot just in case his murderous intent changed its focus toward me. I advised radio of the situation and started the supervisor. I then began attempting to talk to the subject, which proved no easy task since we were about fifty feet apart and he would not leave his car and I certainly was not about to leave mine.

I addressed him on the P.A. in my patrol car. He held up a book by C.S. Lewis. I tried to talk to him further but got no response. His psychiatrist and my lieutenant arrived and we decided to approach the man to try to talk him down. My backup unit was covering us from a distance. I was covering the bad guy and was concealed somewhat by the passenger side blind spot of his car. My lieutenant was standing between the doctor and his patient in the driver side blind spot of the vehicle so that if he tried shooting at the doctor, my lieutenant would take the round and I would end the confrontation with a well-placed barrage of gunfire.

The negotiations did not go well though they went on for some time. I remember watching as the subject became visibly agitated. When he rolled up the window of the car I got a bad feeling. He put the revolver into his mouth and began shaking. A few seconds later he removed the weapon from his mouth, pressed it against his chest and fired. He fell limp but was still alive. I rushed in from my side and secured the weapon. The lieutenant and doctor rushed in from the other side but nothing could be done for the man. Within thirty seconds he had bled to death through the hole he had punched in his own heart.

A night or two later, while the moon was still nearly full, the radio broadcast a call on a signal 50 (person shot) with no further information. Since I was close to the quiet, upper-class neighborhood that the call came from, I was quick to respond. In less than a minute I was at the address given by radio. It was a large estate in a cul-de-sac where there was no real crime problem. The front door to the house was slightly open.

I asked radio if they had any additional information and received the standard response, "No." Backup was very close so I decided to make a limited entry. I very quietly entered the foyer and cleared the rooms on either side. I could hear muffled sounds from upstairs like people talking. I made my way to the foot of the stairs. The sounds became clearer and I could make out two distinct female voices. Both sounded stressed but not in a way that led me to believe that Evil was present. I crept up the stairs (perhaps not the most sound tactical maneuver but I have learned to listen to and trust my instincts, and that's what they told me to do).

When I got to the top of the stairs, I could see at the far end of the dimly lit hallway that there were two women in what appeared to be a bedroom. One woman was talking on the phone and one was on her knees straddling something on the bed. As I crept closer, the faint smell of gunpowder became stronger and I actually noticed smoke in the air. I took the woman on the phone by surprise as I crept up behind her. So much so that when I spoke, she screamed. As it turns out, she was on the phone with the 911 operator and had been since the call came in. (How's that for "no further information available"?)

The woman on the bed was the mother of the late teenage boy that she was straddling. She was attempting CPR and was crying and screaming at the boy. As I drew nearer, I could see a large hole in his chest just under the sternum, which, I found out soon after, came from his .50 caliber percussion pistol. He was already beginning to turn blue and showed no signs of life. As she gave compressions to his chest, the sound of the air rushing out of the gaping wound made sounds strangely like a moan, giving her false hope for her only son's revival.

He was dead. I tried to convince her at the time but she just yelled at me, saying that if he died, it was my fault for not doing anything. I stood by and accepted her rantings without reply because by that point in my career I was used to being the verbal punching bag for distraught individuals. I am OK with it, under certain circumstances and this was one of those circumstances. She soon calmed down but never apologized to me. That's OK too. Police officers have to realize that when people are extremely upset they lash out at anyone who is near, especially if it's a stranger. Most of the time it's better to let them scream at you and get it out of their system because responding only fuels the fire. Above all, don't take it personally. It is cathartic for them and doesn't hurt you.

I guess that her comments nagged at me enough to make me call the M.E the next day to make sure that there was indeed nothing that I could have done for the boy. He assured me that the enormous projectile had destroyed nearly the entire heart immediately. As for the boy, it turns out that his dad (who was divorced from his mom) had missed an appointment to see him and had shown increasing disinterest in his son over the last few months. He loved his dad dearly and it appears that the father had destroyed the young man's heart long before the piece of lead got its turn.

#24.4 Tragic Loss

Ironically, just as this book was nearing completion, I was at home on a Saturday afternoon enjoying my niece's fifth birthday party when the phone rang. On the phone was a fellow police officer and long time friend who told me solemnly, that minutes earlier a good friend and beat partner had committed suicide by shooting himself in the head.

Several years earlier, he had been one of my trainees. He was assigned to my shift right out of training, where we worked together until his death. I remember that when he first started working I thought he was just another college boy who wasn't cut out for police work. I didn't hold out much hope for his ever becoming a sheepdog. Within six months or so of morning watch policing, he began to prove me wrong and he developed into one of the finest officers my department ever had.

No one I know had even the faintest hint that he would consider taking his own life. He was young, recently married, healthy and intelligent. He seemed to have everything going for him, but he was obviously hiding something that none of us saw. Whatever it was, I am sure that we could have helped to fix it if he had given us the chance. We will never know the answers to all those questions that run amok in our brains when someone close to us commits suicide. No matter what we do, we can't fix it now and we have to deal with the loss in the best way that we can.

In these situations we must endeavor to keep in mind some points I made in the beginning of this book. We all have our own unique perspectives and those perspectives are the filter through which we view the world. When a person commits suicide, he is likely not looking through the same filter that we are. Negative emotions sometimes worm their way into our thoughts and in most instances, they do not serve any constructive process. It is difficult, if not impossible, to know what was going on in a man's mind at the point in time when he chose to end his life. Quite frankly, by the time all is said and done, I believe it is irrelevant.

The real victims of suicides are the survivors. We have to cope with the senseless loss of someone close. As with any loss, it is better not to focus on the grief caused by the loss itself, but to find joy and happiness in the memories that we share. We often take life's precious gifts for granted and suffering a loss can help to put the world back into its proper perspective. There are things in life that are truly valuable, like family and friends, and the positive actions and interactions in our lives that make the world a better place. There are also things that, when put into their proper perspective, just aren't so important, like money, a new car, fancy clothes, or what color to paint the bathroom.

If you should ever find yourself seriously thinking of dispatching yourself into the hereafter, if you care anything for your friends or your family, you owe it to them to reconsider and to get help resolving your problems.

There is a legend in my department involving an officer and a supervisor, both of whom I knew and both of whom are still in the land of the living. When the officer was a relatively young man, he approached his sergeant seeking advice in dealing with some severe personal problems. The officer poured his heart out to his supervisor explaining how his life was miserable since his wife was leaving him and taking his children and he was financially destitute, etc. etc. The officer was nearly in tears as he ran down the list of woes he was suffering. When he asked his supervisor what he should do, he got the following response:

"Son – I was in Viet Nam where I watched men die and had to kill to stay alive. You are about the sorriest excuse for a man I have seen yet. The way I see it, there's only one solution for all your problems…"

The supervisor unholstered his department issue sidearm and handed it to the distraught officer and simultaneously said, " …bullet to the brain."

Those who knew the supervisor personally will argue until doomsday over whether he was serious or was deploying a shrewd countermeasure. Whatever the intent, the officer underwent a change in perspective and did not opt for a premature departure. (Any plan that works is a good plan.) The officer called the supervisor later and asked what the supervisor would have done if he had taken the pistol and shot himself.

The supervisor said, "I'd've written in the report that you wrestled it from me."

Chapter 25

_____

If I Drive Fast, Am I A Racist?

Throughout the rest of this book, I have intentionally refrained from referring to any of the manifestations of Evil by anything other than gender. That is why this chapter comes last. The point was to perform an experiment. I hope the reader will answer a question honestly and in doing so obtain some insight into his or her own character that perhaps was not evident before hand. That question is; as you read my stories about my interactions with Evil, did you apply a particular race, religion, age or other physical quality to the Evil? I think that any honest person would have to answer in the affirmative. Now, the real test will be for you to think back and see if there was a pattern in the physical characteristics that your imagination gave to Evil.

Was it always a white person or was it sometimes black, Asian or "other"? Was the assigning of physical characteristics by your imagination something that depended on the setting of the story? Did you ever imagine that Evil was well dressed, well educated, clean cut, old, or someone that may have looked like you?

In your mind you have a preconception of what Evil looks like and that is perfectly normal. That preconception will depend upon your life experiences and the good and evil that you have experienced at the hands of other people. Those experiences help to make you who you are and I would never suggest that you discount them. I do, however, want the reader to realize those "prejudices" for what they are, and in knowing that they exist, take steps to ensure that even though they are a permanent and necessary part of your psychological makeup, you do not need to let them affect your view of and consequent treatment of people that you do not know. Though it is human to judge, do so justly and on the merits of the person you are judging, not on the merits of your past interactions with people who remind you of that person or a particular group to which you think that person may or may not belong.

Though I have been a victim of racism more times than I care to remember, and I honestly think that everyone has at least once in life, I will never understand the attitude of the racist. Since that topic alone could be the subject of an encyclopedic volume, I will limit my comments on it to the topic at hand. That is racism and its role in law enforcement.

The title of this chapter makes a point. That point is that there are many opinions as to what racism is and, to some, the concept is completely foreign. I must say that, growing up, I was constantly bombarded with images from the civil rights movement and stories about slavery and the mistreatment of not just blacks in America, but of the Native Americans, Jews and of the Chinese as well. I did not understand how people could be so cruel to each other and vowed not ever to let my prejudices get the best of me.

I thought that racism was a term that described a few old time southern white folks that tried to "keep the black man down" and that for the most part, racism was a thing of the past. As I learned and grew, my definition of racism was refined extensively. I discovered that no race, religion or human subcategory since the dawn of history has had a monopoly on being racist or being the victim of racism. Almost every conceivable group has been both perpetrator and victim of racist practices at some point in their evolution. Sadly, we all have quite a bit of evolving left to do before eradicating that unique manifestation of Evil.

Racism, in my opinion, is putting someone down *or holding someone up* not based on their own achievement or proven worth, but based upon something so insignificant as where they were born or what they happen to look like. It is self-defeating for a corporation, business entity, government or individual police officer to limit themselves by having such a narrow view of the world.

To be effective, an administrator should seek the best employees who do the best work. Not the best employees who are white or the best who are black or the best who are Muslim, Buddhist, Christian, etc. Likewise an effective police officer cannot allow himself (or herself) to be swayed and thereby limited by opinions or preconceptions.

We should all look forward to the day when race becomes nothing more than what it actually is; a physical trait used to describe someone's appearance.

That is why I tell all my trainees to treat everyone the same. That is, assume that everyone is a perpetrator (until you can prove otherwise) but also treat everyone, including perpetrators, equally and with respect. If you assume that only guys with leather jackets commit crimes, then you automatically miss all the criminals who left their leather jackets at home.

Also, just because you think someone is a criminal, it doesn't mean that you have the right to take them to jail. Our system is based on proof beyond a reasonable doubt, not on feeling. One example is a recurring argument with some of my fellow police officers over a section of Georgia law entitled "Possession of tools for the commission of a crime". The law (GA code 16-7-20) states that, "A person commits the offense of possession of tools for the commission of a crime when he has in his possession any tool, explosive, or other device commonly used in the commission of burglary, theft, or other crime with the intent to make use thereof in the commission of a crime."

Certain officers have construed this to mean that if I stop a car full of suspicious characters and I see a pair of gloves, a flashlight, a rock, a screwdriver or even a slim jim (car unlocking tool), that I somehow have the right to arrest that person based on the fact that I "know" they are going to commit a crime. This interpretation scares the bejesus out of me because it leaves the interpretation of good and Evil to someone's biased opinion rather than to provable fact.

The code section clearly states in the final thirteen words, "…with the intent to make use thereof in the commission of a crime." Unless you have access to a mind reading machine, how do you know what a person's intent is before they actually act upon it. Therefore I submit that to charge someone under this code section, that person must first commit, or attempt to commit some other crime.

If I do not commit, or take a substantial step toward committing, a crime first, then how can anyone possibly know that I intend to use my flashlight and screwdriver (which I carry regularly in my car) to commit a crime rather than to repair a radiator hose? To progress logically, in a free republic, how can it be legal, moral or proper for me to carry a flashlight and screwdriver and not some for other guy who happens to look more suspicious than I do?

Such are the subtleties of prejudice. I have seen such injustices perpetrated by black officers, white officers, Asian and Middle

Eastern officers. Always done with "good intent", I would bet that innocent people have been deprived of their freedoms more often than not under such circumstances. That is why I tell my students that our integrity as a group (Police Officers) must be maintained by every one of us. We must accept the fact that sometimes the bad guy gets away and that sometimes, if we can't prove the existence of Evil in a particular circumstance, in the interest of Good, we must let Evil go. If the person is truly Evil, he will be caught again before long and the end result is the same.

"Good" must remain constant or it becomes what it seeks to destroy - Evil. To continue forward, the next logical step is that the staunch defenders of "Good" must be held to a higher standard. While I will be the first to admit (and in doing so perhaps earn the moniker of hypocrite) that I will not write a simple traffic ticket to another police officer, I will not hesitate to prosecute an officer who makes a victim out of an innocent person. In other words, victimless crimes such as speeding (without accident or injury) do not in my opinion qualify as Evil. True crimes are those which create victims. From petty theft to homicide, any officer convicted of these crimes should suffer more severely than the average person.

I commented on criminal police officers in a previous chapter and will leave it at that. The following accounts are but a few of my personal bouts with racism. Some are funny. Some are scary.

The first incident that comes to mind started one afternoon in heavy, rush-hour traffic. I happened to roll up on an auto accident that was blocking the road and making bad traffic even worse. It was a minor collision with no injuries but the driver of the vehicle that was at fault was also drunk. I went through the necessary motions to make a good DUI case and placed the man under arrest. I discovered soon after that his driver's license was already suspended for numerous DUIs and that he had been declared by the state to be a "habitual violator". In the state of Georgia, driving while you are a habitual violator is a felony in and of itself.

My perpetrator was in big trouble and he knew it. He also was okay with it and was one of the most polite and well-behaved felons I ever had the privilege of arresting. The final phase of the DUI arrest necessitated the administering of a breath test to the arrested person and at the time, I was not certified to operate the breath-testing machine. Consequently, I had to call upon an officer who was certified to run my test for me.

The officer I asked to help was a veteran officer whom I also considered to be a friend. That particular officer was very large, (almost 7 feet tall) and very black. He was also very soft spoken and even tempered. My drunk arrestee was about 5 foot 5 with a well-cultivated beer gut and a body that was obviously suffering from years of neglect.

I drove the drunk-driving Evil to the precinct and sat him down in the holding area to wait for the officer who was to run my test. By that time, he and I were like best buddies and he was nothing but smiles and politeness. That all changed when the black officer appeared.

The officer went about his business preparing the machine to give the breath test. My suspect's demeanor changed noticeably. The kind and smiling face had grown a rather disturbing scowl. He was watching the black officer like a junkyard dog would eye a fresh hunk of meat.

Evil turned his look to me, smiled again and said, "Hey bud, watch this." I immediately began to feel a combination of pity and disgust for the poor bastard who was about to bite off a whole lot more than most people could chew. The pity was short-lived as his actions were no one's fault but his own. I knew that the spectacle that was about to unfold before me was bound to be entertaining and I was not disappointed.

Evil walked over to the officer and stood in front of him. There was a counter and a heavy screen between them but immediately to Evil's left was an open doorway that the officer could reach through if need be. Evil said with Chihuahua like determination, "Hey bud." When the officer looked at him, Evil extended the middle finger of his right hand and thrust it toward the screen that separated the two men.

I remember thinking to myself, "Oh boy. Here it comes."

With his characteristic coolness, the officer paused, looked at the midget Evil, and said in one of the deepest voices a human can have, "What's that supposed to mean?"

Evil in his immense stupidity responded with, "It means I'm goin' to kick your ass, nigger." I shook my head and chuckled, not at the racial slur but at the impending violence this idiot was about to bring down upon himself.

I took out my ticket book to begin writing the charge that Evil was most surely about to commit, knowing full well that my presence would be neither needed nor requested in the imminent conflict.

In one step, the officer fluidly moved from behind the machine and through the door. He stood towering over the foolish little man. The officer then said, "What?"

Most normal men would have cowered back to the corner from whence they slithered when faced with such a formidable foe, but not my little Evil. He immediately removed his stereotypical red flannel shirt to expose the black t-shirt underneath while simultaneously saying, "You heard me. I said I'm goin' to kick your fuckin' ass ……"

Before he could finish the word we all knew was coming next, the officer's sledgehammer-like fist had impacted Evil's left cheek with frightening precision, knocking him onto the linoleum floor. He lay there stunned and bleeding, just long enough to realize that he had been bested by of all things, a black man.

The officer had already begun to walk away assuming that the breath test had been canceled and Evil had been sufficiently subdued. I was walking over to the man on the floor to re-handcuff him in preparation for the ride to jail when Evil screamed, "I'm not through with you yet!"

I put the handcuffs on Evil and helped him to his feet, at which point he began running down the hallway toward the other officer screaming, "I said I was goin' to kick your ass and I mean it!" He actually ran up behind the other officer and literally kicked him in the butt since his hands were cuffed behind his back. This action on Evil's part elicited a reaction from the officer that was identical to the first. In one sweeping motion, the same fist came at Evil with blinding speed and even more blinding force than before and the scene I remember went in slow motion from that point.

Evil, with hands secured behind his back, spun toward me clockwise with a look on his face that I can only describe as precious. Since he had no use of his hands to break his fall, his look became more fearful as he neared the all too familiar linoleum. He crashed faced first into the floor and was down but not out. As I was stuffing him into the patrol car to transport him to the hospital, he was still howling like the rabid dog he had become. All I could do was shake my head and wonder why.

#25.2 In the Name of Rodney King

My next story juxtaposes the "stereotypical" racist encounter. It takes place a short time after the "Rodney King incident" when a young man in the metro Atlanta area who had obviously become "disenfranchised," saw fit to begin a pattern of raping and brutally beating white women. He had a profile for choosing victims. There was a particular physical type that he liked. When he found a woman who met that profile, he would follow her home. When he was sure that his prey was alone and vulnerable, he would attack. Some he beat unconscious with his bare hands. Some he cut with knives or stabbed with kitchen forks. All of them he brutally raped. He would tell his victims, "This is for Rodney King."

He attacked three or four women in my jurisdiction and, if I recall correctly, at least two of them were on the beat that I was working at the time. Before his barbarous rampage ended with numerous consecutive life sentences in another jurisdiction, he would have forever destroyed the lives of roughly eighteen women and their families.

I met him one night. It was after midnight and I was staking out an apartment complex on my beat in an area where he had attacked previously. It was late fall or early winter, near Christmas, so I was also looking out for the many thieves who had been hitting the complexes in my beat. They always steal more during the holidays. I guess scumbags have Christmas trees too.

The particular complex I was in at the time is a relatively small one. It has four buildings that are arranged in a sort of rectangle with residential streets running along the north and east sides. The apartment complex is gated, which makes the residents feel safe but really only serves to keep the police and fire departments out and gives Evil the same sense of security afforded to the residents.

I was conducting my surveillance from a concealed vantage point in the southeast corner of the parking lot. I thought it was a bit strange when I saw an SUV driving slowly through the parking lot. It was coming in my direction from the front gate. What was unusual was that on the street that is adjacent and parallel to the parking lot, there was a car that was going the same speed and direction as the SUV, but was several yards behind it as if intentionally trying to stay in the SUV's blind spot. As it turned out, the driver of the SUV was a female who matched our bad guy's profile. She left one of the local bars alone and Evil followed her, as was his way.

She finally parked her truck in the only available space in front of her apartment building. Her mistake was that she sat in her truck for an inordinately long period of time. While she sat in her truck doing whatever victims inevitably do to give Evil time to properly orchestrate and execute his attack, Evil parked his car on the adjacent street. The first time I laid eyes on him he was creeping through the narrow band of trees that separated the apartment complex parking lot from the street. He was wearing all black and would run from one place of concealment to the next. Each lunge brought him closer to his intended victim. He never moved his gaze from his intended prey. That is one reason I was able to sneak right up to him without being noticed. It was probably the first time in his life that he was the prey.

Evil had made his way to within two parked cars from the female in the SUV when I got within arm's reach of him. I broke the silence with one of my favorite phrases (which I generally deliver with a slight southern drawl), "What er you doin'?"

Evil was obviously startled. He spun around in his crouched position, looked at me, and then, without missing a beat, began doing deep knee bends. Simultaneously he said, "I'm just goin' out for a jog." Not bad for an improv, but it would take more than that to trick me.

I put Evil in handcuffs and gave him the opportunity to talk himself out of his predicament. That particular, age-old strategy nearly always ends with Evil having enough rope to hang himself. In this instance, Evil made the noose, put it around his head, and even started to pull.

He told me that the girl he was following was his ex-girlfriend. They had broken up not too long ago because her white family could not accept that she was dating a black man. He happened to be out at a local bar when he saw her with another man. That led to an argument and she had left the bar mad at him. He wanted to try to make up with her. He even gave me a fictitious name for the female in question.

I know several officers who would have let the man go at that point with no more questions asked. His story was that convincing and he was confident when he told it. However, I have always held to one rule and it has treated me well. Nable's first rule of policing: Operate on the assumption that everyone you talk to is lying. Then you do everything in your power to try to prove that they are lying and if you can't, then they might be telling the truth.

Most people (and consequently most officers) are relatively law-abiding and trustworthy. For that reason, most people tend to think that most people are relatively law-abiding and trustworthy. I'm not saying that it is necessarily a bad way to be, but if you want to be good at finding Evil, you have to expect to find it…even in the most unlikely places.

With that in mind, the next logical step for me was to make contact with the female in the truck. Sometime during my initial encounter with the man in black, she had exited her vehicle and gone inside. I doubt that she ever even noticed me or the creature who nearly changed her life forever.

While another unit stood by with Evil, I first went to the truck. When I ran the tag it came back "not on file" as was common in those days. All the doors were locked and the interior was unusually clean. The last place I looked was through the front windshield to see under the front passenger seat. There, barely visible, was a membership card from one of the local video rental chain stores. I could just make out the last name on the card. I went to the front gate where there was a computer screen that listed all the lessees in the apartment complex. My hope was that the name I had seen on the card would be on the computer. It was.

I typed in the code next to her name so that the computer would dial her apartment. She answered. I identified myself and asked her a few quick questions. I confirmed that she was the woman in the truck in question and got her name. I also had time to confirm that she did not know the subject I had stopped and she stated that she had not ever dated a black man. Then the computer phone timed out and broke our connection.

I feel it appropriate to make a special note here. If you are a civilian, remember the rule I quoted a few chapters ago. Just because someone tells you they are the police doesn't mean that they are. Before you give personal information or invite a stranger into your home, take a few moments to confirm their identity. It is as easy as calling 911 and asking if they have an officer out at your location. If you are a police officer, understand that the person you are contacting doesn't know you. Be patient and work with them to help them become satisfied that you are the good guy so you may then work together to crush Evil.

Except for a brief telephone conversation afterwards to confirm the "victim" information, I never spoke to the woman again. She seemed wholly unimpressed that she had just escaped a fate likely worse than death. I sent the arrest report down to the detective division because I was certain that he was the man the media now referred to as the "Buckhead Rapist" (named after an upscale Atlanta area where his attacks were concentrated).

Our crack, sex crimes investigative unit claims they never got the report. I found that out a few months (and a few rapes) later when I was subpoenaed to an adjoining county for his first trial. Our detective had also been subpoenaed to give evidence in some of the rapes that happened in our jurisdiction to support the case they were making in the other county. When the detective saw me enter the witness room, she said, "Hey what are you doing here?" I said, "I was the one who arrested him in our county."

#25.3 Your-Honor?

My next story is not nearly so amusing but it does represent the only time in my life that I have seen a judge in a court of law treat someone differently and adversely, in my opinion, just because of his skin color.

I had written a middle class black man from Alabama two traffic tickets. One was for expired tag and one was for no proof of insurance. The expired tag was no big deal. It's a non-moving violation that carried at most a $66 fine. The no proof of insurance was a little more serious, but not much.

Our regular judge would customarily dismiss both tickets if the person who had received them came to court with current and up to date documents; even if they had been acquired after the tickets were written. On the day in question, however, we had a substitute judge whom I had never seen before and have not seen since.

There was a white man who had been given the same exact tickets by another officer whose case came up before the tickets I had written to the black man. The white man stood up in front of the judge and was asked if he had gotten insurance on his vehicle since he had received the citations. The man replied that he had gotten insurance on the vehicle and that he had left the proof in his car in the parking lot. The judge told him to go get the proof of insurance and come back to the courtroom with it and the charge would be dismissed. The man left the courtroom.

My case was called. The man to whom I had written the two tickets stood up in front of the judge and said that he had gotten insurance on the vehicle but did not have insurance when I had stopped him. At the time, Alabama residents were not required to have insurance on their cars but he had since become a Georgia resident, so our insurance laws applied to him. Instead of imposing the customary fine on the man, the judge ordered me to place him in handcuffs and transport him to the jail after court was over to post bond for his no insurance ticket. I tried to protest but was silenced by the judge.

Moments later, the aforementioned white guy came back to the courtroom and stood in front of the judge. The judge asked him for his insurance card and the man said, "Your honor, I lied. I haven't got insurance."

I stood up preparing to take the man into custody fully expecting that order from the judge. Imagine my astonishment when the judge said something like, "Don't worry about it. Just pay the fine and go get some insurance, OK?" Not only was I stunned by that development but I was also ashamed to be a representative of the system that day.

As I transported my subject to jail, I told him what he had to have known already, and that was that he had been screwed. I went so far as to tell him that I would gladly testify for him if he filed a complaint against the judge and that I would gladly assist him in any way that I could. I never heard from the man after dropping him at the jail.

I am assuming that at least some people are nodding their heads and thinking to themselves that those sorts of things happen all the time – especially in the South. I can honestly say that that is not the case. Such incidents are truly the exception and not the rule.

Some people also think that whites are the only racists. I suggest that those people research the FBI hate crime statistics. According to the FBI UCR statistics for the year 2001, in reported hate crimes where the race of the offender was known, African Americans perpetrated roughly twice as many hate crimes *per capita* than whites. (Black Americans were the known offenders in 1,882 cases and represent 12.8 % of the population or 35.4 million people. That equates to one hate crime for every 18,809.7 people. White Americans were the known offenders in 6,049 cases and represent 82.2 % of the population or 226.8 million people. That equates to one hate crime for every 37,493.8 people. The exact ratio is therefore 1.99 to 1.)

Please don't misunderstand my point. I am not trying to say that any one group is more or less Evil than another. It is quite possible that if you look at statistics from other years, those numbers may change drastically. I also understand that there are many unseen variables that may be unaccounted for. The simple fact of the matter is that people are bad. Not all people are bad but someone in every group of people is bound to be bad. Evil knows no boundaries. It affects all nations, all religions, all cultures and all professions without exception. Evil is universal. Evil appears in places that you don't expect it to appear and it may not appear in the places or in the forms in which you expect.

Most racists share the same psychological makeup, and if you take race out of the equation, they would be hard to differentiate from one another. Whether you are speaking of a member of Hamas, the KKK, the Black Panthers or any other racist group, if you read their vitriolic diatribes and eliminate any references to race or religion, they all say virtually the same thing. They are militant, hate-filled, ignorant, warmongers and the world would be a better place without them.

Their leaders are particularly dangerous. They take a group of people who share a common plight. They use the common plight to unite the alleged "oppressed". Then they focus on another group and convince the first group that their condition is a result of the actions or even the mere existence of the second group. From that point, it is not hard to convince people that the oppressors should be punished and thereby push the followers to destructive behaviors. This psychology is evident in the methods of Adolf Hitler, Slobodan Milosevic, Malcolm X, Pol Pot, Osama Bin Laden, and the list goes on and on.

Some truly insidious perpetrators of racism are the ones who do not openly promote violence but who use their own racism to polarize communities and perpetuate the racist "status quo" just so that they can maintain their own positions of power. A prominent example of this type of pathology is found in many of today's "community leaders". A few years ago in Georgia, a person of the type of which I am speaking, who has a reputation for blaming all sorts of bad things on white people, actually got on national television and said that white people were responsible for floods that had decimated largely non-white communities. The thought that white people control the weather and can somehow direct floodwaters made most people who are even remotely possessed of intelligence laugh him off his stage, but his rhetoric likely reached some of his "followers" and helped perpetuate his special form of Evil.

If we ever hope to do away with racial strife, then we must acknowledge the fact that references to race should be eliminated. We need to stop referring to ourselves by our skin color. In this country we should not separate ourselves into groups of White Americans, African Americans, Hispanic, Muslim, Asian, Christian, Native, European, Tall, Short, Fat, Smart, Stupid or Whatever Americans. We are all Americans and that is the only thing that counts. Until we have the strength to unite as one people and rise above the petty little differences manifested in our respective subcultures, then we are all working to promote continued racism (Evil) and we are all to blame.

Until we, as a nation, can learn to accept personal responsibility for ourselves and our actions or inactions, we are doomed to perpetuate the environment that allows the racist to flourish. In this great nation, every person is free to become whatever he or she is capable of becoming. It is up to the individual to become the "captain" of his or her own soul. If you find yourself blaming others for your condition or your predicaments, then perhaps you should take a step back and look at yourself. You can choose to waste your time blaming others for your lot in life or you can look into the mirror and see the real culprit. Once you realize who the real culprit is you can begin to make positive changes, not only in your life, but in the lives of those around you.

There are no universal, karmic, bank accounts where eternal tellers meticulously track debts paid or owed to individuals, cultures or civilizations. I am responsible only for me. You are responsible only for you. We are responsible for our own children, but only until they reach an age where they can be responsible for themselves. At that point, they become a reflection of their parents and their upbringing.

The only debts a person owes are those debts that person incurs. Punishments do not extend to the criminal's heirs. Rewards, however, reach to succeeding generations.

Out of Service

When an officer is not available to answer calls he is "out of service". When we finish our shift for the day the same is true. Thus, this is my closing comment or parting shot.

I truly hope that the reader has gained something from my writing. If nothing else, I hope I have either renewed lost vigor, or instilled vigor into those who never had it, to join in the search for Evil.

Searching for Evil is a task we must all perform together for the benefit of each other and of mankind as a whole. We all shoulder this responsibility equally, and must forever defend the enduring principles of Good. Those principles are not dictated by popular mandate, nor exclusive to a privileged few. They are universal and unchanging, divine truths that are impervious to the mind of man.

Searching for Evil is like taking out the trash…no matter how much we carry off today; tomorrow there will be more. The battle is never ending.

"The only thing necessary for the triumph of Evil, is for good men to do nothing." (– Edmund Burke)

"What about the perfect donut?" you ask.

Let it suffice to say that I am still searching…

…and I am savoring the quest.

Pig Latin

Acronyms

- D.R.T. - Dead Right There
- P.O.V. - Privately Owned Vehicle
- F.T.O. – Field Training Officer
- M.V.I. - Mobile Vehicular Investigation
- P.O.P. - Pissin' Off the Police
- D.A. - District Attorney or Dumb Ass (the terms are interchangeable)
- S.D.T. - Sudden Deceleration Trauma
- P.I.T. - Pursuit Intervention Technique
- E.M.S. - Emergency Medical Services
- V.T.O.L.- Vertical Take Off and Landing
- E.V.O.C. – Emergency Vehicle Operations Course
- S.S.U.S.P.V.O.T. – Pronounced "SUS-pah-vot". Super Secret Undercover Stealth Patrol Vehicle Of Trickery. Synonym for unmarked car.

Terms

- Automatic weapon – This term describes a weapon that when the trigger is pulled, it fires ammunition continuously until the trigger is released or until the ammunition feeding device is empty. Commonly referred to as a machine gun.
- Bark Poisoning - Metaphorical reference to death by direct impact with a tree.
- Beat – Area of operation for a police officer. While the officer is on duty, that area is his responsibility. The word can also refer to an act of physical violence. The two definitions are unrelated.
- Blinky Blinkies - Colored lights on a patrol car that flash or revolve.
- Cap – Hat or top. Also a term that when used as a noun refers to a bullet or a round of ammunition. (Example: Let's go bust a cap in his ass.) When used as a verb, it means to shoot at something. (Example: I think somebody just got capped.)

- Choir Practice – Meeting after work to drink beer. Adapted from the movie "The Choir Boys".
- Contact and Cover – One of the single greatest safety tactics for suspect encounters. If two or more officers are present, one officer is designated to "contact" the suspect while the other officer is designated as the "cover" officer. If three or more officers are present then there may be more than one of each (contact or cover officers) depending on the situation. There should always be at least one cover officer. The cover officer maintains distance to allow him to see any threat that may materialize and it is his responsibility to deal with that threat. The contact officer should not have a weapon in hand. The roles may be dynamic, shifting between officers, but should be clear. With one officer on scene, that officer must decide if he is contact or cover. Most times he should sustain a cover function until help arrives, if possible.
- Crispy Critter - Any body that is burned beyond recognition.
- Egg McMagnum - Metaphorical reference to suicide where the subject wishing to terminate his or her existence places the barrel of a pistol into his or her mouth and pulls the trigger.
- Emergency Pants - Spare pair of underwear kept strategically placed in case the current pair becomes "soiled".
- Enroute – French word that means "on the way". Police use it to sound professional.
- Extra Gun - A smaller, secondary weapon carried by officers for use in the event that their primary duty weapon becomes unusable or inaccessible. Real police carry extra guns. An alarming trend is that fewer and fewer officers carry them these days. Also an alternate term for a trainee.
- Field Training Officer – One who trains officers in the "field". "FTO program" refers to that period of time when a new officer rides with an FTO to learn how to be a police officer.
- Geometric Progression – A method employed when searching around corners or obstacles that may conceal Evil. A person performing a geometric progression will distance himself from the object to be seen around and move slowly in an arching pattern until he can see around the obstacle. Sometimes called "slicing the pie" imagine that the object of your search is in the center of a circle and an obstacle lies between it and you. Move slowly around the circumference of the circle until the center is visible.

- Jesus Gun - a small and easily concealable firearm often carried by "real" police in a secret location. This is a backup, backup gun. If this gun ever comes out, someone is going to meet Jesus.
- Melon - Head
- Non-Essential Personnel (NEP) – A term used to described individuals in an organization whose functions are not necessary in the day to day operations of that organization. Synonym – Supervisor
The acronym NEP is also used as the root of certain words like iNEPtitude and NEPotism.
- Perp - Abbreviation of perpetrator
- Pursuit Intervention Technique – A maneuver developed by professional racecar drivers that was later adopted by the police. One driver uses the front corner of his vehicle to impact the opposite rear corner of a target vehicle. If performed correctly, the impact then sends the target vehicle spinning out of control.
- POH-lease - Correct pronunciation of the word "Police".
- Port-a-perp - Slang for paddy wagon or any other vehicle or device designed specifically for the trans**porta**tion of **perp**etrators.
- Prairie Doggin' - Metaphor used to describe to the imminent expulsion of solid waste. The solid waste material protrudes slightly past the sphincter much like a prairie dog sticking his head outside of his den.
- Reasonable, Articulable Suspicion – Suspicion that is both reasonable and articulable.
- Recap – Abbreviated form of the word recapitulation, which basically means repeat. Also a term that describes shooting something again. (First you cap it. Then you recap it.)
- Recto-Cranial Impaction - Heap up Ass.
- Screen Test - Metaphorical reference to an outdated, archaic, obsolete, and no longer used disciplinary procedure performed by an officer against a perpetrator which involves the placing of a handcuffed perpetrator into the rear seat of a patrol car which has a barrier or "screen" which separates the front seat area from the back seat area thereby separating the officer from the perpetrator. The vehicle operator then accelerates to a reasonably high speed and promptly slams on the brake causing the unseatbelted

perpetrator to fly unexpectedly face first into said barrier. This test is not graded, it is strictly pass - fail.

- Semi-automatic weapon – This term describes a weapon that when fired, has a mechanical action that automatically reloads but does not fire the next round of ammunition from the ammunition feeding device. Morons in politics and the media often call this an automatic weapon.
- Sphincter Factor - Refers to the tightening of the sphincter muscles in tense or extremely stressful situations. The higher the sphincter factor the more tense the situation.
- Sudden Deceleration Trauma - It's not the fall that kills you, it's the sudden stop.
- TAC - Secondary radio channel for use when the primary channel is occupied or for less important radio traffic.
- Target Rich Environment - Any area where there is an abundance of criminals.
- Traffic – A word that refers to a volume of vehicles on the roadway or to the conversation that is broadcast over a police radio.
- Universal translator – Term used by insensitive police to describe a baton or nightstick.
- Warning Shot - Any shot that misses the intended target.
- Woo Woos - Siren. (Generally used in conjunction with the blinky blinkies.)
- Wood Shampoo - Another metaphorical reference to an outdated, archaic, obsolete, and no longer used procedure whereby an officer armed with an outdated, archaic, obsolete, and no longer used wooden "night stick" repeatedly strikes a deserving perpetrator about the cranium (which can extend to the neck, torso and extremities if the perpetrator is exceptionally hairy).

Radio Signals

This first group of signal numbers is in use by many of the metro Atlanta area police departments and has been for 25 years or more. Slight variations sometimes exist between the departments because of changes made over the years. The list was originally alphabetical and described the most commonly encountered radio traffic.

1. Abandoned auto
2. Silent alarm
3. Audible alarm
   (The primary difference between a signal 2 and a signal 3 is that the signal 2 would be reported to the police by an alarm monitoring company while the signal three would generally be reported by a citizen who heard the alarm ringing.)
4. Ambulance (Refers to the vehicle itself or also to the fact that an ambulance is on its way to a particular call.)
5. Street lights
6. Burglar in a residence
7. Burglar in a business
(For signals 8 - 15, 19 & 20, the signal by itself means to call that particular location on the phone. When the letter "G" is given after the signal it means to go there in person.)
8. North Precinct
9. South precinct
10. Chief's office (This one is usually bad)
11. Garage (This would refer to the government contract vehicle repair facility, not just to any garage)
12. Home
13. Detective division
14. Identification division (The guys that take fingerprints and photographs and stuff.)
15. Radio (This refers to the communications room not just any old radio.)
16. Cancel call

17. Switch to TAC (TAC is short for tactical channel and is a separate radio channel for radio traffic that does not need to be on the main channel.)
18. Radio repair shop
19. South precinct court
20. North precinct court
21. Call tow truck
22. Vandalism
23. Disorderly child(ren)
24. Demented person (This signal comes up in regular conversations quite frequently.)
25. Discharging firearm
26. Discharging fireworks
(Signals 25 and 26 are often followed by a "Yahooo", especially in the South.)
27. Dog(s) barking
(Don't ask me how or why, but a signal 27 also means "I'm eating".)
28. Drunk
29. Drunk and disorderly or fighting
30. Drunk driver
31. Electrical wires down
32. Escaped prisoner
33. Fire (something's burning)
34. Gambling
35. This has meant different things over the years but doesn't mean anything right now.
36. Hold-up in progress
37. Illegal parking
38. Illegal drugs or alcohol
39. Information for officer
(Signal 39 is also the default code for any call that doesn't fit any other signal.)
40. Investigate animal
41. Investigate auto accident
42. Investigate burglary
43. Investigate hit and run auto collision
44. Armed robbery
(Signal 44 differs from a signal 36 in that a 44 is an armed robbery that has already occurred and a 36 is one that is occurring.)

45. Investigate larceny (theft)
46. Investigate person struck by an auto

47. Investigate person injured
48. Investigate person dead
49. Investigate person raped
50. Investigate person shot
51. Investigate person stabbed
52. Stolen goods
53. Suicide or attempt
54. Suspicious person
55. Trouble unknown
56. Missing person
57. Loud noise
58. Man beating woman (There's not a signal for a woman beating a man. Draw your own conclusions.)
59. Meet officer
60. Molesting a woman or child (There's not a signal for molesting a man. Draw your own conclusions.)
61. Money transaction (This signal is hardly ever used but generally refers to a merchant transporting a large amount of cash that wants a police escort.)
62. Mysterious blank signal that perhaps was originally related to a 35
63. Officer down/needs help
(On the morning watch a signal 63 means something like "I've been shot twice. I need more ammo so I can keep shooting back. Someone is guaranteed to go to the hospital, the morgue, the jail or any combination thereof.)
64. Panhandling (Begging. Or if you're a whiny liberal, a less fortunate individual that really would rather be working but just can't find a job right now.)
65. Public building alarm (That is an alarm in a government building.)
66. Peeping Tom
67. Person down
68. Person screaming
69. Person armed
70. Prowler
71. Public indecency
72. Reckless driving

73. Rush call (That means go real fast.)

74. Selling alcohol on Sunday (It's still illegal in the South. Draw your own conclusions.)

75. Shooting air rifles (That means shooting with them not at them.)

76. Person sick

77. Snatch thief (Person who steals by snatching or a report of such a crime.)

78. Lookout (A description of a person, place or thing to be looked for is called a "lookout".)

79. Stealing of/from an auto

80. Stray animal

81. Roadway or sidewalk obstruction

82. Wagon call or prisoner transport

83. Wanted person (This signal is used over the radio to let an officer know that a given person has a warrant for their arrest. The idea here is that if the officer is too stupid to keep the perp from hearing the radio, then the perp won't know that the officer knows he's about to go to jail.)

84. Direct traffic

85. Wrecker (tow truck) is on the way

86. Bomb threat

87. Traffic stop

88. Not used…..but to a neo-nazi it is a signal that means "Heil Hitler"
(H is the 8th letter of the alphabet so "HH" would be 88)

89. Welfare check (Not the tangible bank draft issued by the government to those underprivileged people who really would rather be working but just can't find a job, but rather a check of one's welfare or well being.)

10 - Codes

The "10 - codes" are not in use in my area but many law enforcement agencies and military personnel still use them. For that reason I have reprinted them here.

10-0 Caution
10-1 Unable to Copy-Change Locations
10-2 Signal Good
10-3 Stop Transmitting
10-4 Acknowledgement (Generally followed but sometimes preceded by words like "Over" and "Roger")
10-5 Relay
10-6 Busy, Unless Urgent
10-7 Out of Service
10-8 In Service
10-9 Repeat
10-10 Fight - Disorder Reported
10-11 Dog Case
10-12 Stand-By
10-13 Weather – Road Report
10-14 Prowler Report
10-15 Burglary
10-15 A Burglar Alarm
10-16 Domestic Problem
10-17 Armed Robbery
10-17 A Robbery Alarm
10-18 Quickly
10-19 Return to _____
10-20 Location
10-21 Call _____ by Telephone
10-22 Disregard
10-23 Arrived at the Scene
10-24 Unit Available
10-25 Report in Person (Meet)
10-26 Underage Consumption

10-27 Drivers License Information
10-28 Vehicle Registration Information
10-29 Check Stolen – Wanted
10-30 Unnecessary use of Radio
10-31 Crime in Progress
10-32 Subject with Firearms
10-33 EMERGENCY
10-34 Open Alcohol
10-35 Loud Music
10-36 Correct Time
10-37 Investigate Suspicious Person/Vehicle
10-38 Stopping Suspicious Person/Vehicle
10-39 Resume Normal Operations
10-40 If Not Stolen, Check With Owner
10-41 Beginning Tour of Duty
10-42 Ending Tour of Duty
10-43 Murder Reported
10-44 Suicide or Suicide Attempt
10-45 Harassment
10-46 Assist Motorist
10-47 Emergency, Road Repaired at _____
10-48 Traffic Light Out at _____
10-49 Speeding Auto
10-50 Accident
10-50I Accident with Injuries
10-50P Accident with Pedestrian
10-51 Wrecker Needed
10-52 Ambulance Needed
10-53 Road Blocked at _____
10-54 Livestock – Carcass on the Road
10-55 Intoxicated Driver
10-56 Intoxicated Pedestrian
10-57 Hit and Run
10-58 Direct Traffic
10-59 Convoy or Escort
10-60 _____ Will Leave This Station
10-61 Obscene Phone Calls
10-62 Damage to Property
10-63 Prepare to Make Written Copy

10-64 Traffic Stop
10-65 Mechanical Breakdown
10-66 Escaped Prisoner
10-67 Missing Person
10-68 Dispatch Information
10-69 Message Received
10-70 Fire
10-71 Child Abuse
10-71 A Child Molestation
10-72 Recovered Property
10-73 Meal Break
10-74 Negative
10-75 In Contact With
10-76 En Route
10-77 ETA – Estimated Time of Arrival
10-78 Need Assistance
10-79 Notify Coroner
10-80 Chase in Progress
10-81 Give Location – Status Hourly
10-82 Entering Auto
10-83 Work School Crossing At _____
10-84 Special Detail
10-85 Disturbance
10-86 Officer – Operator On Duty
10-87 Forgery
10-88 Present Phone # of _____
10-89 Bomb Threat
10-90 Bank Alarm at _____
10-91 Pickup Prisoner – Subject
10-92 Improperly Parked Vehicle
10-93 Blockade
10-94 Drag Racing
10-95 Prisoner – Subject in Custody
10-96 Mental Subject
10-97 Radio Check
10-98 Prison – Jail Break
10-99 Motor Vehicle Theft
10-100 Nature Call
10-101 Shoplifter

10-102 Send Rescue Unit to _____
10-103 Send Police Unit to _____
10-104 Unable to Locate
10-105 Trailer Inspection
10-106 Serving Subpoena
10-107 Serving Civil Papers
10-108 Child Custody
10-109 Patient Condition
A – Walking Injured
B – Moderately Injured
C – Severely Injured
D – Dead
10-110 Multi-Injury Accident
10-111 Abandoned Vehicle
10-112 Kidnapping
10-113 Drowning
10-114 Theft
10-115 Assault
10-116 Aggravated Assault
10-117 Sexual Assault
10-118 Lewd Acts
10-119 Trespassing
10-120 Contraband
10-121 Lost – Mislaid Property
10-122 Juvenile Problem
10-123 Criminal Trespass
10-124 Deliver Message
10-125 Phone Trap
10-126 Open Door
10-127 Chemical Split
10-128 Threats
10-129 Arson
10-130 Loitering & Prowling
10-131 Criminal Attempt
10-132 Extra Patrol
10-133 Indecent Exposure
10-134 Obstruction
10-135 Accidental Injury
10-136 Littering

10-137 Miscellaneous
10-138 BOLO
10-139 Warrant Served
10-140 Case Follow-Up
10-141 Check Welfare
10-142 Check Houses
10-143 Check Club
10-144 Drop-In Visit
10-145 Retrieving Personal Belongings
10-146 Cruelty to Animals
10-147 HIV Positive
10-148 Passing Stopped School Bus
10-149 Fireworks
10-150 Gambling
10-151 Unlawful Sale of Alcohol
10-152 Car Repossession
10-153 911 Hang-Up Calls
10-154 Secure Your Microphone (for Suspect Information)
10-155 Communications Relief
10-156 Expedite
10-157 Debris in Roadway
10-158 Stalking
10-200 Going Poop (My favorite, and in fact the only, 10 code I use besides "10-4 Roger Over")

Richard A. Nable

Page Of Many Thanks

I would like to offer many thanks to the following individuals for their role(s) in making this book possible. They are presented in no particular order (except for Skip, who is always last).

J. Inman	W. Yates	D. Nable	J. Williams	R. Mclarin
T. Shaw	R. Jamison	J. Head	J. Wright	W. Putman
J. Hall	D. Hendrix	P. Graham	J. Hitt	D. Guy
R. Tharps	G. Gallant	R. Stewart	R. Sliz	J. Flood
J. Vann	S. Cruz	J. Burnette	C. Warren	J. Lee
N. Valadi	J. Agurto	A. Tennant	S. Fairley	D. Wilson
G. Hodge	P. Craine	B. Cochran	C. Kistler	C. Dallape
V. Moran	W. Putman	W. Green	J. Stone	R. Stewart
J. Lockett	B. Shane	K. Bright	C. VanMeter	D. Brown
N. Whybrew	J. Vaughan	D. Lapides	J. Shockley	M. Johnson
		Skip Harrell		

…And to my friend, Joe Glass, in Sydney, Australia.

Printed in the United States
1507300003B/208-210